The Baneberry Disaster
America's Deadly Atomic Catastrophe

Larry C. Johns and Alan R. Johns

America's Deadly Atomic Catastrophe by
Larry C. Johns and Alan R. Johns

Front Cover photograph courtesy of National Nuclear Security Administration Field Office
2nd Printing
ISBN: 978-0-578-22239-4

In memory of our parents,
Ray and Helen Johns, whose motto was,
"To the valiant heart, nothing is impossible,"
and
Shields Warren, 1898–1980, Father of Radiation Pathology,
Alice Stewart, 1906–2002, Mother of Radiation Epidemiology.

Contents

Acknowledgments

THE *BANEBERRY* CASE would not have been possible without the support of my wife, Mary, who supported the cause and shouldered the burden of raising our four children, Charles, Laura, Julianna, and Jason, who grew up with *Baneberry*.

Alan bore the burden of *Baneberry* equally, and his wife Loretta and their three children, Tris, Greg, and Brian shared the adventure.

Without Bill Cleghorn there would have been no *Baneberry* lawsuit, and without Paul Duckworth's help in preparing the lawsuit, we might not have been introduced to Dr. Shields Warren, who never faltered in his conviction that his opinion in the Roberts's case was correct. With Dr. Stewart, Dr. Gofman, Dr. Morgan, Dr. Tamplin, and Dr. Bertell on our team, it seemed inconceivable that justice would not be done.

The manuscript would not have been finished without encouragement and editorial advice from Mary D. Wammack, who worked as a legal assistant on both the *Baneberry* and *Prescott* cases and earned a doctorate in history with a focus on nuclear policy.

During the twenty-five years the *Baneberry* and *Prescott* cases were in court, we met countless Test Site workers, atomic veterans, downwinders, and others. Bennie Levy worked tirelessly on behalf of the workers and Janet Gordon for the downwinders. Dale Haralson, who tried the *Allen* case and headed our team in the *Prescott* case, passed away in December 2015. Dale and so many others are not here to thank for their contributions, including thousands of Nevada Test Site (NTS) workers who made the nuclear testing program possible.

The Baneberry Disaster

Prologue

WE NEVER LEARNED WHY the scientists who planned the December 18, 1970 underground nuclear test named it "Baneberry" after a poisonous berry, from the root word "bane" a cause of death and were stunned by the revelation that the Baneberry test was the United States 666th nuclear test following the first test "Trinity" on July 16, 1945 in Alamogordo, New Mexico. The atomic bomb from God incarnate to Satan!

Our Baneberry investigation began in April 1971. Seven weeks later, Daniel Ellsberg leaked the Pentagon Papers to the New York Times and on June 30, 1971, the United State Supreme Court ruled that the Nixon Administration could not suppress publication of the Johnson Administration's View Nam War strategy. Justice Black in his concurring opinion best summarized the rationale:

"Secrecy in government is fundamentally anti-democratic, perpetuating bureaucratic errors. Open debate and discussion of public issues are vital to the national health."

President Nixon shut down the Nevada Test Site for six months because of the Baneberry debacle and in August 1974 resigned because he tried to suppress the truth about the Watergate scandal.

Heartened by Justice Black's admonition, we embarked on our Baneberry investigation expecting the government to tell the truth, but to our dismay learned that the AEC in collaboration with the Department of Justice suppressed the truth about the Baneberry vent, intimidated our chief expert, Dr. Shields Warren, threatened Harley Roberts' widow with a "gag order." and in a final act of hubris the Justice Department lawyer boasted during the trial that the government would spend "whatever it takes to win." And the government won, although we were stunned that the judge ignored the evidence brilliantly and persuasively presented by Dr. Warren and others.

But we take great comfort knowing that Baneberry was largely responsible for the payment of $333 million to 4,500 Nevada Test Site workers for leukemias and cancers associated with exposure to atomic radiation at the Nevada Test Site. The Baneberry debacle resulted in a stunning victory, but not for Harley Roberts or William Nunamaker.

Ironically in 2016, when we finished writing the Baneberry story, Justice Black's condemnation of "secrecy in government" went unheeded at the highest levels of government. The FBI, Department of Justice, and other agencies suppressed/altered the truth and collaborated with newspapers that were the beneficiaries of the Pentagon Papers case, in an "anti-democratic" effort to bring down candidate/President Donald Trump.

Introduction

IN 1950, LAS VEGAS had one high school, Las Vegas High, only a handful of elementary schools, and Fifth Street Grammar School for fifth through eighth grades. On December 18, 1950, the Las Vegas Bombing and Gunnery Range, a vast government reserve in south-central Nevada, was selected to test atomic bombs. On January 11, 1951, the Atomic Energy Commission issued a press release, warning that A-bomb tests would begin soon, but there would be no public announcement of the time of specific tests.[1]

On January 27, 1951, the first A-bomb was dropped from an airplane on Frenchman Flat at the Nevada Proving Grounds.[2] The two-inch headline, "VEGANS ATOM-IZED," described the reactions of people throughout the Las Vegas valley who saw the predawn flash or heard doors and windows rattling in their homes nearly seventy miles south of the blast.[3]

The first few tests were unannounced. But in the fall of 1951, when the AEC did begin announcing upcoming tests, witnessing an A-bomb blast was an initiation into the atomic age. We perched on the roof of our home on North 12th Street to watch the flash of light over the Sheep Range north of town and wait for the rumbling as the sound waves traveled south to Las Vegas.

The A-bomb tests seventy miles away were intriguing but impersonal, until the AEC began civil defense training to prepare Las Vegans for atomic warfare. At North Ninth Street School, where my mother taught second grade, my twin sister Linda and I, and older brother Ron, participated in "Bert the Turtle, Duck and Cover" exercises, crouching under our desks or lying face down on the playground, shielding our eyes and wrapping our arms around our heads.

Soon after testing began, the AEC became part of our community. Anyone who lived in Las Vegas during the 1950s had a family member, neighbor, or acquaintance who worked at the Test Site or attended school with kids whose fathers worked there. Most Las Vegans participated in, or lined up on Fremont Street to watch, one or more of the three Helldorado parades that proceeded up Fremont Street to the Union Pacific Depot on Main Street. Floats celebrating the atomic bomb were featured in the Sunday Beauty Parade, the last of the three parades.[4]

In May 1953, the Las Vegas High School yearbook, the *Wildcat Echo*, displayed an A-bomb blast on its cover.[5] Las Vegas High students were taken out to the football field to watch the flash and mushroom cloud rise over the mountains north of town. Each test series was publicized in the local newspapers. A-bomb tests became so commonplace we paid little attention.

From January 1951 through October 31, 1958, a hundred atomic bombs were exploded in the atmosphere at NTS. In addition, nearly two dozen nuclear devices were detonated in tunnels on Rainier Mesa or in shafts drilled hundreds of feet below Yucca Flat.[6]

There were a few incidents involving atomic testing at NTS that most Las Vegans recall. On May 19, 1953, fallout from an A-bomb test dropped radiation on St. George, Utah. The event was reported in the local newspapers, but there was no television coverage; our first television station began broadcasting in August 1953. The AEC assured us that radiation levels in St. George were not harmful and we believed them.[7]

In the spring of 1955, the AEC began civil defense experiments at NTS to measure the blast effects of an atomic bomb. A fabricated home was constructed at NTS with furniture, appliances, and mannequins of adults and children. The devastation was described in the newspapers and sparked interest in building bomb shelters.[8]

In the fall of 1956, Utah sheep owners, who claimed their sheep were exposed to lethal levels of radiation from aboveground tests in 1953, took their case to trial in Salt Lake City, Utah. On October 23, 1956, the federal judge ruled against them.[9]

In early November 1956, Dwight Eisenhower was re-elected president amidst concerns from noted scientists that fallout from atmospheric tests was polluting the atmosphere and would cause an epidemic of cancers. In 1958, President Eisenhower and Soviet Premier Khrushchev signed a moratorium suspending nuclear testing. The last NTS nuclear test before the moratorium was on October 30, 1958.

Although testing was suspended in 1958 and thousands of displaced NTS workers sought other employment, Las Vegas continued to grow. By 1960, the population was 72,000—three times its population in 1950. Las Vegas had two high schools and one under construction. North Las Vegas had its own high school, Rancho High.

On the evening of January 17, 1961, three days before John Kennedy was sworn in as our new president, Dwight Eisenhower's farewell address to the nation was televised. It was a perplexing speech to a high school student interested in politics, who had participated in the Sun Youth Forum and who would attend Boys State at the University of Nevada in Reno a few months later. Eisenhower's warning about the "military-industrial complex" made little sense to a conservative Republican teenager who had grown up in Las Vegas during the 1950s.

Those who lived through the tranquil 1950s and the turbulent 1960s that followed have vivid memories of the Cuban Missile Crisis, the assassination of President Kennedy, the Vietnam War, the Civil Rights Movement, and the Haight-Ashbury "hippie" counterculture. Fortunately, college, law school, and romance were a wonderful distraction, until I returned to Las Vegas in the fall of 1968, to practice law and start a family. Nuclear testing at the remote Test Site was of little interest, nor could I imagine it would be.

On December 18, 1970, exactly twenty years after NTS was selected as the continental testing site, an underground nuclear test, code named Baneberry, was detonated 912 feet below Yucca Flat. Baneberry, the 666th United States nuclear test, would change my life and the lives of many others.[10]

I learned much from the Baneberry lawsuit about physics, geology, radiation, cytogenetics, and leukemia, especially the horror of leukemia to those afflicted with it and their families. As Alan and I traveled the long Baneberry journey, I learned something I had not expected, something William Pitt warned about in 1770: "Unlimited power is apt to corrupt the minds of those who possess it … where law ends so tyranny begins." I think that is what President Eisenhower was trying to warn us about in his farewell address in 1961.

The Baneberry case was a small piece of a puzzle put together in the 1980s by the actions of individual citizens, courageous scientists, "dreaded" lawyers, a judge in Utah, a jury in Oklahoma City, members of the press, and representatives of the people. When the mosaic was finally pieced together, a frightening picture of an American tragedy was on display for all to see and, hopefully, all to remember.

Baneberry, in retrospect, was perhaps an impossible quest for justice, a dream, at times an un-ending nightmare, but a fascinating, enlightening, disillusioning, and life-altering experience.

NOTES

1. *Las Vegas Review-Journal*, January 11, 1951.
2. The Nevada Proving Grounds was renamed the Nevada Test Site in the mid-1950s.

3. *Las Vegas Review-Journal*, January 28, 1951. Nearly every day from January 28, 1951, through February 6, 1951, banner headlines and photos of the predawn blasts were on the front page of the *Review-Journal*.

4. Ibid., May 18, 1953.

5. We had three copies of *The Wildcat Echo*. My older brother Alan and older sister Judy attended LVHS in 1953; my father taught American history at LVHS.

6. *United States Nuclear Tests July 1945 through September 1992*, DOE/NV-209, REV 15, December 2000.

7. *Las Vegas Review--Journal*, May 19, 1953; *Las Vegas Sun*, May 19, 1953.

8. Ibid., May 6, 1955.

9. Bulloch v. United States, 145 F. Supp. 824 (1956).

10. *United States Nuclear Tests*, 62–63.

[1]

To the Dark Tower

January 16, 1979

"ALL RISE. The United States District Court for the District of Nevada is now in session. The Honorable Roger D. Foley presiding."

The judge ascended the bench, sat down, and banged the gavel. "You may be seated." He looked down at Alan and me and then over at the lawyers seated at the government's table. "This is the time set for the trial of the consolidated cases of *Dorothy Roberts versus the United States of America and Louise Nunamaker versus the United States of America.* Are the parties ready to proceed?"[1]

Dorothy Roberts and Louise Nunamaker looked forlorn and frightened as they heard their names echo across the vaulted courtroom that morning. They glanced nervously at each other and then over at the two young lawyers seated next to them at the plaintiff's table. Dorothy and Louise were the widows of two men who died of leukemia in 1974, less than four years after the men were contaminated by radiation when underground nuclear test Baneberry vented on December 18, 1970.

When we came to court that morning, we had been involved with Baneberry for over eight years but still did not know who gave it that ominous name: Baneberry, a poisonous berry. The root word of Baneberry is *bane*, which is universally defined as a cause of death or ruin, or a deadly poison. The nearly ten-kiloton Baneberry nuclear device, the size of the Hiroshima bomb, was buried 912 feet below the surface at the Nevada Test Site. The blast was supposed to be totally contained to prevent the release of radiation into the atmosphere. In fact, any release would violate the 1963 Nuclear Test Ban Treaty.

But Baneberry did not take orders from the United States of America and did not give a damn about international treaties. Within minutes after it exploded, it ripped a hole to the surface and pumped nearly 7 million curies of radiation up a column of dust and gas into a huge hammerhead-shaped cloud. The radioactive cloud hovered over the test basin three miles east of a base camp in Area 12 where hundreds of workers watched in awe. Had the

AEC cleared the workers out of Area 12 before the test, as in four previous underground tests that week, Dorothy and Louise would not have been in the courtroom that morning. Baneberry, the final test that week and the last test of the year, was scheduled for Friday. The AEC decided to take a chance and left 900 workers in Area 12.

For ten minutes, the black column of radioactive dust and gas continued to feed the ever-expanding Baneberry cloud. Then, suddenly, a large part of the column plummeted to the ground a couple miles south of the Area 12 Camp and began moving up the hill toward the camp.[2] When the test manager in charge of the Baneberry test could no longer ignore Baneberry's movement to engulf the hapless workers, a small band of security guards was mustered to race to the camp to try to evacuate them before they were contaminated.

Dorothy's husband, Harley Roberts, was one of those guards. He and the Baneberry cloud spent nearly an hour together in Area 12 Camp as he rushed the workers out. Harley received the highest radiation dose of the eighty-six men exposed to the Baneberry cloud that day.[3]

Louise's husband, Bill Nunamaker, was one of the men who did not get out before the Baneberry cloud settled on his body and he inhaled its radioactive gas. Bill Nunamaker's radiation dose was only a tenth of that of Harley Roberts's but high enough to require multiple showers to scrub the radiation off his skin and swab out his nasal passages with Q-tips. Yet both men died of acute myeloid leukemia less than four years after their rendezvous with the Baneberry cloud. Their widows suffered through their long and agonizing deaths, watching the bone marrow cancer suck the life out of the men they loved.

The years after Louise buried her husband were hard, but the toll was much worse on Dorothy. She was only fifty-two when she took Harley back home for burial in Bicknell, Indiana, in April 1974. Baneberry took her husband and their life savings. She was left to battle her disabling diabetes with only $178.00 a month in Social Security benefits to pay medical bills, monthly expenses, and a $16,000 hospital bill for Harley's last illness. And, in 1977, things got worse for Dorothy. The IRS threatened to seize her small mobile home for nonpayment of $1,500 in back taxes Harley Roberts owed. Harley and other security guards had taken a deduction for travel pay to the Test Site, which the IRS disallowed.[4]

When Dorothy and Louise came to the office at 8:15 the morning of the trial, neither had slept, worrying about how they would handle their appearance in court and dreading interviews with the reporters they knew would be waiting on the front steps of the federal courthouse.

To avoid the media, we were dropped off near the back courthouse entrance and raced inside to the elevators. But as we waited for the ding of the elevator, a reporter spotted us and bolted over in time to snap a photograph of Dorothy, Louise, and Alan.[5] When the elevator doors opened, we scurried inside to avoid an interview.

We entered the courtroom, escorted our clients through the swinging bar of the court, and seated them at the plaintiffs' counsel table. On our side of the courtroom, our secretary, Kathy Trout, came in and sat in the front row right behind us.

At the government's table, several attorneys were already seated. Bill Elliott was nearest to us. He was from the Justice Department in Washington, D.C. and lead trial counsel for the government. He scowled a sort of acknowledgment as he glanced our way through narrow slits wrapped in folds that hung over his eyelids. When Elliott first joined the defense team in 1977, we tried to be cordial, particularly Alan, who got along with nearly everybody. But during the trial, Elliott's arrogant attitude and contempt for "the Baneberry widows" surfaced in a newspaper article. A reporter asked him how much the government intended to spend to defend the case. "As much as it takes to win," he boasted.[6]

Seated next to him was John Thorndal, head of the local private law firm prospering from the hundreds of thousands of dollars in legal fees it had racked up to carry out Mr. Elliott's pledge.[7] Well over a dozen lawyers and staff from Thorndal's firm, the U.S. Attorney's office, and the local office of the Atomic Energy Commission milled around in several rows on the government's side of the courtroom.

Every nerve pulsed in the pit of my stomach as I sat there. I felt like a sprinter in the starting blocks waiting for the gun. It had all come down to this. The fate of the women made widows by Baneberry was now in the hands of one frail, elderly federal judge, who would hear the evidence and ultimately decide some of the most complex scientific issues of the age. At stake was the United States' thirty-five-year love affair with the atomic bomb and the credibility of the Atomic Energy Commission, which had assured Nevadans and all Americans that its atomic testing program caused harm to no one.

The Baneberry test was headline news in both Las Vegas newspapers on Saturday, December 19, 1970, the day after it erupted.[8] But at the time, it was of no interest to Alan and me. We were furnishing our law office and preparing to open for business on January 2, 1971. Little did we know that a few months later Baneberry would disrupt our fledgling legal practice and become a dominant part of our lives for the next twenty-five years.

This is my story about Baneberry and how it beguiled my brother Alan and me into embarking on a quest to hold the Atomic Energy Commission responsible for the deaths of Harley Roberts and Bill Nunamaker. Baneberry was an alluring and irresistible challenge for two young lawyers who had grown up in Las Vegas with memories of the town before the AEC came in 1951 and who believed that the AEC could be held accountable, like anyone else, under what we thought was the best and fairest judicial system the world had ever known.

NOTES

1. *Baneberry Collection*, MS 19, Special Collections, UNLV Libraries, University of Nevada–Las Vegas. The Trial Transcript, hereinafter "TR" is 5,404 pages in length. Unless quoted, the trial testimony is summarized.

2. Films and videotapes of the Baneberry vent were classified. We had to file motions to compel their release. In 1975 the court allowed us to view the films and videotapes at the AEC building. But we were subject to a protective order that precluded us from copying or reproducing the films or communicating information to anyone about them. On October 6, 1977, the AEC released to the press a black-and-white photo of the Baneberry vent cloud (*Las Vegas Review-Journal*, October 6, 1977). In the photo the portion of the Baneberry cloud that plunged to the ground is on the left or west side and looks like a wolf's head. Rainier Mesa, where Area 12 Camp and the tunnel complexes were located, is behind and left of the column. On March 8, 1979, the government showed selected portions of the films at trial (*Las Vegas Review-Journal*, March 9, 1979).

3. *Baneberry Collection*, EX 66. References are to trial exhibits. EX 66 is the *Baneberry Summary Report*. Figure 1 tabulated the exposures of the eighty-six men exposed at Baneberry but did not identify them. On June 27, 1977, after we filed multiple motions to compel the government to produce the radiation readings for the eighty-six men, the court ordered the government to supply a list of each man exposed and his radiation dose. EX 91 disclosed Roberts's and Nunamaker's radiation doses.

4. *Las Vegas Review-Journal*, May 22, 1977.

5. Ibid., January 17, 1979.

6. *Los Angeles Herald Examiner*, March 11, 1979.

7. *Las Vegas Sun*, May 25, 1979. In hearings before the House Oversight and Investigations Subcommittee in May 1979, William Shaffer, deputy assistant attorney general, testified, "the government spent more than $500,000 in 46 days of [the Baneberry] trial."

8. *Las Vegas Sun*, December 19, 1970; *Las Vegas Review-Journal*, December 19, 1970.

[2]

Thar She Blows

December 18, 1970

AT 6:45 AM, Harley Roberts pulled next to the trailer at security station BJY and slammed the door of his pickup truck. He stepped briskly over fresh patches of snow left from an overnight dusting and walked up to the trailer. As he opened the door, he heard his brother-in-law, Ernie Dyer, in a heated argument with the shift captain. Ernie's face was bright red. "Orders are orders, Dyer," the captain shouted. "Calm down. There's nothing you can do about it."[1]

Harley walked over and stood next to Ernie. The two men were quite a contrast. Ernie Dyer was nearly six feet, 170 pounds, bald, with penetrating blue-gray eyes. Harley was five nine, 145 pounds, with thinning brown hair and sparkling blue eyes. Ernie was assertive with a shrill, cocky, somewhat sarcastic voice. Harley was laid back, and his voice was jocular with a deep, nasal tone.

They were both fifth-generation Hoosiers whose great-great-grandfathers settled in western Indiana before the mid-1850s. Both came to Las Vegas in the 1960s to join the security force at the Nevada Test Site. Ernie came first. He and Harley's sister, Dixie, were living in Phoenix in April 1961, when he saw an ad in the newspaper for a security job at NTS. He drove to Las Vegas for an interview, passed the physical exam, and was hired immediately. Dyer was one of five in the first security training class; Bill Cleghorn was one of the others. Dyer and Cleghorn came to NTS in May 1961 to help secure the site for the resumption of nuclear testing that had been suspended since October 30, 1958.[2]

The Test Site was the home of the most amazing man-made spectacle the world had ever seen. Tens of thousands of soldiers and civilians had been part of the nation's grand nuclear experiment. The broad test basin was littered with concrete foundations sprouting twisted metal, residue of fifty atomic bombs detonated on steel towers as high as 700 feet above the desert floor. Trenches where tens of thousands of soldiers huddled waiting for the shock wave from the blasts were still visible, although sagebrush and Russian thistle had conquered much of the landscape. The huge tunnel portals on the Rainier Mountain Range were closed, but the rails and rail cars still waited for crews to return to cut drifts deeper and deeper.

On September 1, 1961, the Soviets detonated the first nuclear device since the October 31, 1958, moratorium. On September 15, 1961, President Kennedy responded with the United States' first underground nuclear test, Antler, detonated in a reopened tunnel in the Rainier Range.[3] The nuclear arms race was on again.

But tunnel tests were not enough to satisfy the hunger for experimentation. The largest drill rigs in the country were hauled onto the Test Site to drill shafts over seven feet in diameter and up to 1,000 feet below the desert floor to emplace nuclear devices.[4]

Reopening the Test Site for underground tests in tunnels and shafts required the expertise of geologists, hydrogeologists, physicists, geophysicists, and other scientists, if the multikiloton blasts were to be completely contained. The excavation workforce needed engineers, muckers, miners, drillers, heavy equipment operators, laborers, plumbers, teamsters, and various support personnel. The Test Site was transformed from an atmospheric laboratory into a catacomb as thousands of workers descended on the site to dig, dump, and detonate a nuclear device in every crack and cranny that could be carved quickly and filled with a nuclear device.

Harley and Dorothy Roberts had stayed in close contact with the Dyers after Ernie went to work at the Test Site in 1961. When Ernie and Dixie came to Indiana for Christmas in 1961, Ernie bragged to Harley about his new job with good union wages and a pension. He tried to talk Harley into moving to Las Vegas to join him at the site. But Harley was not interested. He liked his small-town lifestyle. He fished and camped with his wife and son, played golf with a group of friends, and competed on a town basketball team. Other than a short stint in the military and his job at a defense plant in Detroit during the war, he had lived his entire life in western Indiana.

Over the next four years, the Dyers frequently returned to Indiana. They were persistent and wanted the Robertses to join them in Las Vegas. By the fall of 1965, Harley was ready for a change. His mother and sister had now followed the Dyers to Las Vegas. He had operated his own small service station, worked as a route-man delivering soda pop, and for the past couple years had run an insurance agency. Yet despite a lifetime of hard work, he had not saved much for retirement. At forty-five, he was still in excellent physical condition. He figured he could work at the Test Site until he was sixty-five. In twenty years, he and Dorothy could move back to Indiana with some savings, a company pension, and Social Security benefits.

Harley applied for a security job at the Test Site. In the fall of 1965, he came to Las Vegas for an interview and passed his physical exam. On New Year's Day 1966, Harley, Dorothy, and their fifteen-year-old son, Randy, drove into Las Vegas.

When Harley reported to security station BJY shortly before 7:00 am on December 18, 1970, he had been working at the Test Site for nearly five years. He was a good sounding board for his more vocal brother-in-law; this morning was no different. Ernie walked Harley to the other end of the trailer to get away from the captain.

"What's got you so pissed off?" Harley half whispered.

"Does it show?" Ernie scowled and without waiting for a reply related the events during the long night. "I got here at six last evening and asked the captain when we were going to sweep Area 12. You know what he said? 'Ernie, they're leaving Area 12 open for this shot.' I couldn't believe it. How could they possibly leave nearly 1,000 workers only a few miles from the shot point? If the damned thing blew, it would dump radiation on them before they could clear out.

"I asked him to call headquarters to make sure. He said he had already confirmed the orders and was not going to call and question them. I kept bugging him until he finally called. He put the blame on me, said the night shift sergeant was demanding that he confirm that they weren't going to evacuate Area 12 for this test. He put the phone close to my ear so I could hear the chief tell him the orders were correct and were going to be carried out.

"Harley, you know we swept Area 12 for four previous shots this week. This shot is a lot closer to Area 12 Camp than any of the others."

"Yeah," Harley affirmed.

"That's what I told the captain. He blew me off; reminded me that none of the prior tests vented, so why should we worry about this one."

"I guess he's got a point," Harley noted.

"Yeah. Anyway, I let it go. We went out to sweep east from the guard station outside Area 12 Camp up through Areas 8 and 15 and then south to the station here at BJY. After we finished around midnight, me and the captain went at it again. I flat told him it was crazy to leave Area 12 open and demanded he call and try to get the orders changed. He was getting pretty hot and wouldn't call. So, I pointed out we only had the two guards posted near Area 12 Camp. If it vented, there was no way in hell they could move a thousand workers out of there.

"He wouldn't budge, so I tried another angle. I asked him to call headquarters to see if we could put sixteen guards up at Area 12 Camp just in case. He knew I wouldn't shut up until he called. So, he finally called and got the same bullshit response. I asked him to try to get permission to put eight men up there. He asked, but they told him to drop it. We went out and finished our second sweep at around three. At six o'clock, we cleared the arming party to go up and activate the device. I've been bitching ever since."

Ernie sighed and continued. "You know everybody had a bad feeling about this Baneberry test all along. They had problems drilling the hole; a lot more than any test anybody can remember. They had to postpone the damn thing several times. It just doesn't make sense to cram all these tests into the last week of the year and end with this one."

When Ernie finished, the rest of the day-shift guards had checked in at the security trailer at BJY. Dyer told them to stand by for shift change.

From the north window of the trailer, the Baneberry site, where the nuclear device had been lowered 912 feet down the hole, was in plain view nine miles away. As the sun crested above the eastern mountain range, the broad test basin, patched with fresh snow, sparkled in the bright winter sun. The Rainier Range to the northwest also had a light blanket of snow. Carved deep into the mountains were the massive tunnel complexes filled with hundreds of workers nearing the end of their shift. The tunnel portals were not visible, but Area 12 Camp, perched on a plateau at the base of the range, was in plain view, as the roofs of its metal buildings reflected the sun.

Area 12 Camp was built to provide housing and facilities for the thousands of workers who poured shift after shift in and out of the tunnels. There were over 300 rental trailers for temporary housing. In addition, the camp had a cafeteria, movie theater, recreation hall, library, baseball field, tennis and basketball courts, and a fire station.

A quarter mile east of Area 12 Camp, two security guards were posted in a shack on Rainier Mesa Road. Bob Yager and George Holly had worked all night ahead of the countdown. They had a clear view of the Baneberry site down the hill three miles away.

Tom Hayes, a radiation safety monitor, or "Rad-Safe monitor," employed by Reynolds Electrical and Engineering Company, REECo, sat in his pickup truck at the same location. A few minutes prior to shot time, Hayes put on his protective gear, rubber boots, rubber gloves, full-body coveralls with orange vest, and hood. He also had a facemask with air filters to avoid inhaling any radioactive dust and rolls of masking tape to seal the seams of his gear to prevent any skin contact with radioactive material.

At the Area 12 cafeteria, hundreds of day-shift workers were finishing breakfast and preparing to board buses up to the tunnel portals to relieve the night crew. Bill Nunamaker, shop foreman at T Tunnel, was sipping a final cup of coffee. He had driven nearly a hundred miles from Las Vegas that morning.

The main entrance to the cafeteria faced southeast, with a view of the Baneberry site and the entire test basin below. The basin was pockmarked with craters from hundreds of underground tests; the largest was the mammoth 1962 *Sedan* crater nearly 1,300 feet in diameter and 300 feet deep. It was a landscape like none other on earth. But the high-desert vegetation had already reclaimed much of the cratered ground.[5]

Behind the Area 12 cafeteria, atop a pole fifteen feet above the surface, sat a radiation detection device. Hardwired to the operation control center, CP-1, nineteen miles south, it was the only permanent radiation-measuring device in the one-square mile Area 12 Camp.

Dyer and Roberts moved over to the window at 7:25 am to listen to the countdown. Nine miles south of BJY, Frank Cluff, the Baneberry test manager, and his advisory panel were at the control point, CP-1. They were seated around a conference table talking and staring at screens displaying images of the Baneberry site transmitted from closed-circuit cameras around surface ground zero.

Cluff and his panel had met for a readiness briefing at 2:30 pm the day prior to Baneberry. At that meeting, orders were given to clear all personnel from areas one quarter mile east of Area 12 Camp, where security guards George Holly and Robert Yager were posted. But Area 12 Camp and the tunnel complexes in Area 12 were left open. At that meeting, fallout predictions were discussed if Baneberry were to vent. One panel member, V. Urban commented, "If Fred's Folly were to erupt tomorrow, I will try to guess." He went on to make predictions about where the vent cloud might move.[6]

When the panel met again for a final briefing at 5:15 am on December 18, 1970, all areas one-quarter mile east of Area 12 Camp had been swept during the night. But no one reported that Sergeant Dyer had repeatedly called to challenge the decision to leave Area 12 Camp open or that he had requested permission to place a guard force near Area 12 Camp in case Baneberry vented. Cluff and his panel were confident that Baneberry posed no "apparent threat to either personnel or the Test Ban Treaty" and directed the device be armed at 6:00 am.[7]

When the countdown reached zero, Dyer and Roberts looked north out the trailer window and saw a cloud of dust rise over the Baneberry site as the chimney above the vaporized cavity 900 feet below the surface transmitted the force of the explosion to the surface. From their guard shack, Yager and Holly looked three miles down the hill at the Baneberry site and saw a circular plume of dust swirl around ground zero. Seconds later, their building shuddered. Workers in the tunnels also felt the shock wave pass through the rock under their feet and waited for the all clear. In the Area 12 cafeteria, the dayshift crews felt the ground move and knew it was time to get ready for the eight o'clock shift change.

At CP-1, the test manager and his advisors watched the screens blur as the cameras around ground zero bounced up and down from the force of the underground blast and then stabilized, recording a 200-foot-diameter circle of dust leap a hundred feet into the air. The test manager's primary duty was to assure that the underground test was completely contained. If he failed and the test vented radiation into the atmosphere, it was his responsibility to make sure the workers were evacuated to avoid radiation exposure.

Two minutes after the shot, the captain chided Dyer, "See, I told you Dyer, nothing to worry about." Dyer and Roberts walked away from the window. There was a collective sigh of relief all over the Test Site. The scientists in charge of the test began preparing to drive up to the Baneberry site to collect data from instruments housed in trailers stationed on a grid several hundred yards south of surface ground zero.

A minute later, the test basin silence was shattered by a thunderous sound as a column of dust and smoke shot a thousand feet above the Baneberry site and kept climbing. At the control point, the images on the screens bounced again, as the cameras shook from the force of the eruption. After a few seconds, the cameras began to stabilize, showing black smoke pouring from a 300-foot-long fissure. To the film crew aboard a helicopter circling the site at about 10,000 feet, fire seemed to erupt the full length of the 300-foot crevice.[8]

Deep below the surface, the core of the Baneberry nuclear device exploded in the wet clay deposit in which it had been placed, producing a super-heated, gas-filled cauldron and isotopes measuring in millions of curies. Roiling and churning against the walls of the spherical cavity, the radioactive stew of pressurized gas probed the substrata until it found a weak point. A fault line tangent to the cavity provided a seam and pathway upward. The pressurized gas ripped open the seam and followed the crack several hundred feet upward, then blew open a 300-foot-long crevice to the surface, spewing gas and charred dust high into the atmosphere.

In the trailer at station BJY, everyone ran to the north window to watch the enormous column climb 8,000 feet above the desert floor and then top out in a huge hammerhead-shaped cloud. Most of the men in the trailer that morning came to NTS in the 1960s and had only seen pictures of the spectacular A-bomb blasts in the 1950s. Baneberry, with its black column and distorted billowing top, resembled the surface tests, although it was detonated far below ground.

In the Area 12 cafeteria, someone yelled and hundreds ran outside to watch the column rise and billow. As they stared, the column and cloud cast a massive shadow over the test basin just south. For most, it was their first glimpse of an atomic test, and they were riveted by the spectacle, paralyzed, waiting for orders. The explosion had not been contained. Now the test manager had to try to figure out where the radiation released into the atmosphere would go. He ran outside the trailer and watched helplessly as the radioactive cloud nearly eighteen miles north of his trailer swelled.

Test Manager Frank Cluff was a meteorologist, uniquely qualified to gauge the movement of the Baneberry cloud. There were wind instruments and radiation detection devices scattered across the site to help him make the right decision. The first radiation measurement came from a device 1,000 feet west of surface ground zero. It maxed out at 1,000 R or 100,000 mR and probably registered 10,000 R or more. But 1,000 R was enough to kill anyone exposed to that dose. Fortunately, the nearest people were the two security guards and the RadSafe monitor three miles west near Area 12 Camp. But trailers on a grid nearby were filled with instruments to collect data from the test. The intense gamma radiation penetrated them and fried equipment and data.

The test manager waited. Five minutes after the venting, an instrument on a thirty-foot tower 1,500 feet west of ground zero reported surface winds heading southwesterly. But at that point, the rising cloud was 8,000 feet above the ground. The test manager was not concerned.

At 7:40 am, while the column was still feeding the ever-expanding cloud at its top, a large chunk of the column plummeted several thousand feet to the valley floor. A photographer aboard a helicopter circling the site filmed the collapse and the cloud of radioactive dust that settled over the basin. Within minutes, the falling dust cloud formed two arms that looked like huge black snakes and began slithering up the mesa toward Area 12 Camp.

At 7:43 am, the 800-foot chimney of rock and dirt collapsed into the spherical Baneberry cavity, producing a dust cloud and crater several hundred feet in diameter and seventy-five feet deep. Normally, the cratering of a device seals off any further radioactive release from the cavern below. But Baneberry defied the norm. Nine hundred feet below the surface, pockets of compressed radioactive gas continued belching radiation to the surface. This lasted for the next twenty-four hours until the last bubble was depleted.

The test manager was transfixed as he received reports of the progress of the swirling surface cloud hovering in the basin south of Area 12 Camp. At 7:45 am Rad-Safe monitor Troy Ellis and four other monitors were on Stockade Wash Road at the head of a caravan of thirty-five to forty-five cars and three buses proceeding east to Area 12. Ellis called to tell his supervisors that the cloud was heading straight toward Area 12 Camp and asked permission to set up a roadblock to intercept all vehicles heading east into Area 12. He was told the cloud was not going to Area 12 Camp. Along with nearly two hundred other workers, he drove on into Area 12.

Just after part of the column plunged to the desert floor, Yager and Holly called to report that the cloud was moving up the hill toward them and asked permission to move west to the Area 12 Camp entrance. The request was denied. Although not a meteorologist or one those "critters that are supposed to chase winds," Yager knew why the radioactive dust cloud was moving up the hill toward his location. Having spent a lifetime in the outdoors fishing and camping, he knew that as the sun began to warm the desert basin, the surface winds were going to head uphill "like the dickens." It was a phenomenon well known to firefighters. He stood on the plateau and watched the cloud climb toward him.[9]

At 7:35 am, Walter Adkins sat in his bus in the parking lot outside the Area 12 cafeteria as Bill Nunamaker and others boarded for the ride up to T Tunnel. When the bus arrived at T Tunnel at 7:50 am, Nunamaker went to his shop just inside the portal.

On any other morning, Adkins would have driven his bus back down to Area 12 Camp. But the T Tunnel supervisor could see the Baneberry cloud approaching and instructed Adkins to stand by. Adkins turned his bus around facing downhill and got a first-hand view of the cloud as it moved up the canyon toward him.

At station BJY, Dyer was tired and frustrated. He had pleaded with his supervisor to evacuate Area 12 and had worked nearly fourteen hours when *Baneberry* vented. At 7:43, he and the others watched a large chunk of the column fall to the ground blocking their view of Area 12 Camp, sealing off the direct route from BJY into Area 12.

By 7:47 am, the test manager's last hope that the surface winds would turn away from Area 12 Camp was dashed. The wind instrument recorded surface winds moving westerly toward Area 12 Camp. The test manager needed a miracle to stop the cloud from blanketing the camp.

Rad-Safe monitor Tom Hayes, at the same location as Yager and Holly, called his supervisor at 7:50 and asked permission to move a quarter-mile west on Rainier Mesa Road to the entrance to Area 12 Camp. His request was denied. Hayes watched the grayish-tan wall of fine ash particles move toward his position and called again at 8:00 am. He was told to hold fast until the readings were above background. While Hayes was on the phone, his Geiger counter began to click as it picked up the first readings. When the instrument pegged out on its lower scale, 20 mR gamma, he switched to the higher scale, 20–200 mR gamma, as the readings rose to 50 mR.[10]

At CP-1, the test manager had ignored calls from the Rad-Safe monitors and reports from crews aboard helicopters that the cloud was moving toward Area 12 Camp. But he could not ignore the radiation readings Hayes reported from his station on the road a quarter mile south of Area 12 Camp. For five minutes Cluff hesitated. But at 8:05 am, when no doubt remained that the Area 12 Camp was Baneberry's target, test manager Cluff gave the order to conduct an emergency evacuation to remove the 900 workers trapped in Area 12 Camp and the nearby tunnel complexes.

On December 10, 1970, the *Test Manager's Operation Plan for Baneberry*, signed by Frank Cluff, outlined all pre and post-Baneberry activities. Item 18 was directed to Reynolds Electrical and Engineering Company (REECo), the prime contractor at NTS that employed all Rad-Safe monitors. It stated: "No.18. — H-30 min. [7:00 am] — REECo Rad/safe will provide standby teams of monitors to be used in an emergency situation as directed by the TM."[11]

Even earlier than the test manager's Baneberry Plan, on April 1, 1969, the AEC adopted *Chapter 0544 EMERGENCIES IN AEC OPERATIONS*. Its stated objective was "to provide maximum practical protection of AEC and AEC contractor personnel."[12] It required that emergency plans be prepared and periodically tested. REECo was to prepare "written emergency plans for the evacuation of personnel in Area 12 Camp" and designate an "Area 12 Camp coordinator to carry out the evacuation."[13]

At 8:05 am on December 18, 1970, when the test manager finally gave the order to start the evacuation of Area 12 Camp, there was no evacuation plan for Area 12 Camp and no designated Area 12 Camp evacuation coordinator. More important, REECo did not have teams of Rad-Safe monitors standing by thirty minutes before shot time to conduct an emergency evacuation.[14]

Without any of the above, Cluff gave the order to evacuate Area 12 to AEC security chief Chan Griffin, who directed Wackenhut Services Inc. (WSI), the security contractor at NTS, to implement the order immediately. Sergeant Ernie Dyer, the highest-ranking WSI field officer in the forward area, was ordered to gather as many men as possible and carry out the evacuation.

The only emergency warning device in the one-square mile Area 12 Camp was a siren at the fire station. But the firemen on duty did not turn it on. In fact, it was not activated until 8:40 am, after Dyer arrived and demanded that it be turned on.

Even without orders, the workers in Area 12 Camp saw the looming cloud and realized they had to get out fast. The Area 12 cafeteria chief knew what to do. He shut down the registers, closed the cafeteria, and told everyone to get the hell out of the camp. Guards Holly and Yager, stationed at the entrance to the camp, blocked the route east and funneled the fleeing workers west onto Stockade Wash Road away from the cloud.

When the order to evacuate was conveyed to the T Tunnel supervisor, the workers raced out of the portal and boarded buses or jumped into their vehicles and headed down the canyon and into Area 12 Camp. Walter Adkins's bus was full, as he headed into the oncoming cloud. Fine grayish particles fell like snowflakes, covering the bus. Some of the passengers tried to seal the windows by sticking paper in the cracks. When they arrived in Area 12 Camp, the cloud had already settled there. They carpooled in private vehicles and headed out.

When Dyer received the order just after 8:05 am, he left one man at station BJY and mustered thirteen security guards to assist him. Because the cloud blocked the ten-mile direct road into Area 12 Camp, Dyer and his men took a circuitous twenty-five-mile route, driving seventy miles per hour on icy roads and arriving in Area 12 Camp at around 8:30 am.

When Dyer passed Rad-Safe monitor Hayes's location at 8:30, Hayes's Geiger counter had maxed out at 200 mR gamma. He switched to a Pic6A instrument that fluctuated wildly between 500 and 800 mR gamma. Hayes assumed the instrument was saturated by high readings in the cloud and called for another Rad-Safe monitor to come by and take readings. Rad-Safe monitor Ron Perry arrived at 9:00 am and recorded a reading of 1,500 mR gamma.[15]

As mentioned, the only radiation device in Area 12 Camp was the probe atop a fifteen-foot pole behind the cafeteria, hard–wired to the control point. Like Hayes's Geiger counter, it was designed to measure only gamma radiation. Handwritten notes taken down at CP-1, showed that gamma readings reached a maximum of 700 mR at around 9:00 am.

It was cold that December morning, and all the security guards wore standard uniforms of heavy flight jackets with an imitation fur collar that collected radioactive particles from the cloud. And since the guards were not expected to enter a radiation field, they did not wear hats or gloves to prevent the swirling radioactive particles in the cloud from collecting in their hair and sticking to faces and hands. Jack Cupples, one of guards who evacuated Area 12 Camp that morning, tied a handkerchief around his face, bandana style, to try to reduce the amount of radiation he drew into his mouth and nose.

At his command post on the main road below the Area 12 cafeteria, Dyer took charge. He ordered the guards to fan out over the one-square-mile camp and clear personnel from all buildings. Harley Roberts and one other guard were ordered to clear all personnel in trailers on the far eastern end of the camp.

Roberts left his truck at the command post and sprinted a quarter mile down the hill to Rainier Street. In the grayish fog-like haze, he raced from trailer to trailer beating on doors ordering the occupants out. Passing the window of one of the trailers he saw his face reflected. It was ghostly white with an almost ashen hue from the dust that covered his entire face. At another trailer window, he caught a fleeting image that haunted him for his remaining days. His head appeared to be x-rayed against the glass panel. Absent hair, skin, and flesh, only the skull stared back at him.

Roberts cleared over seventy-five trailers in about forty-five minutes. Breathing rapidly, he sucked the radioactive gas and dust deep into his lungs and was assaulted from every angle by the penetrating gamma rays. At 9:15 am, he raced back up the hill and reported to Sergeant Dyer that all trailers in his sector were clear. He was the last man to report. The other guards had completed their assignments ten minutes earlier and left the camp.

After Dyer set up his command post and ordered the guards to begin the evacuation, he went down to the fire station to find out why the emergency siren was not sounding the evacuation warning. The firemen curtly told him they had not received any orders and would have to check with their chief. Dyer demanded they get the chief on the phone. They were defiant, so Dyer called AEC security. Minutes later, the fire chief ordered his men to "turn on the damned siren." By the time the siren went off, the evacuation was already well underway.

When Roberts reported back to Dyer at 9:15 am, he was ordered to head west on Stockade Wash Road and then up G Tunnel Road to make sure all personnel in G Tunnel were out. Dyer headed back down to the fire station and told the firemen to leave. They again refused until they got orders. After the earlier episode and over fifteen hours on the job, Dyer's patience was spent. Though tempted to order the firemen out at gunpoint, he called AEC security again. A minute later the order came. The firemen shut off the evacuation siren and left in a huff.

By the time the evacuation was complete, the Baneberry cloud had passed over Area 12 Camp. The metal roofs no longer sparkled in the bright morning sun. Everything was covered with ash and dust. Dyer pulled out of Area 12 Camp at 8:30 am. Ordering the security guard and Hayes to precede him, Dyer's pickup truck was last in a line of over 400 vehicles winding west up Stockade Wash Road to Area 17 Camp. He remained at the end of the convoy until all vehicles had reached the Area 17 checkpoint.

NOTES

1. Based on personal interviews with Harley Roberts and Ernest Dyer.

2. *United States Nuclear Tests, July 1945 through September 1992*, DOE/NV-209-REV 15, December 2000, 16–23. *Antler*, the first shot after testing resumed on September 15, 1961, blew out the tunnel portal and released radiation offsite, as did tunnel tests *Feather, Platte*, and *Des Moines*.

3. *United States Nuclear Tests, July 1945 through September 1992*, DOE/NV-209-REV 15, December 2000, 16–17.

4. Ibid., 16–26. *Operation Nougat* consisted of forty-four underground tests beginning with *Antler* on September 15, 1961, and ending with *Sacramento* on June 30, 1962. The next test at NTS was *Sedan*, the first of the *Plowshare* tests designed to determine the feasibility of using nuclear blasts to dig a canal across Central America.

5. *United States Nuclear Tests, July 1945 through September 1992*, DOE/NV-209-REV 15, December 2000, 24–25. The crater from the 104-kiloton Sedan underground nuclear test, 320 feet deep and 1,280 feet in diameter, released radiation off-site, as did crater or surface tests *Johnnie Boy, Small Boy*, and *Little Feller II.*

6. *Baneberry Collection*, EX 2. Test Evaluation Panel Readiness Briefing Notes, p. 3. Urban's Report, EX 27, projected the fallout pattern and dosage estimates for offsite populations but did not consider the possibility that workers in Area 12, just three miles from surface ground zero, might be exposed to the radioactive cloud.

7. *Baneberry Collection*, EX 3, Readiness Briefing Notes, 5:15 am.

8. We did not see films of the Baneberry venting until 1975, after we filed multiple motions to compel their release. On October 6, 1977, the AEC released a photo of the Baneberry vent showing the huge hammerhead-shaped cloud. *Las Vegas Review-Journal*, October 6, 1977.

9. *Baneberry Collection*, TR.

10. The Geiger counters Hayes and all Rad-Safe monitors carried on December 18, 1970, measured only penetrating gamma radiation, not Beta particles present in the cloud.

11. *Baneberry Collection*, EX 9.

12. Ibid., EX 5.

13. Ibid., EX 7.

14. Ibid., EX 49. A list of all REECo radiological safety personnel on duty the day of Baneberry disclosed that there were 109 personnel, including fifty-nine Rad-Safe monitors in the field. But only one, Tom Hayes, was posted near Area 12 camp at shot time.

15. A standard chest x-ray delivers a gamma dose of about 30 mR.

[3]

The Luck of the Draw

AT 9:25 AM, Roberts left Dyer and drove out of the camp. As he left, the last remnant of the Baneberry vent cloud was moving up and over the Rainier Range. It was as if Harley Roberts had been Baneberry's primary target, and when he left it had no reason to linger.

Following orders, Roberts drove several miles up Stockade Wash Road and turned right to check out G Tunnel. A half mile up the narrow canyon, he met a security guard who told him all personnel were out of G Tunnel. Roberts turned around and followed him back to Stockade Wash Road and joined the long line of vehicles heading west up the mountain road. At the top of the hill, Rad-Safe monitors were stopping everyone to take readings with their Geiger counters. Roberts waited his turn.

As monitor Troy Ellis ran his instrument over Roberts's pickup truck, still coated with a layer of ash and dust, Roberts rolled down his window and heard the Geiger counter clicking wildly.

"Better have you step out and move away from the truck, so I can take a reading on you," Ellis ordered.

Roberts got out and Ellis motioned him over to the side of the road. Ellis held his Geiger counter thirty inches from Roberts's upper body and turned on the instrument. It whirred frantically as the needle hit the right side of the dial on the instrument. Ellis switched to the highest scale. It whirred again to pure static as the needle pegged at its maximum reading of 200 mR gamma.

"Man. You're hot as hell," Ellis exclaimed. "You need to be decontaminated as soon as possible. Get in your truck and proceed past the convoy and report to Area 17 Camp. I'll call ahead so they'll be looking for you."

Ellis had been monitoring evacuees for over an hour. All other security guards involved in the evacuation, except Dyer, had already passed his checkpoint. None had readings nearly as high as Roberts. Ellis called his supervisor, gave him Roberts's name and badge number, and told him the readings pegged his instrument and that Roberts needed to be deconned as soon as possible.

Harley figured he was hot. He had been in the cloud for nearly an hour. But so were the other guards who helped evacuate the camp. He assumed they were about as hot as he was. He jumped in his truck, sped past the long line of cars, and pulled into Area 17 Camp. He walked up to the security trailer, cracked the door, and told the captain, "Better stay away from me. A Rad-Safe guy said I'm hot as hell and need to be deconned."

The captain in charge at Area 17 Camp was not involved in the evacuation of Area 12. His job was to organize the convoy of vehicles and move them to the decontamination facility at CP-2 for monitoring. He seemed unconcerned by Harley's comment and waved him off. Roberts closed the door and walked over to join several other security guards standing nearby.

After about ten minutes, the captain opened the door, rushed over to where Harley and other guards were standing, and said he just got orders to post a guard at Dead Horse Flats to close off incoming traffic from the north. He picked Roberts to post the blockade and said he would get a Rad-Safe man to join him. Roberts did not remind the captain that a Rad-Safe monitor had told him he was "hot as hell" and should be decontaminated. He obeyed the order.

Roberts was teamed up with Rad-Safe monitor Willie Virgil, who had recently completed his training. Virgil grabbed his equipment and jumped in Roberts's pickup. They left Area 17 at around 9:50 and took the road up through the canyon into Area 19 to Dead Horse Flats. Radio reception was poor. Roberts drove around for several minutes to find a spot with fair reception. He parked his vehicle in the middle of the road and called headquarters to report that the roadblock was in place.

After they settled in for what they knew would be a long day, Roberts told Virgil about the evacuation of the camp and that a monitor on Stockade Wash Road told him he was hot as hell. When Virgil heard this, he said he should take some readings of Roberts and his vehicle. Roberts got out of the truck and Virgil told him to move twenty to thirty feet away from the vehicle. There, Virgil turned on his Geiger counter and held it chest high about thirty inches from Roberts. It made the same sound Harley had heard hour earlier. Virgil told Roberts he was registering around 300 mR gamma, and his vehicle was reading around 90 mR gamma. But Virgil seemed unconcerned about Roberts's readings and did not ask to use his radio to report them to his supervisor.

For the next six hours Roberts and Virgil sat in the truck. Virgil told Roberts he reported for duty that morning at 8:00 am and watched the cloud moving toward Area 12 Camp. He and two other monitors spent fifteen minutes hunting for instruments and were stationed on Stockade Wash Road, several miles west of Area 12 Camp. Virgil was never in the cloud that passed over Area 12 Camp and was not exposed to any radiation.[1]

At around 10:00 am, ten minutes after Roberts left Area 17 Camp, Dyer pulled in next to the security trailer. He opened the door and confronted the captain in charge. He demanded to know what the orders were for his guards. Dyer had worked seventeen straight hours. He was tired and angry. His men had carried out an evacuation that should have been done by Rad-Safe personnel. The captain called headquarters and spoke to WSI Captain Tackett. Dyer and his security force were given top priority and were directed to proceed immediately to CP-2 for decontamination. "Damn right," Dyer said angrily. "We got the dirty work no one else would do. They better take care of us."

Dyer stormed out and rounded up eleven of the guards who helped him evacuate Area 12 Camp. Two were missing, Harley Roberts and Carl Peterson. Dyer told his men to get in their trucks and follow him down to the CP for decontamination. With sirens blaring, they passed the convoy slowly snaking its way down Pahute Mesa Road. Dyer got on the phone and called Captain Tackett to see if he had any information about Roberts and Peterson. Ten minutes later, Tackett called to tell him that Peterson had been located and was behind them on the way to CP-2. But no one knew where Roberts was.

The REECo Rad-Safe decontamination pad was situated at CP-2, near CP-1, where the test manager and his advisors were located. When Dyer and his men arrived, the Rad-Safe monitors were waiting. They ordered the guards to remove their clothing, wrote down readings of their clothing, and placed them in plastic bags marked with each guard's name. The film in their identification credential was removed and placed in a box for processing. Then the guards themselves were monitored. All readings far exceeded the 25 mR gamma reading for required decontamination. They were told to swab out their nasal passages with a Q-tip. A Geiger counter was run over the Q-tips and the readings recorded for each.

Then they were ordered into the showers. When the showers were turned on, ice-cold water streamed out. The guards complained but were told the boiler was broken and they would have to take cold showers. Hair thick with ash and dust, faces chalky, and nasal passages encrusted with radioactive particulate, they entered the cold showers and soaped, scrubbed, and swabbed and gargled to wash out noses and mouths.

After ten minutes, the guards emerged and wrapped themselves in towels to get warm. The Rad-Safe monitors ran the instruments over them and placed the Geiger counters on their necks to see if radioactive iodine was concentrating in the thyroid glands. The readings were still far in excess of

25 mR. They were told the radiation levels were still too high and ordered back to the showers.

While Dyer and the guards were showering, their pickup trucks were being monitored in the yard. All vehicles were impounded and kept at CP-2 for over a month to scrub the exterior and vacuum and wash down the interior to bring the radiation back to safe levels.

After Dyer completed his first shower, he refused to reenter the showers until he called headquarters to find out where his missing guard was. He called Tackett and asked where the hell Roberts was. Tackett said they were still looking for him. Dyer commented scornfully that Roberts could not have just disappeared and the captain better get on the horn and find him. Tackett promised he would and to send him in for decontamination.

Dyer rejoined the other guards for his second shower. The guards went through the same showering and monitoring process multiple times. Several guards joked that Carl Stevens, one of the palest guards on the force, was turning blue from the ice-cold water. Finally, after additional showers, the monitors said they could not bring the radiation levels down any further. They dried off, put on paper coveralls and booties, then boarded a bus and were transported twenty-five miles to Mercury Medical for more monitoring and decontamination.

Meanwhile, the great convoy began arriving at CP-2. Most of the 900 workers in Area 12 had gotten out before the cloud settled there. Those who did not were only in the cloud for a few minutes before leaving. But eighty-five men, including Dyer's security crew, had readings above 25 mR gamma when they arrived at the decon pad and also had to take cold showers and swabs.

Walter Adkins, the bus driver who drove from T Tunnel down the canyon directly into the cloud and Area 12 Camp, took several showers before he was released. Bill Nunamaker, T Tunnel shop foreman and on Adkins's bus, also took several showers before he was released in a paper suit. His vehicle was impounded for a month. After Nunamaker was released from the decon pad, he carpooled to town. When he got home, dressed in paper coveralls and booties, he told his wife, Louise, he was "right in the middle of it."

As soon as Dyer and his men arrived at Mercury Medical, Dyer called Tackett to find out if Roberts had been found. Tackett said he was still looking. Dyer threatened to contact the AEC manager directly, if Tackett did not find him. Dyer and his men took several warm showers at Mercury Medical and were monitored for radiation levels. When they finished, it was nearly 4:00 pm. Dyer called Tackett again, but Roberts was still missing.

Dyer and his men were told they needed more testing and would be bused to Las Vegas for a whole-body scan. At 4:15 pm, just before boarding, Dyer again called Tackett. Roberts had been located up at Dead Horse Flats, and someone was being sent to relieve him.

Ernie Dyer called his wife, Dixie, in Las Vegas and told her he was heading to town for more tests, and Harley would not be far behind. Dorothy Roberts, who was with Dixie, finally got word about Harley. It had been an agonizing day for her. She heard about the Test Site blast from a neighbor midmorning and drove over to Dixie's house to wait for news about Harley and Ernie.

By 5:30 pm, all guards involved in the evacuation of Area 12, except Roberts, were in Las Vegas at the U.S. Public Heath building, and by 7:00 pm they were home. Dyer was exhausted after his twenty-four-hour shift.

While Dorothy waited anxiously for news about Harley, he was manning his post at Dead Horse Flats. At 3:30 pm, he received word on his radio that relief was on its way, but the relief was for Rad-Safe monitor Virgil. At 4:00 pm, Bill Earnest, a long-time Rad-Safe monitor, arrived in his Rad-Safe vehicle. Virgil told Earnest he thought his Geiger counter was saturated and inoperable and asked Earnest to survey Roberts.

Earnest knew his instrument had just been calibrated and was accurate. Following standard procedure, he had Harley step away from his vehicle and remove his jacket. He moved his instrument up and down Harley's body. When it pegged on the lower scale, he switched to the highest scale. The readings for Roberts were still above the maximum 200 mR gamma at thirty inches from his lower legs. Earnest moved the instrument thirty inches from the upper body, and the clicking was much more intense.

Earnest was primarily interested in the upper-body readings, because it was in Roberts's breathing zone. He took separate readings of the jacket with the fur collar and compared them to the body readings. Based upon his training and experience, he estimated Roberts's gamma readings were around 1 R or 1,000 mR, the equivalent of thirty-three chest x-rays.

Earnest called in the readings and informed his superiors that Roberts should be relieved immediately for decontamination. Earnest turned his truck over to Virgil, who drove down to CP-2, and got in Roberts's truck. They waited nearly an hour for relief to arrive.

Harley Roberts arrived at CP-2 at around 6:00 pm. Only one Rad-Safe monitor was still at the decon pad, and he was getting ready to leave. It was Troy Ellis, who had monitored Roberts at 9:30 am that morning on Stockade Wash Road. Ellis was surprised to see Roberts and asked him where the hell he'd been all day, reminding him he told him he was hot as hell when he checked him earlier. Roberts explained that he told the captain at 17 Camp he was hot but was ordered up to Dead Horse Flats and had just been relieved.

Ellis made him remove his jacket and clothing, took readings, said they were still very high, and placed them in a plastic bag marked with Roberts's name and identification number. He placed the Geiger counter to Roberts's neck for a thyroid reading. The needle immediately pegged the right side of the scale. Readings of his hair were even higher. Ellis swabbed the inside of Harley's nose, wrote the down the readings, and put the swabs and the written readings in another plastic bag.

Roberts was the eighty-sixth man ordered into the showers that day. When the blast of cold water hit him, he complained, but Ellis told him everyone had taken cold showers that day. Roberts soaped and scrubbed face, hands, and body and swabbed out his nasal passages. He was in the shower ten to fifteen minutes. After his first shower, readings were again taken, recorded, and placed in a plastic bag.

After his third shower, his readings had come down, but his hands were still over 50 mR gamma and the nose swipes recorded readings of 100 mR gamma.

Ellis wrote down all of Roberts's readings at CP-1 and filled out forms that were turned over to his supervisors. Those forms and readings disappeared.2 Ellis gave Roberts a paper suit and rubber booties and told him he was going to personally drive him down to the Mercury Medical facility for further decontamination. On the way, Ellis described the Baneberry operation as mass confusion and said he was glad it was over.

At Mercury, Roberts was monitored again and sent in for a warm shower. It felt so good he did not want to get out. His radiation readings were recorded, and he was told to bend over a brick-like structure so they could check his thyroid level. When he was released, he was told his hands were still reading over 25 mR gamma, and there was nothing more they could do. He was given a pair of rubber gloves to wear to bed that night and some paper coveralls.

Before Roberts was discharged from Mercury Medical around 10:30 pm, he called Wackenhut. The normally mild-mannered Roberts had had enough. He demanded they find him some cloth coveralls. It was cold, and he was not going to wear a damned paper suit to bed. He was picked up fifteen minutes later and driven to the barracks. When he hit the bunk, he was exhausted.

Except for Harley Roberts, all eighty-six men deconned that day joined their families in Las Vegas that night. The drinkers drank a little more than usual. The lovers were a little more arduous, the thinkers a little more contemplative. In bars and bedrooms, the events of the day were relived. Every version was different, but all conversations ended with the same questions: what went wrong, and why?

Those questions were also consuming the AEC's top command and the scientists who planned Baneberry, all part of the atomic oligarchy. One thing was certain. There was no way the vent cloud could be squeezed back into that underground cavern. As the sun set early that December day on the eve of the winter solstice, the radioactive cloud was moving relentlessly across eastern Nevada, Utah, and into the U.S. heartland on its way to Canada and into the air stream to circle the globe.

International treaties were violated. Millions of dollars of equipment were hopelessly contaminated. Workers at NTS were exposed to radiation at levels they did not understand. Some wondered whether they had been injured and might develop cancer or some other illness.

But this was the least of the AEC's concerns. It had already moved into damage-control mode. Before the venting had abated, REECo contacted its radiation consultants. The AEC was mustering a force of its own, rounding up scientists to sit on a panel to evaluate the cause of the vent, assess the radiation doses, dispel any claim of injury or damage, and assure the public and the media that everything was okay.

As the diffusing Baneberry cloud distributed radiation across the country, the radioactive particles and gas it dumped on Area 12 was bombarding the lungs, blood, and organs of the men who participated in the day of the bane. Baneberry-day ended at midnight on December 18, 1970. But the cataclysmic struggle between radiation and living tissue in the bodies of the men exposed had just begun.

NOTES

1. *Baneberry Collection*, EX 91.
2. Ibid., TR; Las Vegas Sun, January 25, 1979.

[4]

The Bulldog

April 1971

WHEN WE OPENED our law office in January 1971, the practice of law was a noble profession we were honored to join. There were fewer than 150 members of the Clark County Bar Association, and we knew most of them.

Mike Hines, a long-time lawyer and one of Alan's first bosses, hosted a party at his ranch each year to welcome the new members. It was the event of the year, where the new lawyers were introduced to the judges and the leading members of the bar. Considering the amount of alcohol consumed, it is amazing that those who attended Mike's parties could navigate their way home after the affair. But those were the days before Mothers Against Drunk Driving, so the miscreants could quietly negotiate their citations with the judges who attended the same party.

In mid-April 1971, a call came into our office. The caller asked to speak with either Alan or me. Alan was in court, so I took the call.

"This is Bill Cleghorn," the caller announced. "I was referred to you guys by your former boss, DA George Franklin. He said you were good lawyers and might be able to handle this case."

"Well, that was nice of George," I responded, wondering why George, now in private practice, had not taken the case himself. "What's your case about?"

"You probably read about the Baneberry underground test that blew out last December and exposed all those workers at the Test Site to radiation. I'm president of the Independent Guard Association of Nevada, the union for the guards. Our guys had to go in and evacuate all the personnel in the base camp and got the highest radiation doses. They made a written request on the AEC to give them information about their radiation readings but were ignored. We're considering filing a lawsuit.

"I don't know what you guys know about it, but Baneberry was a mess. Everybody out there knew it. Anyway, would you be interested in handling the case? We're going to interview some other lawyers. So, if you're not interested say so," Cleghorn ended.

"I'll talk to my partner," I responded. "But I think we'd be willing to meet to discuss the matter. Do you want to make an appointment?"

At precisely 10:00 am the next morning, Bill Cleghorn arrived. He was ushered into my office, where Alan and I were waiting. Bill was around 6' 4", over 200 pounds, and in good physical condition; the type of security guard the AEC needed to protect its nuclear weapons testing program.

Bill opened his briefcase, pulled out a manila file, and launched into a discussion about the Baneberry event. Fourteen guards were exposed to radiation, all were decontaminated that day, and all but one went to the U.S Public Health facility for additional tests. The guards wrote to the AEC requesting their radiation doses, but the AEC did not respond.

We asked Bill if the guards gave written statements. He said they did, but their statements were taken and classified, and the guards weren't allowed to make copies.

Bill handed us two articles in our local newspapers about the Baneberry venting.[1] He also gave us an article with an AP photo of the Baneberry cloud rising over a mountain range east of the Test Site with the headline: "600 Flee Nuclear Spill."[2] But the most interesting news story he supplied was by Colin McKinlay, *Los Angeles Times* staff writer, headlined: "Nevada Nuclear Blast Goes Wild, 500 Workers Evacuated." In the article, McKinlay interviewed an AEC spokesperson, who stated, "Exposure levels are not estimated at being above permissible dosage levels .... We don't know how much gamma radiation they got or what they inhaled or got internally."[3]

Baneberry released more radiation into the atmosphere than any test since the resumption of underground testing in September 1961. Bill knew this to be a fact, because he came to the Test Site in June 1961. He also mentioned that President Nixon had suspended nuclear testing until an investigation was completed. An official report was to be issued by the AEC in a few weeks.

When Bill Cleghorn asked if we were interested in the case, Alan and I looked at each other and one of us responded that we would consider it. Bill said he would get back to us. After he left, we discussed the matter but did not expect to hear from him again.

Nearly a month went by. Then, on May 13, 1971, Cleghorn called to tell us the AEC was going to hold a press conference the following day to announce the results of their investigation. He said he could not attend, but one of the guards would pick up whatever material they handed out and drop off a copy at our office.

At around 4:30 pm on May 14, 1971, copies of the *Baneberry Summary Report and AEC Press Release, May 14, 1971* were delivered to the office.[4] The press release assured the public that there was no hazard to anyone exposed to the radioactive Baneberry vent cloud and announced that testing would resume at the Test Site.

The *Baneberry Summary Report*, a sixteen-page stapled document with a bright yellow cover, stated that the vent was an accident that could not have been anticipated. Significantly, it confirmed that two Test Site security guards received the highest radiation doses and included Figure 1, which graphed the radiation doses of the eighty-six men exposed. There were four categories, Beta, Gamma, Lens of the Eye, and Thyroid Dose, but names and individual doses were not given.[5]

On May 19, 1971, five days later, we saw an article by James Barrows, *Sun* staff writer: "AEC Ignored Advice of Five Scientists." Barrows reported that five scientists were against the Baneberry test and that it was improperly planned and engineered. He focused on the radiation readings of two security guards who got "exposure to the lens of the eye almost equal to the exposure limit."[6]

In late May 1971, we agreed to handle an estate matter with the prospect of our first good fee and hoped that Cleghorn had found other lawyers to take the case. But in mid-June he called and came in. Cleghorn was out of patience. Requests for radiation records had been ignored by the AEC. He wanted us to file a lawsuit to force the AEC to produce the records. We suggested he make a formal request as president of the Independent Guard Association of Nevada (IGAN).

On June 20, 1971, *Feature* magazine in the *Las Vegas Sun* displayed photographs of failed, leaking underground nuclear tests at NTS prior to Baneberry and questioned the AEC's claim that it did not anticipate that the Baneberry test might vent.[7]

On June 21, 1971, Cleghorn, as president of IGAN, made a written request upon the U.S. Public Health Service for radiation readings of all security guards sent there for testing on Baneberry-day, December 18, 1970.[8]

NOTES

1. Las Vegas Sun, December 19, 1970; Las Vegas Review-Journal, December 19, 1970.
2. Unknown, December 19, 1970, copy in author's possession.
3. Los Angeles Times, December 19, 1970.
4. Summary report: Baneberry Collection, EX 66. Press release: Baneberry Collection, EX 65.
5. Ibid., EX 66.
6. Las Vegas Sun, May 19, 1971.
7. Las Vegas Sun, Scene Feature Magazine, June 20, 1971, with photos of vents of Platte, Eagle, Des Moines, and Eel.
8. William Cleghorn to U.S. Public Health Service, June 21, 1971. Copy in author's possession.

[5]

The Georgiadis Curse

October– December 1971

AFTER SENDING THE LETTER TO U.S. Public Health Service, Bill Cleghorn called us several times to report there had been no response. By early October, he insisted we meet to discuss what could be done to get the radiation records.

When we met, Bill ranted about the mistreatment of the security guards and wanted us to file a lawsuit against the AEC. The Independent Guard Association of Nevada would bring the case on behalf of the fourteen security guards. In his view, as president of IGAN, he had a duty to protest the AEC's use of security guards to enter a radiation zone to evacuate the camp. At the very least, a lawsuit would force the government to produce the radiation records for his men.

When he finished, we explained that the union, by itself, could not file the lawsuit he wanted to bring. It could demand information on behalf of individual members, which it had. Only the individual guards exposed to radiation could file a lawsuit against the Atomic Energy Commission. But before they could bring a suit against the AEC, each had to fill out a federal tort claim stating the basis for his claim and demand a monetary amount as damage.

We told Bill we had not met any of the guards and had no idea how they felt about the matter. Cleghorn assured us he had talked to all of them, and they wanted to pursue it. But his assurances were not enough. We had to meet with each to make sure they wanted us to file a claim in their behalf. Bill understood and said he would contact them to make an appointment with us.

Although we had met with Bill several times, the subject of our legal fees had never been discussed. Bill asked what kind of a retainer we would need to file a lawsuit. We told him we would have to meet with the guards and then decide whether to proceed with the case. At that point, we would discuss legal fees, but we also made it clear that we were not willing to underwrite the costs and expenses of litigation against the government. Cleghorn said he would get the union to pay the costs.

Over two weeks passed. We assumed the union board was not willing to pay costs and the individual guards had lost interest in pursuing the case. But we learned Bill Cleghorn was determined that something be done and had a strong ally in Ernie Dyer, the sergeant in charge of the Area 12 Camp evacuation.

In early November, Cleghorn called and asked us to prepare a retainer agreement to cover our court costs. He was confident the executive board would approve it and the guards would call our office to make appointments to meet with us.

Over the next week, Alan and I discussed whether we should get involved in a lawsuit against the AEC. The *Baneberry Summary Report* claimed the vent was an unforeseeable accident, but news articles questioned the AEC's claim that it was unexpected. Further, the AEC's refusal to provide radiation records for the guards shrouded Baneberry in mystery. We wanted to know more and could not let it go. And within a few days, guards began calling to set up appointments.

Over the next few weeks, we met with thirteen of the fourteen guards; the fourteenth man was not interested in pursuing the matter. The guards were a very patriotic group of men, most with prior military service. They wanted us to proceed, but some were hesitant to talk about their activities at the Test Site or their specific activities at Baneberry. They had taken an oath not to disclose any information about the Test Site, and their written reports about their activities at Baneberry were classified. Some were concerned they might be prosecuted for divulging classified information.

All guards confirmed that when they joined the guard force, they had a two-week orientation, which did not include a discussion of radiation or its health effects. Their job was to secure and control access to areas where radiation was present, and they were not supposed to enter a radiation zone. Only Rad-Safe monitors, scientists, and personnel with clearance were authorized to pass through their checkpoints.

They all knew that radiation can cause cancer, and a few were concerned for their future health. But nearly a year had passed since Baneberry, and all were in good shape.

We explained that each guard had to file a tort claim against the AEC alleging they were negligently exposed to radiation at Baneberry and asking for damages for injuries they might sustain in the future. All thirteen guards agreed to submit a tort claim and file suit, if necessary, to get their radiation readings.

Ernie Dyer's interview was the longest. He was not reluctant to tell us about his battle with the captain all night before the test, his fight with the firemen, and his efforts to locate Harley Roberts. Nearly a year after the event, he was still angry and critical of the AEC, REECo, and his own Wackenhut superiors for exposing the guards to radiation and leaving Harley at a remote post all day.

Our meeting with Harley Roberts was the most memorable. He was not angry like his brother-in-law and seemed unworried about his radiation exposure. He had a good memory of the events and took us through his activities that day, from his discussion with Ernie when he first arrived at BJY, his graphic description of clearing out the trailers in the camp, the monitors' comments about his readings, to his decon procedures and release at Mercury Medical at 11:00 pm wearing rubber gloves. He mentioned he had diarrhea for several days following Baneberry but thought it was just the flu.

We asked about his life prior to the Test Site. He spoke fondly of living in Indiana and said that although he was only five feet ten he loved basketball and was a good player for his size. He played on town basketball teams until he was forty-five. Hoosiers, he explained, love basketball as much as Texans love football. He was also a good golfer and had won quite a few trophies. Camping and fishing were his favorite family activities back home.

The move to Las Vegas was a big change. He worked four twelve-hour shifts at the Test Site every week, checking badges and clearing out areas before shots. Unless he was called in, he avoided overtime. He spent two of his three days off playing golf or fishing and camping at Lake Mead. He came to the Test Site for the pay and intended to return to Indiana as soon as he retired.

We asked about his health prior to Baneberry. He said he never went to doctors in Indiana. Other than the annual physical exam required by Wackenhut and an occasional sinus flare-up after he came to the desert, he had not seen any doctors. He did not have as much energy as he used to, but was fifty one and probably slowing down a little.

Harley knew he got more radiation than most of the other guards and there was a chance he might develop cancer sometime in the future. When asked if he wanted to file a claim and, if necessary, a lawsuit, he did not hesitate. If nothing else came out of it, he wanted to find out what radiation he received and why they sent the guards into that mess.

After talking to all thirteen guards, we knew Harley had received the highest radiation dose in all categories. His diarrhea after Baneberry raised questions whether his dose was higher than reported in the *Baneberry Summary Report*, since diarrhea is a classic sign of high radiation exposure. But it could indeed have been the flu, as he assumed.

Cleghorn called the office in late November and asked us to send a retainer agreement for the union to sign. We wrote up a simple one-page agreement covering costs and mailed it to Cleghorn. On December 3, 1971, he dropped the signed document off at the office and wanted to know what was next.

Now there was no turning back. "Here's another fine mess you've gotten me into," Alan would chide me repeatedly over the years, as if the decision to take the case was entirely my own. Baneberry had beguiled us both and continued to lure us further and further into its web.

In December 1971, we filed federal tort claims for thirteen of the Wackenhut security guards involved in the evacuation of Area 12. For twelve of the thirteen, we asked for $250,000 in monetary damages each. But Harley Roberts's claim was for $500,000, because the AEC did not decontaminate him promptly, which in our view increased his radiation dose and risk of developing cancer.

The tort claims were served on the United States Attorney in Las Vegas, the legal representative of the United States and the AEC. We did not think the AEC would respond to the claims and we would have to file a lawsuit. But we did assume the federal judge, at the very least, would force the government to disclose the radiation records of the thirteen security guards.

December 1971 marked the first anniversary of Baneberry and the end of our first year of private practice. Divorces tend to slow down around the Christmas holiday; but one memorable client that year was Mr. Georgiadis. He had left his wife in Greece and come to Las Vegas to take a job on the strip. Now he wanted a divorce and brought in rental slips at a local motel, confirming his six-week residence prior to filing. We filed his divorce complaint and had his wife served with the complaint in Greece. We sent along a letter and power of attorney for Mrs. Georgiadis to sign, authorizing an attorney to appear for her in court and not contest the divorce.

But Mrs. Georgiadis refused to sign. Instead, she wrote us a letter. It was a stinging rebuke of her husband who had promised to send her money so she could join him in Las Vegas. For assisting her husband to commit this perfidious act, she devoted an entire paragraph to invective against us. She said she was placing a Greek curse upon us. At the time, we found her letter somewhat amusing, particularly the curse. We had never heard of a Greek curse and had no idea how long one lasted. But coming as it did as we were preparing and filing the Baneberry case, we have wondered over the years whether Baneberry was the curse and Mrs. Georgiadis the priestess who delivered it.

[6]

The King Can Do No Wrong

THE UNITED STATES HAD six months to respond to the tort claims we filed in December 1971. If it ignored them as we anticipated, we then had to file an action under the Federal Tort Claims Act (FTCA) by December 1972.

The Federal Tort Claims Act was enacted in 1946.[1] Although it had been under consideration by Congress for nearly thirty years, the event that seems to have precipitated its passage was when a B-25 bomber, flying in dense fog during World War II, crashed into the north side of the Empire State Building. Although it was unintentional and the United States could not be sued, Congress offered money to the victims. Most accepted, but some rejected the offer and filed suit against the government. When the Tort Claims Act was passed in 1946, it provided a retroactive remedy for the crash victims.

For the first time, U.S. citizens could sue the United States for damages caused by negligent acts of government employees. Its passage ended the immunity our founders inherited from the English Common Law doctrine, "the king can do no wrong," firmly settled in England by the 1200s, when Henry de Bracton explained: "Our lord the king cannot be summoned or receive a command from anyone," citing a judgment of the King's Court in 1234."[2] Over 500 years later, Alexander Hamilton, in Federalist No. 81, restated de Bracton's rationale for the doctrine: "It is inherent in the nature of sovereignty not to be amenable to the suit of an individual without its consent."[3]

On its face, the FTCA appeared to open the courts of the land for suits against the government in a nation that prided itself on the sovereignty of the people and the concept of "justice for all." But the right to sue came with draconian limitations and defenses available only to the government.

First, suits can only be tried in the United States federal courts, before a judge appointed by the president with the advice and consent of the Senate. Federal judges serve for life and can only be removed by impeachment in the House of Representatives and trial and conviction by the Senate. At first blush, it might seem a federal judge appointed for life would be immune from politics and all other influences. But of course, we were not naïve. We knew that a judicial appointment is a highly political matter. A United States senator makes the recommendation from the home state to the president, who then formally nominates the judge. Approval requires a majority vote of the Senate. But the nominations were rarely challenged. The FTCA is an explicit statement that the federal government does not trust the state courts or its judges to preside over suits brought by citizens against the United States government.

Second, trial by jury, the most sacred right our colonial ancestors brought from England to the American colonies and embodied in the Seventh Amendment to the United States Constitution, is expressly denied. Instead, a federally appointed judge decides all facts and law in a trial against the government. The denial of the right to trial by a jury of ordinary citizens was obviously very significant to the government.

When Congress passed the FTCA, it recognized that the federal judges who would decide cases involving government conduct had been nominated and would render their decisions mindful of their political affiliation and their pension benefits. Federal judges sit in a federal courthouse, which is an enclave with its own federal marshals in charge of security and access to the building. The federal judges derive their authority directly from the federal government in Washington and are not answerable to the people in the state where they hold court. Their decisions are reviewed by federal appeals courts and are not subject to scrutiny or review by the state judiciary. The prestige, power, and celebrity of their office come from the United States government and endure for life, including all attendant retirement benefits.

By contrast, a jury of ordinary U.S. citizens represents a cross-section of the community in which they live. They take an oath to "well and truly" hear the evidence and decide the truth of the matter. They do so in virtual anonymity, without celebrity, without opportunity for gain, for a short period time, and for minimal compensation. A verdict by a jury in a civil case in federal court requires a unanimous decision by at least six jurors (and frequently more) based upon their collective conscience. For over a thousand years, the jury has stood as the most incorruptible and impartial system devised by man to determine the facts and arrive at the truth.[4] Congress was unwilling to trust ordinary citizens to judge the U.S. government's behavior.

Other rights taken for granted by parties in ordinary lawsuits were denied or severely limited by the act. One defense is not available to any other defendant. The federal government granted itself "immunity" from liability for acts or conduct carried out by government employees in the "exercise of their discretionary authority." This term was not defined in the act. Over the next fifty years, federal trial and appellate judges wrestled with its meaning and redefined the term.

Whatever the intent of the act at the time of passage, practically everything a government official or bureaucrat does is pursuant to some authority, directive, rule, or regulation. Most of their duties are within the ambit of their limited discretion somewhere down the links of the command chain.

Carried to its logical conclusion, the sovereign immunity defense, interposed to protect the government, allows government officials to do almost anything under the umbrella of a chain of command that runs straight up to the president of the United States. The only notable exceptions are intentional or criminal conduct or garden-variety negligent conduct like an auto accident caused by a postal worker for which the government employee could be sued directly.

Our research led us to *Dalehite v. United States*, the first U.S. Supreme Court case to test the new act. It involved the Texas City Disaster of April 1947. A ship loaded with fertilizer blew up in the harbor at Texas City, Texas, killing over 500 people, injuring 5,000, and nearly leveling the city.[5]

Henry Dalehite's successors filed suit under the FTCA alleging that the government "shipped or permitted shipment to a congested area without warning" of a potentially highly explosive substance, ammonium nitrate, the same explosive Timothy McVeigh loaded into his rented Ryder truck and parked outside the Murrah Federal Building in Oklahoma City in 1995. Although no specific acts of government negligence were alleged, the government had overseen the entire fertilizer export plan, which included this shipment on its way to Europe.

The district judge found in favor of Dalehite's heirs and others and awarded damages of $75,000 for each victim. The government appealed and the circuit court reversed the award. The case was then appealed to the Supreme Court, where six justices acknowledged that "acts of subordinates carrying out operations of government in accordance with official directions cannot be actionable" and that executive or cabinet-level decisions are not subject to question by anyone, including a federal judge. The Supreme Court, by a majority, found that the "decisions held culpable [by the trial judge] were all responsibly made at a planning level rather than operational level and involved considerations more or less important to the practicability of the Government's fertilizer program."

Three Supreme Court justices dissented. They would have held the government liable, commenting about the FTCA, "Surely a statute so long debated was meant to embrace more than traffic accidents. If not, the ancient and discredited doctrine that 'The King can do no wrong' has not been uprooted; it has merely been amended to read, 'The King can do only little wrongs.'"

The next case we studied was Bulloch v. United States, the ill-fated sheep case decided by a federal judge in Utah in October 1956.6 Members of the Bulloch family and other Utah sheep owners claimed their sheep were exposed to lethal radiation from the 1953 atmospheric tests at the Nevada Test Site. They lost their FTCA lawsuit because the federal judge found they had not been able to show that the sheep deaths were caused by radiation from atmospheric testing. Because the judge found the Bulloch plaintiffs had not presented evidence to support their damage claims, he did not decide whether the government had acted negligently in exposing the sheep to radiation from atomic tests. We could only wonder whether the judge had taken the easy road to avoid the "sovereign immunity" issue.

These two decisions were not encouraging. In one, where death and destruction were catastrophic and caused by an explosion, the case was thrown out based upon the sovereign immunity defense. In the other, the judge took the government's side, ruling that the fallout from an A-bomb test in 1953 did not cause any harm. We knew we had to overcome both defenses to win.

We had read *Bleak House* and were amused by Dickens's stirring admonition to "suffer any wrong rather than enter the English Court of Chancery."[7] But it was a novel, a piece of fiction about conditions in nineteenth-century England. Still, as we reviewed the law dealing with the Federal Tort Claims Act, we realized there were a dozen reasons "to suffer any wrong rather than enter" the federal court system to test again the FTCA, and almost no good reason to retest the AEC's atomic program, particularly in Las Vegas.

We pressed on with great trepidation. Fortunately, none of our clients at that point was suffering any acute effects from radiation at Baneberry. But it was too early to be sure there would be no long-term effects, and there was plenty of evidence of government negligence.

Our review of Baneberry and the post-shot exposure of the guards to the Baneberry cloud involved decisions and directives made by AEC officials before and after the test vented. The decision to fire the test came from the top, but the order was carried out by countless underlings down the chain of command. The direct order to Dyer to muster the guards to evacuate Area 12 that morning came from his Wackenhut supervisor Captain Tackett. But that order came from the top AEC security officer at the control point.

The order directing Harley Roberts to the remote Dead Horse Flats station was issued by a Wackenhut captain after Harley told him he was "hot as hell." But the order to decontaminate all the guards involved in the evacuation came from the command center and filtered down the chain to Wackenhut. The failure to locate and decontaminate Roberts, in compliance with that order, was an extension and violation of that order.

Monitoring and recording the radiation exposure the guards received was the responsibility of the AEC test manager. But the procedures for monitoring and determining the doses were carried out by REECo Rad-Safe monitors and technicians who were not government employees.

Since every nuclear test had to be preapproved by the president, we expected the government would argue that the entire testing program—top to bottom—was a discretionary decision, and the government was therefore entitled to claim sovereign immunity from suit.

In late 1971, when the claims were filed, we reviewed the facts and decided—or as Alan would later claim, I decided without any strenuous protest from him—to test again the sovereign immunity defense. The claims were filed, and the ball was in the government's court.

While the government reviewed the claims, we began an intense investigation to understand the inner workings of the Nevada Test Site. Prior to Baneberry, we knew almost nothing about the 1,350-square-mile reserve or the interrelationship between the nearly 10,000 employees who carried out the day-to-day work and the scientists who planned the hundreds of different tests.

We learned that REECo became the prime contractor at the Test Site in 1952 and employed most of the workers, directly or through subcontracts, including nearly 300 radiological safety personnel. The Radiation Safety division of REECo was responsible for issuing the film badges worn by all persons allowed access to the site and employed the Rad-Safe monitors and technicians to measure radiation levels all around the Test Site. Finally, they collected all film badges worn at the Test Site and filled out forms recording radiation exposures. Rad-Safe monitors had specialized training and were equipped with full-body protective clothing and respirators that they were required to wear when entering radiation zones.

After eighteen years of radiation monitoring at the Nevada Test Site and with about 300 fully trained and equipped employees, we were perplexed that Rad-Safe monitors had not been mustered and ordered to enter the radiation cloud to conduct the evacuation of Area 12.[8] The appearance of suited up Rad-Safe monitors with hoods and respirators would have left no doubt in the minds of the workers in Area 12 that the radioactive cloud was dangerous. But on the morning of December 18, 1970, there was only one monitor near Area 12 camp at 8 am. Fully outfitted in his Rad-Safe protective gear and facemask, he hailed the guards and waved them on into Area 12 Camp but never entered the camp or took a reading there the entire time the guards were conducting the evacuation.

The more perplexing question was why one contractor, REECo, which employed directly or through subcontractors most of the 10,000 workers at the Test Site, was also in charge of radiation monitoring and in exclusive control of all instruments used to determine radiation exposures of the workers. Was it likely that one division of REECo would condemn the conduct of another division?

Further investigation revealed that the vast Nevada Test Site was divided into thirty separate areas and that two scientific laboratories designed and carried out nearly all nuclear tests there since testing began in 1951.[9] Los Alamos Scientific Laboratory (LASL), a division of the University of California headquartered in Los Alamos, New Mexico, conducted most of the early tests at the Nevada Test Site. In 1952, Nobel physicist Ernest O. Lawrence set up a separate laboratory, the Lawrence Radiation Laboratory, later Lawrence Livermore Laboratory (LLL) at the University of California, Berkeley. The labs were rivals and competed for federal dollars.

We had no idea why the scientists in both divisions of the University of California could not collaborate and consolidate their efforts, nor any idea what either of them had accomplished in the over 500 atmospheric and underground tests conducted at the Nevada Test Site over the preceding twenty years. All we knew was that the Baneberry test was in Area 8 and Area 8 was LLL territory.

The physicists at LLL who designed the Baneberry test, reputedly top scientists in the field, were employees of the University of California, not government employees. But the test was approved by the AEC and the president. Moreover, as employees of the University of California, we would have to join LLL, a subdivision of the State of California, and face the Eleventh Amendment to the U.S. Constitution, which bars suits by citizens of one state against one of the United States.[10]

We learned that another AEC contractor, Fenix & Scisson, oversaw the design and drilling of the eighty-six-inch diameter Baneberry emplacement hole. These drilling experts should have known about the geology of the formation where the Baneberry device was placed. As a private contractor, they were not immune from suit under the FTCA.

We had enough evidence to support filing suit against the contractors for their negligent acts related to the Baneberry test without naming the Atomic Energy Commission. On February 2, 1972, we filed suit in the U.S.

District Court of Nevada on behalf of each of the thirteen guards, and at Cleghorn's request, also named the Independent Guard Association of Nevada as a plaintiff. We named as defendants Reynolds Electrical and Engineering Company, Wackenhut Services, Inc., Fenix & Scisson, and Forest Tackett, the Wackenhut captain who failed to locate Roberts. We served the defendants and waited for their response.

Since we had never been to the Test Site and were unfamiliar with the sciences related to atomic testing and radiation effects, we hired Ronan & Associates, a consulting firm, to investigate the Baneberry case. In late April 1972, they gave us a report and bill for $1,350. They also delivered two thick publications: *Radiological Health Handbook*, revised edition, January 1970, and *Public Safety and Underground Nuclear Detonations*, June 1971, by Samuel Glasstone.[11]

We forwarded the bill and report to Cleghorn and plunged into our reading. Over two weeks later, Cleghorn told us the union board was grumbling about the $1,350, but he would get them to pay it.

In June 1972, we were flooded with legal documents filed in court in response to the complaint. We knew that once the defendants mustered their lawyers, the case would explode. Faced with all the costs and expenses and countless hours dealing with the legal issues, it was time we took a serious look at the Baneberry lawsuit. We reviewed the documents and the applicable law and by the end of the month had decided we could not pursue the case.

While in the process of drafting a letter to the union and the individual guards to inform them of our decision, Harley Roberts called.

"Larry," he began, "I've been feeling pretty bad for the past few months."

"What's the problem?"

"I just feel tired all the time. I mentioned it to one of the guards, and he recommended I make an appointment to see Dr. Chauncey Smith. He's Chief of Medicine at Loma Linda University."

"Have you seen any local doctors?"

"No. I guess you know I don't like to go to doctors. But Dr. Smith comes highly recommended."

"It's probably a good idea."

"I'm going to have to do something. Dorothy's worried. She can tell I don't seem to have much energy. Oh, I manage to get to work all right. But, I've been taking more sick days lately and I avoid overtime whenever possible."

"Have you told anybody at Wackenhut that you're not feeling good?" Larry asked.

"No. But I'm getting concerned. We work long hours and I work solo a lot of times at some of the checkpoints. If I get caught sleeping, it's automatic discharge."

"Have you made an appointment to see Dr. Smith?"

"Not yet. I thought I better let you know. I'm going to schedule it during my vacation in July. That way the company won't know anything about it," he ended.

A couple weeks later, Harley called and said he had an appointment with Dr. Smith at Loma Linda Hospital on July 20, 1972. He was there for five days and met Dr. Smith and several specialists. When he got back to Las Vegas, he made an appointment to see us but did not want Dorothy present. We met on July 27 and had him sign a medical authorization so we could get copies of his Loma Linda records.

Harley looked pale. He said they did lots of blood tests and described how they stuck a big needle into his hipbone for a bone marrow study. It was quite painful. Dr. Smith told him he had something called "leukopenia" and that the bone marrow test showed it was abnormal. He mentioned to Dr. Smith that he had been exposed to radiation at the Test Site in December 1970. Dr. Smith made a note of it and told him to make an appointment to return in August for a recheck of his blood.

We sent the medical release to Loma Linda Hospital in July but did not get the records until early September. By that time, Harley had returned for a follow-up visit on August 25th.

The medical records of the June hospitalization disclosed much more than the doctors had told Harley. The bone marrow test showed he was missing a chromosome. Dr. Irvin Kuhn, the hematologist, concluded, "One should bear in mind the possible preleukemia state and therefore I would recommend repeat blood studies every month for four to six months or more unless the etiology [cause of the disease] is found."[12]

Preleukemia is the phase of the leukemic process preceding manifestation. On September 15, 1972, Harley called with good news. He got a letter from Dr. Smith reporting that his August blood test results were normal. But in September the results turned negative again. Christmas at the Roberts home was filled with apprehension, as Harley braced himself for the next round of blood tests.

We never finished the letter we were drafting in June. We could not drop Harley's case while he was fighting for his life. Baneberry was drawing us deeper and deeper into its web.

Notes

1. Federal Tort Claims Act, Public Law 601, §28 U.S.C. 1346(b) (1946) governs federal tort claims actions. Collectively, hereinafter referred to as FTCA.

2. Sir Frederick Pollock and Frederic William Maitland, The History of English Law, Vol. I, Legal Classics Library, (1982). Henry de Bracton's Summa, published between 1250 and 1258, "is the crown and flower of English Medieval jurisprudence." In it, he cites over 500 decisions. Regarding the notion that the "king can do no wrong," it was never established law. In fact, "the king can do wrong; he can break the law; he is below the law, though he is below no man and below no court of law" (514–16).

3. The Federalist, Legal Classics Library (1983, 318): "This is the general sense and general practice of mankind; and the exemption, as one of the attributes of sovereignty, is now enjoyed by the government of every state in the union."

4. Pollock and Maitland, The History of English Law, Vol. I, Legal Classics Library (1982, 140–41): "We must look to the Frankish inquisitio, the prerogative rights of the Frankish kings. . . . He [the king] orders that a group of men, the best and most trustworthy men of a district, be sworn to declare what lands, what rights, he has or ought to have in their district. He uses this procedure for many different purposes. He uses it in his litigation:—he will rely on the verdict of the neighbors instead of battle or the ordeal. . . . The procedure which he employs in support of his own rights he can and does grant as a favour to others. . . . All this we see in the Frankish empire of the ninth century; we see it in the Neustria which the Normans are invading

Yet on the whole we may say that, but for the conquest of England, it would have perished and long ago have become a matter for the antiquary."

5. Dalehite v. United States, 346 U.S. 15 (1953).

6. Bulloch v. United States, 145 F. Supp. 824 (D. Utah 1956).

7. Charles Dickens 1853, Bleak House. Complete Works, Centennial Edition, 1967. Vol. I, p. 3. London: Heron Books. A more complete quotation: "This is the Court of Chancery; . . . which gives to monied might the means abundantly of wearying out the right; which so exhausts finances, patience, courage, hope; so overthrows the brain and breaks that heart; that there is not an honorable man among the practitioners who would not give—who does not often give—the warning, 'Suffer any wrong that can be done rather than come here!'"

8. We did not learn until years later, as we prepared the case for trial, that the Test Manager's Baneberry Plan required that REECo have teams of monitors standing by thirty minutes prior to shot time or that the AEC required REECo to prepare specific written emergency plans for Area 12 Camp.

9. Sandia Laboratories in New Mexico was involved in some tests.

10. U.S. Constitution, amendment XI. "The Judicial power of the United States shall not be construed to extend to any suit in law or equity, commenced or prosecuted against one of the United States by Citizens of another State, or by the Citizens or Subjects of any Foreign State."

11. Bureau of Radiological Health, U.S. Department of Health, Education, and Welfare, Radiological Health Handbook, revised edition, January 1970. Washington, D.C. Samuel Glasstone, Public Safety and Underground Nuclear Detonations, June 1971, TID-25708. Atomic Energy Commission: Washington, D.C.

12. Baneberry Collection, EX 110.

[7]

We're Here to Help You

January 1973–February 1974

BY EARLY APRIL 1973, Harley Roberts was struggling to work his four twelve hour shifts each week. He called Dr. Smith, and he and Dorothy drove to Loma Linda on April 17. Dr. Smith ran blood tests and was amazed Harley could continue working. He filled out a total disability form for Harley to submit.

We met with Harley after he returned from Loma Linda. He was nearly in tears explaining his financial condition. He was a proud man who knew they would have to depend upon Dorothy's income. She took daily insulin injections and worked as a change girl at the nearby Safeway store.

Harley was born in 1920 and grew up during the Depression. He knew hard times, but this was worse. He and Dorothy thought about selling their home and moving back to Indiana but decided they needed to stay close to Dr. Smith for medical treatment. They also wanted to be near Harley's mother and sister in Las Vegas. Their son Randy was in the Marine Corps.

Harley was soon largely housebound except for Saturday night card games with the Dyers and occasional fishing trips to Lake Mead. He had not been able to play golf for nearly a year, and his disease had progressed to the point that B-12 injections and blood transfusions were all that kept him going.

By June 1973, Dr. Kuhn classified Harley's condition as preleukemic. When we told Harley, he knew what that meant. Leukemia was a death sentence. We learned that the AEC's Oak Ridge Hospital was a leading research facility in radiation-related cancers and leukemias and asked Harley if he would be willing to go there if the government would pay the expenses. Harley was desperate and eager to try anything. We contacted government counsel to inquire whether the AEC would consider sending Harley to Oak Ridge for a comprehensive examination and recommendation for supportive treatment.

After negotiating for several weeks, the AEC agreed to pay Harley's expenses for the trip and evaluation by their doctors. Harley asked if they would pay Dorothy's expenses. We made the proposal, but the AEC refused.

In mid-August Dorothy drove Harley to the airport. He was admitted to Oak Ridge Hospital on August 16, 1973, and discharged on September 1, 1973. The Oak Ridge doctors knew Harley had filed a lawsuit against the AEC. He saw many physicians, and each asked him about his radiation exposure at Baneberry. Harley said he felt like he was the enemy.

We made requests upon government counsel for the records of Harley's hospitalization at Oak Ridge, but the records were not produced until nearly two months after he was released. Even then, they were not produced to us but were sent to Dr. Smith at Loma Linda, who sent us copies. When we examined the records, we noted references to oral communications between the AEC and the AEC doctors at Oak Ridge regarding Harley Roberts's radiation readings and readings of urine samples after his exposure at Baneberry.

The Oak Ridge doctor who reviewed the thyroid readings sent by the AEC acknowledged that the bioassay (urine sample) results "were unclear because . . . [they] did not know exactly what [iodine radioisotope] was measured." To us, this statement confirmed that Harley's internal exposure from inhalation of radioactive gases was the unknown element and possibly the most significant component of his radiation dose.

The reports varied wildly regarding Harley's dose from exposure to the Baneberry cloud on December 18, 1970. An extensive handwritten report by one physician ignored all documented radiation readings for Roberts. He stated that Roberts received a "brief estimated 10–15 millirem [mR] exposure" and referred to the "exposure in question," implying that Roberts may not have been exposed to radiation at all. Another physician referred to exposure to "100 Rods of radiation" (100 *Rads* or 100,000 mR) for which there was no support in any of the records that came from Loma Linda or anywhere else.

From our review of the Oak Ridge record, it was unclear what radiation dose the Oak Ridge doctors relied upon for their analyses. But the bone marrow studies they performed showed that of twenty bone marrow cells examined eighteen contained only forty-five of the forty-six chromosomes. The head physician at Oak Ridge, Dr. Gould Andrews, prepared a summary concluding that although radiation could not be ruled out, he felt the dose was too low to have caused the condition.

In late January 1974, the government lawyers called and told us it was imperative they take Harley Roberts's deposition as soon as possible. We assumed the doctors at Oak Ridge had told them Harley's condition was grave and he might not have long to live. Harley's deposition was set for February 20, 1974.

On February 20, we met Harley in the lobby of the AEC building. He was so pale we wondered how he had managed to drive unaided from his home. Alan, Harley, and I were seated on one side of a long conference table with government lawyers aligned on the other side. Harley was sworn in and answered a series of general questions about his background, education, and life before coming to the Test Site.

When the government lawyer finally got around to asking about his health before and after Baneberry, Harley began to bristle. He looked the lawyer in the face and said he was in great shape before Baneberry. When asked what health problems he attributed to his exposure to radiation at Baneberry, Harley looked puzzled, as if he did not know where to begin. He said he was short of breath because he did not have any oxygen in his blood, was down to around 127 pounds, and felt like he was not really living. He had only been sick two days in his life before Baneberry and that was when he had diphtheria as a child. He never had any sign of fatigue until after Baneberry and proudly stated that he played basketball regularly until he was forty-five years old.

When asked whether he had ever been exposed to any toxic substances or chemicals before Baneberry, he said he had not. He was out in the wide-open spaces in Indiana most of his life and wished he had stayed there.

When the government lawyer asked if he was worried about his health, Harley's countenance went from astonishment to anger. He glared at the government lawyer and nearly broke down. After a short pause, he began speaking in almost a whisper. He was sure it was just a matter of time. He probably had a year or two, maybe not even that long; he did not know. The lawyer was reluctant to follow up, but Harley did. He said he could not do anything anymore. He still drove the car a little and had driven himself to the AEC building this morning, but when he got out of the car and the wind hit him in the face, he thought he was never going to breathe again. He said he nearly passed out in the hall. The room fell silent. Now it was the government lawyer who did not know what to say.

When the deposition ended, we asked Harley if he was okay to drive home. Harley said he thought he was and told us he was relieved he had finally gotten to tell his story about Baneberry and explain how it had ruined his life. He was irritated by the questions and referred to the government lawyer as a "smartass jerk."

A week later Harley called. He was feeling terrible. He had just gotten off the phone with Dr. Smith, who told him to drive down immediately and check in that evening through the emergency department at Loma Linda. Dr. Smith would instruct the ER physicians to admit him. Harley and Dorothy left town right after he hung up.

[8]

A Ray of Hope

HARLEY'S EMERGENCY TRIP TO Loma Linda so soon after his deposition was unexpected. The Oak Ridge doctors would not support his case and offered no suggestions for treatment. We needed a radiation expert willing to get involved in a lawsuit against the AEC.

We called Paul Duckworth, our consultant, and told him Harley was back in the hospital and asked him to see if he could get the name of a medical expert to review Harley's case. Paul called back a few days later and gave us the name and telephone number of Shields Warren, a doctor in Boston. Paul said he got Dr. Warren's name from Robley Evans, a well-known physicist, who had studied radiation effects. Paul called Dr. Evans and asked him if he could look over Roberts's radiation information and records. Evans disclosed that he had served as a consultant for REECo since the mid-1960s and had been hired by REECo to investigate Baneberry shortly after it vented. He supplied Dr. Warren's telephone number as one who might be willing to consult on the matter.

We had no background information on Dr. Shields Warren but knew we had to find an expert. We called the number Paul Duckworth gave us and asked the woman who answered whether Dr. Shields Warren was available. She asked the purpose of the call and we explained that Robley Evans had suggested we call Dr. Warren to see if he would be willing to consult on a case involving a Test Site worker exposed to radiation.

"I'll see if he's available," she said and put us on hold. We all but held our breath while we waited to see whether Dr. Warren would accept the call. When we called, we expected Shields Warren to be qualified but had no idea we would be talking with one of the founding fathers of radiation pathology and probably the leading expert in the world on the effects of radiation from atomic testing.

"Hello, this is Shields Warren," a voice responded with a pronounced stutter. "I understand Robley Evans recommended me to you."

"Yes, Dr. Warren. I'm Larry Johns and my brother Alan Johns is also on the line. We are attorneys in Las Vegas, Nevada, who represent a Test Site worker exposed to radiation in December 1970. Dr. Robley Evans is consulting for the AEC in a court case here in Las Vegas involving the radiation exposure. He gave us your name."

"I've known Robley Evans since the 1930s. He's not a medical doctor, but has done a lot of work in radiation measurements. Can you summarize what the case is about?"

"Yes. We represent thirteen Nevada Test Site security guards exposed to radiation when the Baneberry test vented in December 1970. They were ordered into the radioactive cloud to evacuate workers from a base camp. Harley Roberts, the security guard who had the highest reported radiation readings that day, is at Loma Linda Hospital. His diagnosis is acute myelogenous leukemia, and he isn't expected to live much longer."

"What information do you have about Mr. Roberts's radiation exposure on December 18, 1970?"

"The only information we have is from a report the AEC put out in May 1971, five months after Baneberry. It states that a security guard received a gamma dose around 1.00 rem, a beta dose around 4.5 rem, and a thyroid dose around 3.75 rem. We are certain those are the readings for Harley Roberts, since he was in the radiation cloud for nearly an hour and was not brought in for decontamination until eight hours later. Mr. Roberts testified at his deposition that he was monitored shortly after he left the base camp and the radiation monitor told him he was hot as hell. After he was decontaminated around 10:00 pm that night, his hands were still reading 25 mR, and he was issued rubber gloves and told to wear them overnight due to the readings on his hands."

"Both the gamma and beta readings were undoubtedly recorded on Roberts's film badge," Dr. Warren explained. "I was director of Biology and Medicine when the Atomic Energy Commission was created in 1947. In that position, I oversaw health and safety at all the AEC's facilities, including the Nevada Test Site when it opened. In fact, I watched the first aboveground test in Nevada in January 1951."

When Dr. Warren mentioned his connection with the AEC, we were deflated, expecting a polite decline to review a case against an agency he had worked for. But to our surprise he launched into a long explanation, more like a lecture on all aspects of radiation. We were spellbound as we listened and scribbled notes on our legal tablets, trying to absorb the information.

"The film badge is generally a reliable instrument that records the gamma rays and beta radiation that was in the radioactive cloud. Gamma rays have the same penetrating energy as x-rays and would reach all the internal organs of the body. Most would penetrate through the cortex of the bones into the bone marrow, where the leukocytes or white cells are formed. Myeloid leukemia originates in the bone marrow and is derived from the Greek word mye which means "bone," and leukemia from the Greek work leukos which means "white" and refers to the white cells that fight off infection.

"The external gamma and beta readings recorded on Roberts's film badge are only part of the picture. Roberts would have been inhaling radioactive gases while in the Baneberry cloud. His thyroid readings confirm that he inhaled radioactive iodine present in the cloud that concentrated over time in his thyroid gland. Based upon many years of experience, I believe I could make a rough estimate of his external and internal bone marrow dose from the various sources, but it would be helpful if you could provide additional information. I also need all of his medical records both before and after his exposure to radiation in December 1970," Dr. Warren told us.

"We have records of annual physical examinations by the Test Site doctors from 1966, when he joined the force, that show he was in good health prior to the test. For several days after his exposure, he complained of diarrhea and mild fatigue, which he thought at the time was the flu. In July 1972, he went to Loma Linda University and was diagnosed with anemia. The doctors ordered bone marrow studies, which showed that he was missing a chromosome in the C group."

"That is extremely interesting," Dr. Warren interrupted. "Radiation has been known to cause chromosome mutations since the early 1900s. Dr. Boveri, the German embryologist, was the first to publish studies suggesting such a relationship.

"I assume you are aware that in the late 1920s Dr. Hermann Muller performed experiments for which he was later awarded the Nobel Prize demonstrating that fruit flies subjected to radiation showed chromosome mutations and deletions. It has been generally accepted since that time that radiation can cause an abnormal number of chromosomes in the daughter cells.

"The fact that Mr. Roberts was exposed to radiation in December 1970 and tests a year and a half later showed that he was missing one of the C chromosomes in his bone marrow stem cells is evidence that his radiation exposure may have caused the chromosomal mutation. There is evidence that the absence of a C chromosome is a precursor of myeloid leukemia. Once the missing C chromosome is found, the patient progresses to leukemia within a few years, as appears to have been the case here. Roberts's exposure to radiation at Baneberry in 1970 may have caused his condition."

When we heard this, we were thrilled and tempted to comment, but Dr. Warren continued.

"I have been interested in radiation effects since medical school. I began my own studies of radiation effects and published many papers on the subject in the 1930s. After the bombs were dropped on Hiroshima and Nagasaki, I was commissioned to organize a team of Navy doctors and hospital corpsmen to travel to Japan and work with the Japanese doctors to study the survivors at Nagasaki. We were later joined by a team of Army doctors, headed by Dr. Stafford Warren, and expanded our studies and worked with Japanese doctors in Hiroshima.

"Within a year and a half, there was pretty clear evidence that leukemia would develop and by 1950 there had been a significant increase in leukemia among the Japanese survivors. The study of the survivors of the atomic bombings confirmed my prediction that there would be a sharp increase in leukemia that peaked around four to six years after the bombings."

As stellar as Dr. Warren's qualifications were, we knew that Harley had been examined by doctors at the AEC's Oak Ridge Hospital and were concerned that once he learned that the AEC's doctors had examined Harley, he might be reluctant to challenge their findings.

"Mr. Roberts was sent to Oak Ridge Hospital last August," we interjected. "The doctors there confirmed the missing C chromosome and diagnosed his condition as preleukemia. Dr. Gould Andrews's summary does not rule out the possibility that the Baneberry exposure could have caused his condition but suggests that his radiation dose, as reported, was probably too low."

"Well," Dr. Warren responded, "Dr. Andrews and the AEC doctors at Oak Ridge would certainly have been looking to accurately diagnose the disease and should have understood the significance of the chromosome deletion. I would want to have all of their records to review."

"Obviously, we would not expect you to offer any opinions without reviewing all of the records," I interjected. "But we are planning to visit Mr. Roberts in the next few weeks. May we tell him that we have been in contact with you and that you are willing to consult on the case? It should be encouraging for him to know that you are interested in the matter."

"Certainly," Dr. Warren responded. "You may tell him that I am reviewing it. I have studied many patients with leukemia, and the last stage is very difficult for the patient and the family. I would request that when you visit him you ask his doctors to perform an autopsy, and prepare slides of his bone marrow, since it is very important that a correct diagnosis be made. As a pathologist, I would consider an autopsy imperative."

"We will see him soon," we said, "and will talk to his doctors and explain the need for an autopsy. May we mention your name and tell them that the request came from you?"

"Yes, and I would also request that following the autopsy, the bone marrow slides be sent to my laboratory here for my own review. Although I would have no reason to doubt the findings, I would be more comfortable in giving my own opinion based upon my review of the slides."

"We very much appreciate your willingness to review this matter. If you require a consultation fee, please let us know."

"I would be willing to review the records for $500. Please assemble the dose records, medical records, and other information and send it here to me. I will not have a chance to review this matter now, so unless there is some urgency, we may want to wait until after the autopsy has been performed, so I can review the slides."

"We'll send all the records we have and make sure the autopsy slides are sent to you."

"Very well. I will wait for the records. I will be on vacation for two weeks, but should be available in late April, if you have any questions."

"Thank you for agreeing to consult on this matter," we ended.

"Not at all. Goodbye," he said.

Dr. Warren had been gracious and utterly unembarrassed by a pronounced stutter, which produced delays during the phone call. But his mild impairment allowed him to make a much more deliberate explanation of each point and made it easier for us to take notes and understand the complex medical issues.

We were ecstatic that an expert of the caliber of Dr. Warren was willing to review the case. His summary of his qualifications, particularly his involvement with the Japanese survivors and former position with the Atomic Energy Commission, could leave no doubt that we had found the perfect expert to review the case.

In early March 1974, we made plans to visit Harley at the hospital in Loma Linda.

[9]

The Ides of March, 1974

I WAS NOT LOOKING forward to driving over to Loma Linda Hospital to see Harley. Alan and I agreed we could not both go, so I volunteered. There's an old saying that a lawyer should not get emotionally involved in his client's case. It is a fine-sounding legal axiom I probably heard in law school from some old professor cautioning his students to remain detached and totally objective about their clients' cases. But it was too late for trite legal crap. Harley was a warm, friendly, down-to-earth sort of guy. He was unpretentious and humble, except about Hoosier basketball, which he boasted was the best in the country.

Alan and I got to know Harley well in the years after he came in for his initial interview in November 1971. We shared his anxious moments and saw his depression deepen as his health steadily declined. He was not a man who expected a lot out of life, but neither had he planned on dying and leaving his wife Dorothy alone and nearly destitute.

It had been less than a month since Harley went over to the AEC building to tell his story about Baneberry in the deposition. Now he was back at Loma Linda. We had practically memorized his medical records. His diagnosis on admission a few weeks earlier was cold and impersonal but laid out his story. "The patient is a 53-year old Caucasian male, with a myeloproliferative disorder and history of exposure to radiation at the Nevada Test Site. Diagnosis: acute granulocytic leukemia." His medical records detailed the progression of his disease from the first faint hint of general fatigue to full-blown leukemia. They were punctuated by mysterious medical terms such as "blood dyscrasia," "sideroblastic anemia," "myeloproliferative disorder," "leucopenia," "pancytopenia," and "hypodiploidy," words that were now part of our vocabulary.

After talking to Dr. Warren in late February, we knew that Harley's leukemia had just about run its deadly course. There had been many other hospitalizations, and he had rebounded. But not this time. Dr. Warren had insisted on an autopsy, and we knew what that meant. I had to face Harley and wondered how I would react if he asked me about his condition. Did I have an ethical duty to tell him he was dying? Could I conceal from him that Dr. Warren wanted to make sure an autopsy was performed? Should I tell Harley the next chapter in preparing his case for trial against the AEC was an autopsy of his remains?

As I passed the Las Vegas J. C. Penney, I remembered how store-window mannequins were taken out to the Test Site and placed in fabricated homes during the 1950s atmospheric tests. We were excited when the AEC told us the tests were intended to replicate blast effects on a typical American family. Later, we learned that the scientists were trying to reconstruct the Japanese radiation doses at Hiroshima and Nagasaki. Those mannequins were an expendable sacrifice for the atomic testing program. Harley was not.

I pulled into Paul Duckworth's driveway a little past 6:00 am. We had hired Paul to assist us in investigating the Baneberry case because of his engineering background and his years working at the Test Site for Livermore (LLL), the lab running the Baneberry test. Paul was watching from the window and quickly jumped in to avoid a cold March breeze.

"Are you ready for this?" I asked.

"Not particularly."

At 9:00 am, we took the Loma Linda exit and stopped for breakfast at the first restaurant. It was balmy and misty, the coastal fog still not burned off by the morning sun.

Loma Linda University Hospital was majestic, compared to the small curbside hospitals in Las Vegas. The Veterans Hospital down the street was equally impressive, another stark contrast to Las Vegas, which had only a small outpatient clinic for the thousands of southern Nevada veterans who had to travel to California or other states for serious medical care.

The cancer ward was a large room with a circular nurses station. Stacks of monitors were feeding information from each of a dozen or more patient rooms on the perimeter. We checked in at the nurses station and asked to see Harley Roberts. The nurse in charge issued us paper masks, explaining that infection was the greatest danger facing terminal leukemia patients. She pointed to a room. A clipboard and chart hung on the door with Harley's full name in bold black ink.

Harley was lying on a small hospital bed, upper body elevated and head propped up with pillows. The yellow walls and yellow glow coming through the small curtained window contrasted with the stark and sterile white bed linens in which a pallid, emaciated face swam. There were tubes and wires everywhere: a plastic oxygen tube was stuck into Harley's nose, a tube ran to a urine bag hanging by the bed, tubes came from under the sheets to dangling IV bottles, and wires ran between the machines and monitors. The stillness was broken only by the slight hum of the oxygen machine, as the flickering monitors silently registered vital information transmitted to the nurses station.

Harley was asleep. Overcome by the sight of his ghastly visage peeping out from the sheets, I debated whether to wake him or return a little later. But it was too late. Harley's eyes cracked open, and he greeted me with his familiar wry smile.

"Hello, Larry," he spoke almost in a whisper, but with that resonant, nasal tone so recognizable to those who knew him.

"Hey, how are you doing?" I asked.

"Well, I'll tell you," he half chuckled, gasped, and then turned deadly serious, "I feel like hell . . . I can't get my breath." It was a long minute before he could continue. "I don't have the strength . . . to even get out of bed. If I could, I'd pull out these damn tubes . . . and get it over with."

I could not find words to respond. Harley was gasping and desperate, and I felt helpless as I watched him struggle. Fortunately, Paul Duckworth changed the subject.

"I'm Paul Duckworth. I've been working on the Baneberry case with Larry and Alan. I worked for LLL out at the Test Site for many years."

"Oh, sure. I recognize you." Harley paused to get his breath. "You came through my checkpoint ... You probably don't remember me. But you know . . . we check badges and log people ... so we remember just about everybody."

"I'm sure you checked me lots of times. I left before Baneberry. I couldn't take the AEC's cavalier attitude about health and safety. Baneberry is just one more example of their incompetence."

"Nobody can believe the bastards ... won't just admit they screwed up," Harley interjected. "Everybody at the site knew ... Baneberry was a mistake."

His voice filled with despair and anger, Paul replied, "I think it was obvious long before they fired it with all the drilling problems they had. I wrote the AEC shortly after the blowout. I asked them to tell the truth about the vent. They never responded, of course. They just don't seem to care. Anyway, I've got a lead on a couple of geologists from the University of Kansas. I hope they will agree to investigate it. It looks like the AEC is going to fight every step of the way."

Finally, able to rejoin the discussion, I tried to lift Harley's spirits. "Harley, we've spoken about your case with Dr. Shields Warren. He's an expert in radiation effects at Harvard University. He thinks we may be able to make a case for you and has asked us to send him all your medical records, including the ones from Oak Ridge. Without him, we'd have a tough time showing that your condition was caused by Baneberry. Of course, he hasn't completed his investigation, so it's too soon to say for sure."

"You know," Harley followed up in a bewildered tone, "I still can't understand ... why the AEC agreed to send me to their ... hospital in Oak Ridge last year if they didn't damn well know they caused this."

"We felt the same way at the time, Harley," I replied. "We thought they were concerned about you and wanted to help. Those Oak Ridge doctors get their funding from the AEC and aren't going to bite the hand that feeds them. It was probably a mistake to send you there. It looks like all they really wanted was to get you to their hand-picked doctors to try to figure out a way to cover their asses."

Harley sighed, "I wouldn't care ... if they had come up ... with some kind of treatment for this. I guess all I got ... was an expense-paid trip to Tennessee."

It seemed like a long time before Harley broke the silence again, pleading, "Fellas, I can't take much more of this. I'm just hanging on for Dorothy's sake ... She doesn't seem to realize ... how bad I am and I just can't bring myself to tell her." Harley turned away to conceal the tears he was fighting.

"You've got to hang on. You can't let them win," I said.

"Larry ... let's not kid ourselves. I'm not gonna be around much longer . . . They give me transfusions. . . but, it only helps for a short time." His voice trailed away as he turned to the wall.

And again, silence. Neither Paul nor I knew how to respond to Harley's matter-of-fact statement that his life was ebbing away. But Harley was not done.

He abruptly turned to face us again and angrily said, "The AEC doesn't give a damn about me ... Dorothy's diabetes is really bad ... We can't even afford for her ... to come stay with me."

Then, with what little strength he could muster, he propped himself up on his left arm, tubes sticking out from under the sheet, clenched his fist, and looked me in the eye. "Larry ... you got to make the bastards pay for this ... They know they caused this ... They can't kill people and get away with it."

"Harley, you know we'll do everything we can," I said.

"If their smart-ass lawyers ... had to go through just fifteen minutes of this," he tapered off and then suddenly snapped, "by God ... I'd give anything to trade ... places with them ... just for one day ... then I could die in peace."

His outburst was interrupted by the nurse who had noticed his vital signs spiking erratically and decided the visit had to end. She said she had to check Harley and we would have to leave for a while. Harley held out his bony hand. I grasped it warmly and was struck by how cold and lifeless his once strong and calloused hand had become. For just a moment, I cradled Harley's frail hand in both of mine. And then, trying not to show our relief, Paul and I headed for the door.

Turning back, I said, "Well, Harley, we'll see you later. We just wanted to see how you were doing and bring you up to date. We're going to see your hematologist, Dr. Kuhn, and tell him we've talked to Dr. Warren. We'll see you in Vegas after you get released."

"Thanks for coming," he said. Then raising his head from the pillow, Harley looked me straight in the eye one more time and spoke with all the strength he could muster, "Don't forget, Larry . . . you got to make the bastards pay."

Harley's last will and testament, "you got to make the bastards pay," was not written on gilded parchment, subscribed and sworn by witnesses before a notary public. But it was Harley's dying command. Over the next twenty-two years, as Harley's Baneberry case wended through the federal court system in the longest roller-coaster ride in the history of the District of Nevada, my darkest moments were inspired by Harley's grim and determined plea.

We pushed open the double doors, discarded the paper masks, and headed to the information desk on the first floor to find Dr. Kuhn. Neither Paul nor I spoke. We were both struck dumb by Harley's unburdening of emotions that had wracked his soul in the years since Baneberry. No team of government lawyers or high-paid government doctors could deter this Indiana farm boy from the plain, unvarnished truth. He knew Baneberry had poisoned him, and he knew the AEC knew it too.

We entered the Hematology Department, approached the desk, and asked if Dr. Kuhn was available. Several minutes later, Dr. Kuhn came out. He was fit and trim and looked younger than I had expected from our phone conversations over the past year. After exchanging introductions, he ushered us down a hall past logging stations and into a small office.

"Have you seen Harley?" he asked.

"Yes. He's very discouraged. He said he just wants it over," I responded.

"He's suffering terribly, physically and mentally," Dr. Kuhn said. "His type of leukemia, we call it acute granulocytic or myelogenous leukemia, they are the same, alters the white cells, the ones that attack infection. His bone marrow is manufacturing white cells but they are nearly all abnormal, replacing the few normal cells he has left. We've given him transfusions, but that's about all we can do. Without the transfusions, he would have been gone long ago."

"Have you had a chance to review the records from Oak Ridge?" Paul asked.

"Yes, and I'm pleased they confirmed my finding that he has a missing a C chromosome. To me that's significant and the most unusual feature of his case. Otherwise, I can't see that they have come up with anything new. I mean, they call it preleukemia, but of course that simply means they know it's progressing toward frank leukemia. I'm really not qualified to discuss whether his leukemia is the result of his exposure to radiation at the Test Site, although it could not be ruled out."

"We've spoken to Dr. Shields Warren," I said. "He's a radiation pathologist at Harvard. He told us it looks like Harley's exposure at Baneberry could be the cause, but that is merely his preliminary view, and he wants all of the medical records."

"Well," Dr. Kuhn noted, "everyone knows of Shields Warren's work. If he's considering the case, I doubt you would need any opinion from me."

"Well, we would be interested in your observations, nevertheless. You may be asked your views at some point, in any case."

"I'm afraid I can't be of much help either way," Dr. Kuhn explained. "As a clinical hematologist, I diagnose and treat blood disorders, including leukemia. Harley's type of leukemia is unique in my experience because he has this missing C chromosome. I believe very little has been published about leukemia cases involving missing chromosomes."

It was time to let Dr. Kuhn know that Dr. Warren had wanted an autopsy. "Dr. Warren is grateful that you discovered the chromosome abnormality right at the beginning. He told me that your initial findings are very important in the case and many specialists might not have done the detailed investigation and follow up you did. He did ask me to make sure that an autopsy is performed and that slides of the bone marrow are taken so that he can review them. He wants to make sure that acute myeloid leukemia is the cause of death, since it is the first type of leukemia that ordinarily shows up after one is exposed to radiation. He will probably call you with the information about where to send the slides."

"That's fine. I'll inform Mrs. Roberts of the necessity for an autopsy immediately after his death. Tell Dr. Warren I'll be waiting for his call. In the meantime, we'll try to make Harley as comfortable as possible. He's constantly fighting respiratory infections. Once it gets him, it will likely progress rapidly to pneumonia, which he will not be able to fight," Dr. Kuhn explained.

"Thank you, doctor, for your time," I said, sensing that he was anxious to get on with his work. "I hope we can call you if we need any information."

"Sure." Dr. Kuhn walked us out to the hall, shook hands, and returned to the lab.

Paul and I left the hospital and headed back to Las Vegas. Neither of us felt like talking. I was haunted by Harley's emaciated, pallid form wrapped in the bed sheet. A light rain began to fall as we entered the freeway, but through the whine of the tires on wet asphalt and the cadence of the windshield wipers, I kept hearing Harley's final words, "Make the bastards pay."

APRIL 17, 1974

IN EARLY APRIL, IT was evident that Harley had indeed developed pneumonia. He declined rapidly. Thankfully, his son Randy was granted an early discharge from the Marines in late March to be with his parents during his dad's final days. Randy knew how much his mother depended on Harley. Taking daily insulin injections placed an added burden on her. Randy drove his mother and grandmother to Loma Linda on Dorothy's days off and whenever Dorothy could be spared from her work.

By the 10th, Dorothy, Randy, and Harley's eighty-year-old mother were at the hospital every day, keeping vigil. By mid-April Randy knew the end was near. Harley was sleeping most of the time, but Dorothy kept hoping he would get better. Harley's mother was facing one of the most difficult things a parent can face, the death of a child. But she bore her suffering silently and did what she could to help Dorothy.

On April 17, after a very difficult night, Dorothy clung to Harley's bed, refusing to leave. By late afternoon, her legs were so swollen and she was so exhausted the hospital staff was threatening to hospitalize her if she did not follow their advice. Randy finally persuaded her to lie down on the cushioned sofa in the hallway and take a nap.

Dorothy collapsed and slept. Randy stayed beside Harley, watching the monitors falter and flatline. Randy found his mother sound asleep on the hallway sofa and gently touched her shoulder. At first, she thought she must be dreaming. But somehow, she responded to the urgency of his touch. She finally opened her eyes and saw Randy stooping over her, his own eyes misty and his voice breaking as he told her. "Mom, he's gone." And she knew what he meant more from his face than the words he spoke. Harley had been more than a father to Randy; he had been a friend and companion.

As soon as Dorothy realized her Harley was gone, panic and shock grabbed her. She rose, burst through the door, and staggered toward his room with desperation, as if she could somehow stave off death or at least arrive in time to say goodbye. She had had no opportunity for a final farewell, unwilling as she had been to admit the gravity of his condition. But when she reached the bedside and saw the expression on the nurse's face, the truth hit her like a hammer. She went numb . . . passive. So complete was her retreat from reality that she could recall almost nothing of the event or what followed over the next several weeks. She signed the consent for an autopsy and arrangements were made. The bone marrow slides sent to Dr. Warren confirmed the Loma Linda pathologist's diagnosis. Harley died of acute myelogenous leukemia, the type of leukemia long known to be caused by radiation exposure.

Arrangements were made for his body to be flown back home to Indiana to Harley's beloved Bicknell for burial. Harley Roberts, like the Baneberry vent cloud, passed over Nevada and into the American heartland. His nightmare was finally over.

[10]

Cracking the Shell of Secrecy

IN EARLY MAY 1974, Dr. Warren called to report that he had reviewed the autopsy slides from Loma Linda. They confirmed that Harley Roberts died of acute myelogenous leukemia. But his next words were quite unexpected.

"I thought I should let you know that I have reviewed all of Mr. Roberts's medical records and his film badge readings, and it's beginning to look fairly certain that the radiation from Baneberry caused Roberts's C chromosome deletion, which in turn led to his leukemia and death."

Dr. Warren spoke in his very deliberate manner, leaving little doubt in our minds that, if anything, he had understated his conviction that radiation from Baneberry was the most probable cause of Harley's death. But he would need more information about Harley's radiation dose before he would prepare a written opinion.

We told him we were scheduling the depositions of the Rad-Safe monitors who took readings of Roberts and would send copies. This could take several months. Dr. Warren said he looked forward to receiving the additional information.

Dr. Warren's call was exhilarating. When we filed the lawsuit in February 1972, it was primarily to protest the AEC's casual attitude in ordering the security guards into a radiation zone but also to force it to produce the guards' radiation exposure records. We had not anticipated that any of the guards would develop health problems.

With Dr. Warren firmly on our side and with newfound enthusiasm, we were determined to find the truth about the cause of the Baneberry vent and pursue the Roberts case to its conclusion, no matter how long, difficult, or costly.

When Dr. Warren called, the AEC's explanation about the cause of the December 1970 Baneberry vent was unraveling. In late 1973, we took the depositions of Baneberry Test Manager Cluff and the scientists who selected the Baneberry site. We learned that the United States Geological Service (USGS) had investigated the cause of the vent and issued a report early in 1971. We also learned that in January 1971 the AEC had completed its investigation of Baneberry, prepared a comprehensive report, and had reviewed films of the vent.

We filed motions to produce the two reports and the films, but the government opposed our motion. The AEC claimed disclosure would compromise national security. We persisted and ultimately prevailed, despite opposition by government counsel, who summed up the government's disdain for us and the public: "This isn't a case where the public has a right to know what the scientists are doing, but this has to do with some highly technical classified information."[1]

We were dumbstruck by the arrogance and could not imagine how the records, reports, and primary data about the geology of the Baneberry site and the films could compromise national security. In our view, a geological formation laid down eons before the AEC began testing A-bombs at NTS could not be classified "secret." Geology, we thought, was an imperishable science, which even the AEC could not alter, distort, or conceal.

Ever since the AEC first came to town in 1951, they had let us know how fortunate we were to have such eminent scientists in our backward community. Now, twenty years later, they asked us to accept, without question, statements by the eminent scientists that either they did not fully investigate the Baneberry geology or did not understand the consequences of detonating a device in the geologic formation they selected.

Although we had long suspected, particularly our consultant Paul Duckworth, that the May 1971 *Baneberry Summary Report* was inaccurate, we were now convinced the AEC was engaged in a cover-up and would try to bury all contradictory information.

The court granted our motion to produce. We were provided a heavily redacted copy of NVO-95, the January 1971 *Baneberry Summary Report*.[2] We were also provided a copy of the USGS report issued in January 1971.[3] But we had to file additional motions before the court allowed us to view the films of the Baneberry vent.[4]

In June 1974, I traveled to Denver to take the depositions of the USGS geologists who had prepared the report. Their testimony established that the *Baneberry Summary Report* was false or very misleading in its conclusions about the geology of the Baneberry site and the cause of the venting.

Armed with NVO-95 and the USGS report, Paul Duckworth contacted two geologists at the University of Kansas, in Lawrence. Ernest Angino was professor and chairman of the Department of Geology. His expertise was in geochemistry. He served as chief of the geochemistry section of the Kansas Geological Survey from 1965 to 1970. John Halepaska earned his doctorate in geoscience in 1970, after completing an MS degree in groundwater hydrology. He was chief of the groundwater section of the Kansas Geological Survey.

Both were eminently qualified to challenge the AEC's contention that the Baneberry vent was unexpected. Between 1969 and 1972, they headed up a study to determine the feasibility of burial of high-level nuclear waste in Kansas. Based upon their investigation, the Kansas Geological Survey recommended against the idea. This was significant, because they had opposed the AEC and beaten them.

Drs. Angino and Halepaska reviewed the geological information and concluded that the AEC's statement in the May 1971 *Baneberry Summary Report* that the "primary cause of the vent was an unexpected and abnormally high water content in the medium surrounding the detonation point" was unsupported by the evidence. They relied upon the USGS report that showed "water content of the clay medium at Baneberry was very high" and that another "nuclear test *(Stutz)*, known to have been conducted in a similar clay medium, gave an unusually high seismic response similar to Baneberry." They pointed out that the USGS report revealed another deliberate omission in the *Baneberry Summary Report*.

> A large fault lies nearly tangent to the Baneberry shot point cavity [and that] the vent path was probably up this fault to its intersection with a tension fracture in the alluvium and thence up that pathway to the surface. Thus, the venting at Baneberry was probably related to a coincidence of structure [a fault], including fracture orientation, and water bearing clay.

They pointed out that NVO-95 also discredited the bastardized May 1971 *Baneberry Summary Report*. NVO-95 contained over thirty charts and tables and acknowledged that there was "high montmorillonite clay content above and below the shot horizon." This "caused the much higher water content than is normally expected at this depth in Yucca Flat." It concluded, "The implications of geology with respect to containment are implicitly recognized by the Laboratories [LLL and LASL], but the explicit implications for this specific case were not fully considered by the entire testing community."

It took only a moment to decipher this cryptogram. The scientists at LLL recognized there was a high likelihood Baneberry would not be contained, but others in the testing community did not.

In late July 1975, we disclosed to government counsel the opinions of Drs. Angino and Halepaska. The government immediately scheduled their depositions. I traveled to Lawrence, Kansas, for Dr. Angino's deposition on September 3, 1975, and to Tampa, Florida, on September 4, 1975, for Dr. Halepaska's deposition.

After our two geologists were deposed, we were confident we could show that the AEC had deliberately misrepresented the geology of the Baneberry site when they issued the May 1971 *Baneberry Summary Report*. It had been a painful awakening. The AEC's decision to issue the May 1971 *Baneberry Summary Report*, with full knowledge that NVO-95 and the USGS report contradicted it, amounted to a gross misrepresentation of the truth.

We began our investigation of Baneberry in early 1971, trusting an agency that had been part of our community for over twenty years. Over the next four years, as we investigated the Baneberry vent, we realized we were dealing with AEC officials and a platoon of government lawyers prepared to do whatever was necessary to protect the AEC's image and defeat our claims in court.

NOTES

1. *Las Vegas Sun*, September 6, 1975.

2. *Baneberry Collection*, EX 62, *Baneberry Summary Report*, January 1971, NVO-95. Unlike the fourteen-page May 14, 1971 Baneberry Summary Report, NVO-95 was seventy-five pages with multiple tables and charts. The copy we were supplied with looked like Swiss cheese, with countless redactions.

3. *Baneberry Collection*, EX 36. *Results of the Exploration of the Baneberry Site, Early 1971*, USGS-474-145. The report was over 110 pages in length, including multiple figures, tables, and redactions.

4. We filed multiple motions to produce the films. On April 21, 1975, the court allowed us to view the films at the AEC offices but under a protective order, which precluded us from copying or reproducing the material or communicating to any person information about the films.2. Baneberry Collection, EX 62, Baneberry Summary Report, January 1971, NVO-95. Unlike the fourteen-page May 14, 1971 Baneberry Summary Report, NVO-95 was seventy-five pages with multiple tables and charts. The copy we were supplied with looked like Swiss cheese, with countless redactions.

3. Baneberry Collection, EX 36. Results of the Exploration of the Baneberry Site, Early 1971, USGS-474-145. The report was over 110 pages in length, including multiple figures, tables, and redactions.

4. We filed multiple motions to produce the films. On April 21, 1975, the court allowed us to view the films at the AEC offices but under a protective order, which precluded us from copying or reproducing the material or communicating to any person information about the films.

[11]

Tell That Lawyer to Go to Hell

DR. WARREN WAS A CAREFUL investigator who wanted as much information as we could obtain before he would give us his final opinion in the Roberts case. It took five months to complete the depositions of Rad-Safe monitors and others who collected the data on dosage.

We called in November 1974 to make sure Dr. Warren had received the information. He said he had but had not worked through the stack of documents. He believed he would be ready to discuss the case with us in early January and would have his secretary call to schedule a telephone conference.

The conference was held in mid-January. We listened to Dr. Warren for nearly an hour as he discussed Harley's medical records, Harley's deposition testimony, and the radiation records. He spoke to us as if we were his medical students and he was tutoring us on the science, as he walked us through every aspect of his analysis and opinion. In addition to the many hours he spent reviewing the material we supplied, he researched the medical and scientific literature. And we received not only Dr. Warren's opinion that Harley's radiation exposure at Baneberry caused his leukemia, but also an education in the field of radiation effects that explained why there could not have been any other cause. We understood why Dr. Warren was revered in the scientific community, considered by many as the father of radiation pathology.

He explained that radiation had long been recognized as a highly potent cause of chromosome abnormalities. Dr. Boveri conducted the first research in the field and established the point in the early 1900s. In the 1920s, Dr. Muller studied the effects of radiation on fruit fly chromosomes, which are very large and easily identifiable, unlike human chromosomes.

Harley's exposure to radiation at Baneberry was sufficient to cause his chromosome abnormality. But unlike Dr. Muller's experiments, which produced immediate chromosome damage clearly visible under the microscope, Harley's chromosome abnormality from radiation at Baneberry, although immediate, was not detected until July 1972, eighteen months later. The bone marrow sample taken at Loma Linda Hospital in July 1972 revealed that Roberts was missing a C chromosome in one of the six pairs of C chromosomes. It was later specifically identified as a C-7 chromosome.

Dr. Warren then quantified Roberts's radiation exposure and explained how it caused the C-7 deletion. The film badge Harley wore showed he had received a whole-body dose of 1,045 mR gamma radiation. This dose was sufficient to cause the chromosome deletion. But there were other measurements of Harley's gamma exposure taken by Rad-Safe monitors throughout the day. The gamma radiation in the Baneberry cloud penetrated his body from every angle during the nearly one hour he was in the Baneberry cloud. However, many studies have shown that only about 70 percent of gamma rays penetrate the cortex of the bone and reach the red bone marrow, where the blood forming stem cells are produced. Therefore, the 1,045 mR gamma reading on his film badge would need to be reduced by roughly 30 percent to arrive at a whole-body bone marrow dose.

The film Roberts wore also recorded a beta dose of around 4,500 mR at the surface of the body. Unlike gamma rays, beta emitters that strike the surface of the body penetrate only about half a centimeter. Still, the beta emitters would add somewhat to Roberts's overall bone marrow dose, since a small percentage could penetrate the skin and the bone cortex to reach the red bone marrow in his skull, sternum, rib cage, spine, and pelvis where a large part of the red marrow is located.

In addition to the external radiation dose, Harley was inhaling radioactive gases in the Baneberry cloud the entire time he was in Area 12 Camp. While measurements were taken of radioactive iodine concentrated in his thyroid gland, there would have been many other radioactive gases present in the Baneberry cloud that were not measured. As Dr. Warren explained, these other radioactive substances in the cloud, like the iodine, would have been inhaled into the lungs and taken into the blood stream to circulate throughout the body, contacting all his cells, including the stem cells in the red bone marrow.

Dr. Warren said that he could not give any firm overall radiation dose to the red bone marrow, but most probably it was about 15 R or 15,000 mR, more than sufficient to cause damage to bone marrow stem cells.

All stem cells in Roberts's red bone marrow probably received radiation from Baneberry. But it was radiation to a single bone marrow stem cell in the process of cell division that caused the damage and initiated the leukemic process. Dr. Warren explained that Dr. Rudolf Virchow, the nineteenth-century German pathologist who is considered the father of pathology, first advanced the theory that leukemia and cancer begin with the alteration of a single cell that multiplies and overpowers the normal cells. Dr. Virchow's theory has been generally accepted since that time.

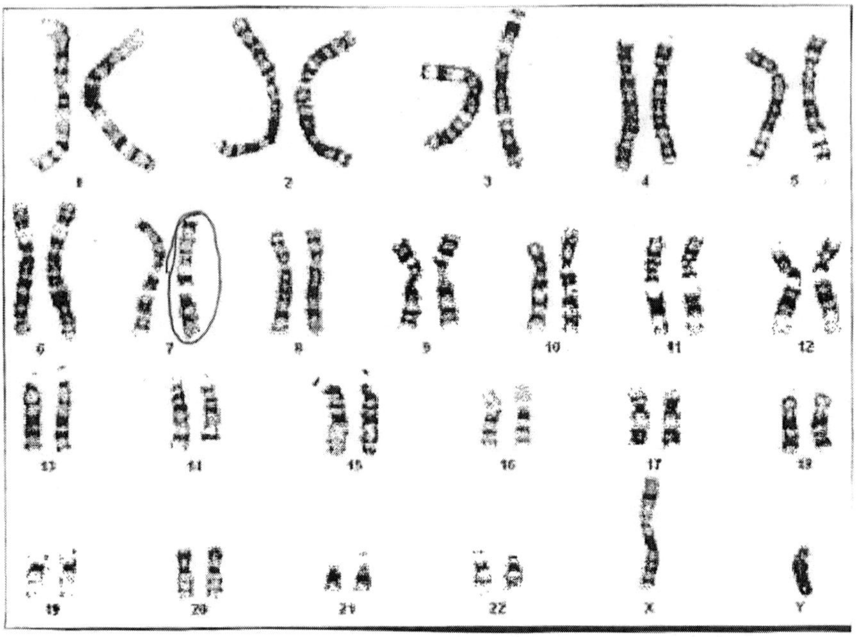

Representative copy of chromosome karyotype work. Harley Roberts had only one 7 chromosome after his Baneberry exposure.

Courtesy of the author.

The bone marrow cell damaged by radiation at Baneberry was in the process of dividing. The twenty-three pairs of human chromosomes in the bone marrow cells can only be viewed microscopically, when the cell is in the process of division. At that point, the chromosomes line up in pairs and are clearly visible and the chromosomes are most vulnerable to damage from radiation.

Dr. Warren assumed we had never seen a picture of the chromosomes in a human cell and had no more than an abstract notion how they are analyzed. He described the different chromosomes as looking like Chinese characters. When visible under the microscope, a photograph of the twenty-three pairs can be taken. For further analysis, each pair is cut from the photo and pasted on a board from chromosome 1 through chromosome 22. The final pair, chromosomes 23, are the sex chromosomes, X for female, and Y for male. The photograph is referred to as a karyotype. We didn't have a karyotype at the time he was explaining the matter, but his explanation certainly gave us a mental image of the violence radiation can do to a chromosome during cell division.

Dr. Warren explained that after the radiation destroyed the C-7 chromosome, one of the two daughter cells would have the missing C-7 chromosome. That abnormal cell has distinct advantages over the normal cell and would reproduce rapidly. Over time, it would overpower the normal cells. The rate of reproduction would be fast, because the bone marrow cells are among the most rapidly dividing cells in the body and in a constant state of division, replenishing all the blood cells that circulate throughout the body.

By July 1972, when a serrated needle was stuck into Harley's pelvic bone to draw out bone marrow cells for examination, the abnormal daughter cell produced on December 18, 1970, had proliferated to such an extent that many cells were detectable under the microscope. The growth rate of the abnormal bone marrow cells examined was consistent with the rate that would have been expected eighteen months after that first cell was altered by radiation from Baneberry.

Of course, the abnormal cells continued to increase and by February 1974, when Roberts was officially diagnosed with acute myeloid leukemia, 90 percent of his bone marrow cells contained the missing C chromosome. As expected in these cases, Roberts survived only two more months and died on April 17, 1974.

Dr. Warren explained that in 1974, there were only a few cases in the literature that described patients with a C-7 deletion. This was because it was not possible to clearly distinguish the C-7 cell until Dr. Caspersson, a Swedish physician, developed a new staining technique called banding for each of the twenty-three human chromosome pairs. Dr. Warren knew Dr. Caspersson and witnessed a demonstration of the new banding technique when he came to Boston in late 1972.

Although there are only a few cases in which the C-7 deletion has been found, they confirm that once it is detected in the bone marrow, the patient progresses to acute myeloid leukemia within a couple of years, followed by death within months. These cases, in Dr. Warren's view, established the connection between the course of Roberts's disease and death and his radiation exposure.

Dr. Warren then explained that in his opinion Harley's leukemia could not have any cause other than his Baneberry exposure. He reviewed with us Harley's medical history before and after Baneberry, which showed that REECo doctors gave him a physical examination when he joined the security force in 1966 and had annual physical examinations prior to Baneberry and one on February 18, 1971, a couple months after Baneberry. His blood studies were normal. He pointed out that the study done in February 1971 occurred so soon after Baneberry that it could not be expected to show any signs of a blood disorder.

In addition to the blood studies, which ruled out any blood disorder prior to Baneberry, Roberts's medical records showed that on December 18, 1970, he was in good physical condition for a man fifty years of age. On that day, he carried out rigorous duties, running from trailer to trailer for nearly an hour to evacuate workers.

Dr. Warren said he had carefully reviewed Harley's work history prior to Baneberry and saw nothing that could have caused a chromosome abnormality. He further explained that the C-7 deletion, once detected, takes no more than a year, two at the most, to cause anemia and other blood conditions. Therefore, it was very unlikely that Roberts had his C-7 deletion prior to Baneberry.

Summing up his analysis, he felt confident that Harley's exposure to radiation at Baneberry was the most probable cause of the chromosome deletion, which set in motion the progression to the anemia and the leukemia from which he died. As he put it, Baneberry left its fingerprint inside the body of Harley Roberts.

After Dr. Warren ended his explanation, he asked if we had any questions. We did not. In fact, Dr. Warren had anticipated all questions that could possibly bear on the relationship between Baneberry and Harley's death. By the time he finished, we were confident that no one could dispute his opinion in the case. Dr. Warren told us he would write up his opinion in the next week or so and mail it to us.

On January 30, 1975, Dr. Warren sent us a five-page, single-spaced letter, entitled *Analysis of Data and Opinion in the Case of Harley Roberts and Opinion of Shields Warren, M.D.* It set forth the basis of his opinion that Roberts's exposure to Baneberry on December 18, 1970, caused his C-7 deletion, which progressed to leukemia and death.[1]

A few days later, Dr. Warren called. His normal calm, professorial tone was replaced by disgust and anger. He said he had received a visit by a lawyer for New England Deaconess Hospital, where the Shields Warren Radiation Laboratory and his office were located. The hospital's counsel informed him that a lawyer from the Justice Department had contacted him after learning that Dr. Warren had given an opinion in a lawsuit against the AEC. The Justice Department lawyer advised hospital counsel that given the substantial funding his hospital received from the AEC, he considered it inappropriate for Dr. Warren to consult and serve as an expert in a lawsuit against the AEC. The Justice Department lawyer stated that Dr. Warren's involvement in a case against the AEC was a conflict of interest.

Dr. Warren reacted with outrage. In his view, the conflict of interest claim masked something more nefarious. In turn, he considered it a blatant effort to stifle his right to testify about a subject to which he had devoted his entire career. For a split second, we thought that the Roberts case had been dealt a serious blow, and we would need to find another expert. But Dr. Warren silenced our fears.

"I told the hospital's attorney to tell the government lawyer to go to hell," he said angrily, and described the government lawyer's tactics as "dirty pool." Dr. Warren assured us that he would testify in the case and no one could prevent him from doing so. His reassurance was not enough, however, to shake our rising panic that the government had nearly derailed our effort to pursue the Roberts case in court.

Until that moment, we had not appreciated the lengths to which the AEC and the Justice Department lawyers would go. It was sobering to learn that they immediately tried to bully Dr. Warren, one of their own. We realized we were dealing with a closed network of AEC-funded laboratories and hospitals and how difficult it might be to find other medical experts willing to testify against them.

TUCSON, ARIZONA, MARCH 1975

In late February, Dr. Warren called to tell us he would be in Tucson for two weeks in early March and invited us to meet with him to discuss the Roberts case. We were honored but a bit nervous that he might also have wanted to meet us to take the measure of the lawyers who had entangled him in the case. I had attended the University of Arizona and was anxious to meet the man who had so courageously defied the AEC and the Justice Department.

I arrived just before 10:00 am at the Arizona Inn near the University of Arizona Medical School. Dr. Warren was dressed formally in a light gray suit and wore spectacles. He struck me as a proper Bostonian who had changed neither his dress nor his manner over the past fifty years as he worked tirelessly to reach the top of his field. After we shook hands, Dr. Warren explained that he came to Tucson every spring so he could break up the long, cold New England winter and swim in the unheated sixty-eight-degree swimming pool. He had allotted precisely two hours to go over the information and answer any questions.

We sat opposite each other at a small table stacked with all his records and files in the Roberts case. He handed me a copy of his single-spaced, twenty page written résumé and told me that he had not updated it in the last couple of years. I quickly scanned through it and calculated that in addition to his education, honoraria, memberships, editorial boards, and professional societies, he had authored well over 400 papers and publications.

I had seen résumés of expert witnesses in other cases. Usually, they had one or two pages, including a few publications. But Dr. Warren's listing of his work was so overwhelming, I had to ask how he had managed to conduct so much research and publish so many articles. He looked at me and said matter-of-factly that he was one of those fortunate people who only require about four hours of sleep a night. This allowed him to start his work well before dawn and continue late into the night.

He must have sensed I was intrigued by the work in which he had been involved, some of which he had mentioned during our lengthy phone conversations. He began with a discussion of the Japanese survivors of the atomic bombings and the role he played in setting up the protocol for the studies. He described in some detail the conditions when he first arrived and the efforts to assist the Japanese doctors treating survivors suffering from acute radiation sickness, radiation burns, anemia, and other blood disorders. It was gruesome, but as a pathologist he had spent a lifetime dealing with disease and death.

Dr. Warren followed up with a discussion of the long-term studies of those who did survive and noted that he was primarily interested in blood studies to see whether they would develop leukemia.

Based upon the protocol he set up, he followed the group and documented the first case of leukemia that he considered to have been a direct result of the bombings. Relying upon that case and other records, he published the first paper predicting an outbreak of leukemia. He could not conceal how proud he was of his role in setting up the protocol and how important the studies were in tying together all the information about long-term radiation effects.

I imagined that the work in Japan must have been part of his standard introduction to his Harvard medical students over the years. It was fascinating for me to connect in a small way with his firsthand experiences after such horrible but momentous events. But in his descriptions, there was no hint of arrogance, just a genuine desire to educate me on the basics of radiation and its effects, using the most poignant and best-known example.

He must have sensed my awe. I wondered whether he was satisfied that he had placed his standing and reputation in the hands of the young lawyer opposite him and whether he felt I was capable of adequately presenting the Roberts case at trial.

He spoke about Harley Roberts with genuine compassion. He had, after all, seen firsthand the devastating effects of radiation that culminated in leukemia and an agonizing death. As Dr. Warren talked, I could not help comparing the approach of this sympathetic man to the Oak Ridge doctors whom Harley had described as cold and impersonal and treated him as the enemy. I was profoundly sorry that Harley was unable to meet him, for Dr. Warren's compassion might have made the suffering a little more bearable.

After commenting about the Justice Department lawyer's attempt to prevent him from expressing his opinion in this case, he mentioned that it was not the first time he had taken a principled stand and asserted his right to express his opinions about radiation risks. In the early 1950s, he related that he had a clash with the Department of Defense. It occurred when he was director of Biology and Medicine at the Nevada Test Site.

"I was in conflict with the military brass during that early period," he explained. "I was concerned that the soldiers were stationed in trenches too close to the atomic tests."

"How did they determine the dose the soldiers got?" I asked.

"That was part of the problem," he answered. "The military had their own radiation monitors who randomly issued film badges to the soldiers and were primarily interested in measuring gamma radiation. I was concerned about all the fission products produced in the explosion. This is the material sucked up into the fireball and then scattered over the area where the soldiers were ordered to march. There was no effort made to measure the radioactive gases and particles inhaled by the soldiers, and it would be impossible for me to determine the health risks to which they would be exposed. It is the same concern I have regarding Roberts's bone marrow dose from inhalation of gases in the Baneberry cloud.

"In the spring of 1952," he continued, "when the military resumed the series of aboveground tests and placed thousands of soldiers within a couple miles of ground zero, I again voiced my concerns and felt that they should not be placed closer than seven miles from the blasts. But the military's demand for active participation by the soldiers overrode my complaints. I registered my objections in writing and resigned my position effective July 1, 1952. I've never regretted that decision. I could not, in good conscience, continue as director and did not want to be held responsible for those soldiers."

It was nearly noon when he finished. He asked if I had any questions. Though I had reviewed his résumé quickly, I noted that it did not include any reference to testimony in lawsuits. In early 1974, that information was not required to be disclosed in a witness résumé. Today, court rules require an expert witness to produce a list of court cases in which he or she has given a deposition or testified at trial. I asked how often he had testified in court.

"Usually," he responded, "if I give an opinion, which I have on many occasions, that seems to end the matter. If my opinion supports the plaintiff, the case is usually settled. If my opinion supports the defense, the case is frequently dismissed. But, over the years, I have testified in court on a few occasions."

It was another matter-of-fact and credible statement befitting a man of his stature. I dared not inquire any further regarding the strength of his opinion in the Roberts case, but I could see why the government had wanted to remove him as our expert witness.

Within a week, government counsel sent a letter asking us to arrange a time for them to take Dr. Warren's deposition in Boston. His deposition was scheduled at the Shields Warren Laboratory at the New England Deaconess Hospital on June 9, 1975.

BOSTON, MASSACHUSETTS, JUNE 9, 1975

I arrived in Boston on Sunday night, June 8, and met with Dr. Warren early the next morning. The first thing he told me was that Robley Evans, the expert hired by the government, had called him late Friday afternoon, June 6, to discuss the Roberts case. Evans said the reason for calling was to tell Dr. Warren he was authorized by the government to disclose information regarding the breakdown of the various radioactive iodine isotopes produced by the Baneberry nuclear explosion. However, Evans conceded that there were no measurements of iodine or other radioactive gases taken in the Baneberry cloud during the time Roberts was present in Area 12 Camp.

Dr. Warren said he sensed that the real purpose of Evans's call was to try to persuade him that Roberts's bone marrow dose was too low to cause his leukemia and to determine whether Dr. Warren would change his opinion. He told Evans that the information regarding the iodine component was helpful but did not alter his opinion that the bone marrow dose was sufficient to cause the C-7 chromosome deletion and initiate the leukemia process. He had studied radiation-induced chromosome damage over many years and remained convinced that the radiation dose at Baneberry, even if less than he had originally thought, was sufficient to cause the C-7 deletion.

Dr. Warren explained to me that he understood Evans's point of view. But Evans was not a medical doctor and was unfamiliar with studies of radiation induced chromosome abnormalities, which might account for his failure to understand what Dr. Warren considered the most important aspect of the case.

Dr. Warren showed me around the laboratory while we waited for the attorneys. At just before 10:00 am, two government lawyers arrived with a court reporter in tow. The deposition lasted until 1:30 that afternoon.

The government lawyers were aware of Robley Evans's call to Dr. Warren and were hoping Dr. Warren had changed his opinion. But they learned that Dr. Warren had not been persuaded to accept Evans's estimated bone marrow dose. However, upon questioning, Dr. Warren did concede that his original estimate of 15 R or 15,000 mR was probably high, due largely to his not having been provided all the information, including a breakout of the radioactive iodine present in the cloud. He remained convinced that Roberts's bone marrow dose from external gamma radiation, combined with the internal dose from gas inhalation, was considerably higher than Evans's lower estimate of less than 1 Rem and "something under my first top estimate of 15 Rem." In either case, it would not change his opinion, because there was abundant evidence that radiation causes chromosome deletions, which was the bedrock upon which his opinion was based.[2]

Following the deposition, Dr. Warren took all three attorneys to lunch at the Harvard Club. Later that afternoon, he drove me to his home on Pilgrim Road in West Newton, where he had on display memorabilia and awards from his life-long study of radiation and contributions to other fields of medicine. He did not have time to discuss them all but did point with pride to an award from Hiroshima University and the Japanese government for his studies of the A-bomb survivors.

Dr. and Mrs. Warren then took me to dinner at a restaurant overlooking the Charles River. Near the end of dinner, the conversation came back to Baneberry. Between a thinking-out-loud comment and question, Dr. Warren wondered if another worker exposed at Baneberry might develop acute myeloid leukemia.

"Having one acute myeloid leukemia in the Baneberry group," he said, "is quite striking, but two cases would be truly remarkable." It was a curious thought that lingered with me on my flight back to Las Vegas. When I got to the office the next morning, I mentioned it to Alan.

NOTES

1. *Analysis of Data and Opinion in the Case of Harley Roberts and Opinion of Shields Warren, M.D.*, January 30, 1975. Copy in author's possession.

2. *Deposition of Shields Warren, M.D.* Copy in author's possession.

[12]

The Second Man

AFTER DR. WARREN MADE his observation about another possible leukemia in the Baneberry group, we asked Bill Cleghorn and Paul Duckworth whether they knew of any workers exposed at Baneberry who were having health problems. They checked around but did not find anyone.

Other than running an ad in the local newspaper, we knew of no way to find the names of the eighty-six workers. Today, attorneys solicit clients through television ads seeking persons exposed to asbestos or pharmaceuticals for the obvious purpose of filing lawsuits in their behalf. But in 1975, it was a violation of the canons of professional ethics to advertise or solicit clients for litigation.[1] "Barratry" is the term that prohibits lawyers from stirring up litigation in this way.

After the Justice Department tried to disqualify Dr. Warren from assisting us in the Baneberry case, we knew it would pounce on a chance to pursue disciplinary action against us before the Nevada Bar Association and seek to disqualify us from pursuing the case if we solicited other workers to join the lawsuit.

From July 1975 through the end of the year, we had no further information to pursue Dr. Warren's speculation that there might indeed be another leukemia. We assumed Harley's leukemia was the only one. But in January 1976, a call came into the office.

"Larry, Bill McGimsey is on the phone," the secretary told me over the intercom.

Bill and I had been friends since grade school. We and another grade school friend, Bill Steele, were roommates at the University of Arizona. Bill McGimsey and I passed the Nevada bar in 1968 and were sworn in in October.

"Hello, Bill, what's up?" I asked.

"I have a lady in my office who drove down from Indian Springs to talk about a real estate matter. She told me her husband worked out at the Test Site and was involved in the big blowout in 1970. I assume she's referring to Baneberry and told her you and Alan filed a lawsuit against the government over that test."

"Is her husband with her?" I asked.

"No. She said he died of leukemia."

"Really? I'd like to ask her a couple questions."

"I'll hand her the phone."

"Hello. This is Louise Nunamaker."

"Hello. This is Larry Johns. Bill said your husband worked out at the Test Site. Was he in the Baneberry test in 1970?"

"Yes. He was there. He came home in paper coveralls that evening."

"Bill said your husband died of leukemia. When did he die?"

"It was December 10, 1974. I'll never forget that date and how much he suffered during the last few months."

"Mrs. Nunamaker, I don't know whether you are aware that we filed a lawsuit for a security guard who was in the Baneberry test. He died of leukemia in April 1974."

"No. I've been in a state of shock ever since he died. I've been living up at Indian Springs and hadn't heard anything in the news about a lawsuit. Could I make an appointment to meet with you? I'd like to find out whether I have a case against the government over my husband's death."

She was only in town for the day, so we met with Louise Nunamaker early that afternoon. She told us her husband died of leukemia and produced a death certificate she kept in her purse. William Nunamaker died on December 10, 1974 of acute myelomonocytic leukemia, Naegeli type.

Louise was positive Bill was in the Baneberry test. She said he took a lot of showers, came home that day wearing a ridiculous paper suit and told her, "Mother, I was right in the middle of it." They kept all his clothing and even the car, which wasn't returned for nearly a month. He went on working for the next four years. Then he "just fell apart," she said, wiping away tears with the tissue she had been clutching.

When we told her about Harley Roberts and the lawsuit his widow Dorothy was pursuing, she asked us to file suit over her husband's death and wanted us to know about her husband and their life together.

We knew from the death certificate that Bill Nunamaker was born in Nebraska in 1913. She did not talk about his life before she met him during World War II. She knew he enlisted in the Navy right after Pearl Harbor and served in the Pacific during the war. They met in 1943, while he was on leave, and married right after the war ended. Bill was an operating engineer, and they moved around a lot. He worked all over the northwestern United States before he came to Las Vegas to take a job at the Test Site. Everybody liked him. He did not talk about his job, but she knew he worked in the tunnels and was promoted to shop foreman. He drove to work every day, because he did not like to leave her alone at night. They had four children, all grown and living on their own. It had been very hard for her without him.

After we met with Louise, we called Dr. Warren and told him there was another leukemia, an acute myelomonocytic leukemia, Naegeli type. He explained that Nunamaker's leukemia was essentially the same as Roberts's. I then asked him how he had known or suspected that there might be another acute myeloid leukemia in the Baneberry group. He said that of course he did not know there would be another leukemia when he made the comment, but since acute myeloid leukemia is the first cancer one would expect to see in a group of people exposed to radiation and Roberts had already been diagnosed with the disease, if there was going to be another acute myeloid leukemia, it would most probably show up in the first four to five years after Baneberry. That was the case with the Japanese.

On February 23, 1976, we again met with Louise. She now insisted we file a lawsuit against the government. We prepared the tort claim form, which she signed, and a two-page "Request for Release of Radiation Data and Medical Reports." They were served upon Mahlon Gates, manager of the Energy Research and Development Agency (ERDA) in Las Vegas.[2]

ERDA did not send the radiation exposure information or the medical records Louise requested. We obtained an autopsy report for William Nunamaker and other medical records and sent them to Dr. Warren for his review. On November 15, 1976, Dr. Warren wrote us, indicating that although the time from the Baneberry radiation exposure to development of acute myeloid leukemia was compatible with exposure and the onset of Nunamaker's leukemia, he did not think the radiation dose was sufficient to induce the disease. His preliminary conclusion was that it was a spontaneous case of leukemia in the group of men exposed at Baneberry. But he agreed to continue his investigation of the Nunamaker case.[3]

NOTES

1. Attorney advertising was not allowed until the U.S. Supreme Court struck down the Arizona Bar Association's prohibition of advertising in 1977, Bates v. State Bar of Arizona, 433 U.S. 350 (1977).

2. In 1974, Congress passed the *Energy Research and Development Act*. ERDA succeeded the Atomic Energy Commission. In 1977 Congress enacted the *Department of Energy Act*. The DOE succeeded ERDA.

3. Shields Warren to Larry Johns, November 15, 1976. Copy in author's possession.

[13]

A Hobson's Choice

BY THE END OF OCTOBER 1975, we had taken over twenty-five depositions to prepare for trial: Frank Cluff, the Baneberry test manager; Drs. Weart and Brownlee, the scientists who signed the *Baneberry Summary Report*; Dr. Lawrence Germain, an LLL scientist who sat on Cluff 's Test Evaluation Panel; Chan Griffin, AEC Security Chief; Richard McArthur, the LLL geologist who selected the Baneberry site; four USGS geologists who authored the USGS report; five Rad-Safe monitors who took radiation readings on the day of Baneberry; Captain Forest Tackett, WSI chief; and a dozen others.

The government also took over twenty-five depositions: Harley Roberts and the other security guards exposed at Baneberry; Paul Duckworth our consultant; Dr. Warren our medical expert; Drs. Angino and Halepaska, our geologist experts; and others.

We had forced the government to disgorge the "secret" documents that discredited the AEC's May 1971 *Baneberry Summary Report* and had viewed films of the Baneberry vent that showed the radioactive cloud blanketing Area 12 Camp. Most important, Dr. Shields Warren was prepared to testify at trial in support of the Roberts case.

The court closed further discovery on December 30, 1975.[1] We expected the case would be set for trial in the spring of 1976. But discovery did not close. On January 30, 1976, the court filed Amended Standing Order No. 24, which required the parties to attend a settlement conference to "fully and fairly" discuss settlement of the case.[2]

Discovery was extended to March 31, then to April 30, and then to June 18, 1976. With discovery set to close on June 18, 1976, we sent defense counsel a letter offering to settle Dorothy Roberts's case for $500,000, the amount Harley Roberts requested in the tort claim he filed in December 1971.[3] The offer was based entirely upon Dr. Warren's opinion supporting Roberts's case. The government had not challenged Dr. Warren's opinion.

In fact, Dr. Gould Andrews, who reviewed Roberts's medical records at Oak Ridge Hospital, reported that he "could not rule out radiation as the cause, although he felt the radiation dose was too low."[4]

Dorothy's offer was high, but we were authorized to reduce it by half if the government was willing to negotiate. We received no oral or written response to our settlement offer until April 28, 1977. During the ten months from June 4, 1976, to April 28, 1977, we were bogged down with motions, discovery disputes, hearings, extensions, and court orders, capped off by an order setting a pretrial conference before the court on February 7, 1977, then reset for March 14, 1977.[5]

On February 10, 1977, Alan and I met with John Thorndal and Bill Elliott to discuss trial witnesses and exhibits. We met again on March 2, 1977. During the meetings, we brought up the Roberts settlement offer but got no encouraging response. When we pointed out they had not identified an expert to counter Dr. Warren, they said they would disclose a radiation expert from Oak Ridge. On March 3, 1977, we sent a letter stating we would object to their adding expert witnesses as untimely, since the trial was set to begin on May 1, 1977.[6]

On March 9, 1977, the proposed pretrial order was lodged with the court.[7] In it, the government identified Dr. Clarence Lushbaugh, an Oak Ridge doctor, to counter Dr. Warren. On March 14, 1977, we filed a motion to strike Dr. Lushbaugh from the government's witness list as untimely, but when we attended the pretrial conference that day, the judge reopened discovery through June 17, 1977, to allow us to take Dr. Lushbaugh's deposition.[8]

On April 6, 1977, as we made final preparations for trial, an article appeared on the front page of the *Las Vegas Review-Journal*: "A-blast, then Leukemia." The article began, "Paul Cooper is dying of leukemia. His doctors say it's because he stood unprotected about 3,000 yards from a nuclear test blast in the Nevada desert nearly 20 years ago."[9]

We saw the news article about Paul Cooper. Dorothy and Louise also saw it and called us. They were saddened that another person exposed to radiation at NTS was dying of leukemia but believed the story would strengthen their claims. We were not so sure.

On April 28, 1977, the government responded to our June 4, 1976 offer to settle Dorothy's case. In the letter, Assistant Attorney General Barbara Babcock, by David Anderson, Chief of Litigation Division, offered to settle Dorothy Roberts's case for $75,000.00. She offered each of the other claimants $250.00 and gave us until May 10, 1977, to accept or the offer would be deemed rejected.[10]

The timing of the government's offer puzzled us. It came just three weeks after the headline news story about Paul Cooper. We called government counsel to discuss the $75,000 offer and inquired whether there was any room to negotiate a higher settlement. We also suggested that any settlement include the Nunamaker case. We were told they would convey our message to Washington.

After speaking with counsel, we called Dorothy, told her of the $75,000.00 offer, and asked her to meet us as soon as possible. Dorothy and her son Randy came in the following day. They were aware of our earlier $500,000 offer and could not understand why the government had offered so little for Harley's life. When Dorothy learned that Louise Nunamaker had been offered nothing, she looked puzzled but said she did not know much about Louise's case.

After telling Dorothy we had spoken to counsel about negotiating a higher settlement, we told her if she did not accept the offer by May 10, it would expire. We could see Dorothy was overwhelmed by the situation and was looking to Alan and me for advice. We could have taken the burden off her shoulders. We could have told her we were unwilling to spend more money and time and she must settle for whatever we could get. But we believed the ultimate decision was hers.

Dorothy asked the question every client asks when a settlement offer is made: "If I accept the $75,000.00 offer, how much will be left for me after all expenses are paid?"

We had never discussed with Dorothy the arrangement we made with the guard union in December 1971. The union agreed to pay all costs, but after they paid the $1,350 Ronan & Associates invoice in 1972, the board reneged and refused to pay further costs. We did not tell Dorothy and Randy that the costs we had paid already exceeded $40,000, and the costs would mount rapidly as we prepared for trial.

The thousands of hours we had devoted to the case over the past six years were incalculable. We had not kept records. We told Dorothy if she accepted the $75,000.00 offer, we would settle our costs for $20,000 and our fees for $20,000, which would leave her with $35,000.00.

Dorothy was not surprised by the cost figure and said we were being generous accepting only $20,000 for all the work we put into the case. She seemed genuinely sorry that we would all be left with so little if she accepted the $75,000. We reassured her we would be satisfied with $40,000, but the ultimate decision was hers.

She asked about our chances if we went to trial. We told her what she already knew: her case was based entirely upon the standing and opinion of Dr. Warren. The government would not have offered $75,000.00 had they not realized he was a formidable witness. But the government had also recently disclosed a doctor from Oak Ridge to counter Dr. Warren. We thought we had a strong case but could not predict the outcome if we went to trial and reminded her again that we had to respond in less than two weeks.

We could see the anguish in her eyes. It was tempting to take the settlement and end the ordeal. She looked at Randy and commented that it would make her life a little easier but only for a short while. After a very long moment, she said she was sorry, but she just could not take the offer. Harley's life was worth a lot more than $75,000, and she had suffered too much to accept so little. As tears welled in her eyes, she said, "I'd give anything if I could talk to Harley. I just don't believe he would want me to sell out so cheaply."

I had never mentioned to Dorothy the last words Harley spoke to me at Loma Linda in March 1974: "Make the bastards pay." Now, three years after Harley's deathbed plea, Dorothy delivered the same message with as much passion.

After our meeting, we called Dr. Warren. He understood her refusal and thought the government would too and would offer more. We also discussed the publicity about Paul Cooper's claim against the VA. Dr. Warren was aware of it. He found it interesting but offered no comment about the merits of Cooper's claim.

Next, we met with Louise Nunamaker. If Dorothy had agreed to settle for $75,000, it would have been a very unpleasant meeting. We would have explained to Louise that the Roberts case was much stronger than hers because of Dr. Warren's opinion. We had no expert to support her case and would not have been willing to expend additional time and money to pursue her lawsuit. Our involvement with Baneberry would have ended in May 1977.

Louise was furious when told the government had offered Dorothy $75,000 but nothing for her. She calmed down when we explained that Dorothy had rejected the offer. We told her we hoped the government would be willing to negotiate a higher settlement for Dorothy and offer to settle her case, but the deadline was May 10. We waited but heard nothing from government counsel. On May 10, 1977, the $75,000 offer expired.

Dorothy was disappointed and bitter. Unable to settle the case and faced with an IRS lien on her mobile home, on May 15, 1977, she wrote a letter to President Carter asking for his help. A few days later, a reporter came to her home to interview her. The interview appeared on Sunday, May 22. In it, she described her nightmare, the IRS's threat to take her mobile home, that "she had lost faith in her government," and "couldn't take much more of it." She said she had written to President Carter asking for his help and commented about Paul Cooper, the soldier exposed to radiation in 1957, which "caused the leukemia that is killing him."[11]

Although we knew it was probably futile, on May 24, two days after Dorothy's story appeared in the *Las Vegas Review-Journal*, we sent Bill Elliott a letter offering to settle the Roberts case for $225,000.[12] In the letter, we took a different tack from relying upon Dr. Warren. We referred to the October 30, 1973 decision by Judge Foley awarding Mrs. McGarry $185,000.00 and her adult daughter $40,000.00. Mrs. McGarry sued the AEC for the death of her husband, Thomas McGarry, a REECo employee electrocuted at the Test Site on December 10, 1969.[13]

Our reference to *McGarry* was a not-so-subtle reminder that Judge Foley had found the AEC liable for the death of an NTS worker. The Ninth Circuit Court of Appeals had affirmed his decision in December 1976.[14] We knew *McGarry* was on appeal to the U.S. Supreme Court but thought it would be decided soon.[15]

By the end of May 1977, any hope of settling the Baneberry case was over, and, by July, the Baneberry case expanded to include Louise Nunamaker's case. Publicity about Paul Cooper and other veterans exposed to radiation at NTS, was, as we had feared, a two-edged sword. The April 1977 article about Paul Cooper was the catalyst for the $75,000.00 offer to Dorothy. But in our view, extensive publicity about Cooper and other atomic veterans dashed any hope for a fair settlement of Dorothy Roberts's case. In fact, the amount offered was punitive, since the government knew we would have to absorb our costs and time, leaving Dorothy with very little.

The Cooper case elevated the investigation into the health effects from NTS radiation from a parochial concern in southern Nevada to an issue of national concern.

We did, however, make one final effort to settle Dorothy's case and Louise's as well. On March 17, 1978, we sent two letters to Bill Elliot. The first offered to settle Roberts for $200,000, which included $25,000 for her son Randy. One basis for our offer was that Dr. Akio A. Awa, a Japanese cytogeneticist who reviewed comments in Dr. Lushbaugh's deposition, stated that Lushbaugh had misinterpreted his findings. Another basis referenced recent investigations challenging the AEC's claim that low-level radiation was harmless. We ended the letter with a calculation of Dorothy's economic damages based on Harley's life work expectancy.[16]

In the second letter, Louise Nunamaker offered to settle her case for $125,000, based upon a calculation of Bill Nunamaker's work-life expectancy.[17] We received no response to either letter.

NOTES

1. DS 202. The docket sheet prepared by the U.S. District Court clerk in Roberts v. United States of America, CV-S-1766-RDF, is a chronological record and summary of all documents and court orders, beginning with the filing of the complaint on February 2, 1972: (1)—2/2/72—filed Complaint. The order closing discovery is DS 202. A copy of the docket sheet is in author's possession. Copy in author's possession.

2. DS 211.

3. Larry Johns to John Thorndal, June 4, 1976. We also offered to settle the claims of the other security guards for $25,000.00 each. Copy in author's possession.

4. *Baneberry Collection*, EX 73. 5. DS 230–270.

6. Alan Johns to John Thorndal, March 3, 1977. Copy in author's possession.

7. The proposed pretrial order was lodged, not filed, and has no docket sheet number but is noted on March 9, 1977.

8. DS 264; DS 265.

9. *Las Vegas Review-Journal*, April 6, 1977. Paul Cooper's battle with the VA began in 1976, and was extensively covered. *Salt Lake Tribune, Parade*, June 19, 1977; *Las Vegas Review- Journal*, July 17, 1977, *Las Vegas Review-Journal*, August 10, 1977.

10. Barbara Allen Babcock to Larry Johns, April 28, 1977. Copy in author's possession. David Anderson was chief litigation counsel for the government in Baneberry until he was promoted. He was replaced by Bill Elliott.

11. *Las Vegas Review-Journal*, May 22, 1977.

12. Larry Johns to William Elliott, May 24, 1977. Copy in author's possession.

13. McGarry v. United States, 370 F. Supp. 525 (1973).

14. McGarry v. United States, 549 F.2d 587 (1976).

15. On October 31, 1977, the U.S. Supreme Court rejected the government's appeal. The *Review-Journal* headlined the decision: "Government Liable for Test Site Death." *Las Vegas Review-Journal*, October 31, 1977.

16. Larry Johns to Bill Elliott, March 17, 1978. Copy in author's possession.

17. Larry Johns to Bill Elliott, March 17, 1978. Copy in author's possession.

[14]

GI Joe and the Smoky Vets

IN EARLY 1976, Paul Cooper, a resident of Idaho, went to see his family doctor complaining of weakness and fatigue. He was referred to specialists in Salt Lake City, Utah, who diagnosed his leukemia. When Paul told them that he was among a large group of young soldiers exposed to radiation during aboveground bomb test *Smoky* at NTS in August 1957, they helped him fill out a claim with the Veterans Administration and attributed his leukemia to his exposure to radiation at the Test Site. The VA denied his claim.

Paul Cooper refiled the claim and began searching for other veterans who had participated in Smoky. It was not long before another veteran, Donald Coe, from Kentucky, came forward. He also had been diagnosed with leukemia. Coe filed a VA claim seeking disability benefits.

By the end of 1976, Cooper and Coe were pursuing benefits, supported by doctors who believed their leukemias were caused by Smoky, a 44-kiloton blast at the Test Site on August 31, 1957, part of the twenty-nine-shot *Plumbob* series conducted between May and October of that year. Dr. Glyn Caldwell, an epidemiologist at the Centers for Disease Control (CDC) in Atlanta, became interested and initiated a study of the soldiers exposed at test Smoky.

After the headline story about Paul Cooper appeared in our local newspaper on April 6, 1977, we called Dr. Caldwell in Atlanta and explained that we represented workers exposed to radiation at the Baneberry test in December 1970 and two had died of acute myeloid leukemia in 1974. We mentioned that Dr. Shields Warren had given an opinion that the acute myeloid leukemia of one of the workers was caused by his exposure to radiation at Baneberry and inquired whether Dr. Caldwell could study the group of men exposed at Baneberry. Dr. Caldwell asked us to send more information for him to review.

On May 4, 1977, we sent Dr. Caldwell a letter with some information and Dr. Warren's deposition and again inquired whether he could perform a study of the Baneberry group.[1]

Dr. Caldwell wrote back on May 31, 1977, indicating he could perform an epidemiological study of the men exposed at Baneberry if we were able to provide the date of birth, race, sex, date of death (if deceased), radiation dose, and any illness (especially leukemia and cancer) for the men exposed.[2]

On June 9, 1977, in reliance upon Dr. Caldwell's letter, we filed a Request for Production of the names, ages, sex, race, and radiation doses of the workers exposed in Area 12 on the day of Baneberry.[3]

On June 19, Dr. Caldwell's study of the Smoky vets was the subject of a multipage insert in the *Salt Lake Tribune, Parade Magazine*, including a full page color photo of an atomic test with a group of veterans in the foreground.[4]

Paul Cooper's claim was again front-page news in Las Vegas on July 17, 1977. The *Las Vegas Review-Journal* carried a photo of Paul Cooper and his wife with an article in which Cooper described his exposure to the radioactive cloud at test Smoky.[5]

Within days after the story appeared, Dr. Caldwell telephoned. He said he had been contacted by an attorney from the Justice Department who told him "it was inappropriate for me [Larry Johns] to ask and for the center [Dr. Caldwell and the CDC] to agree to conduct a study" of the Baneberry workers. Of course, we were reminded of the Justice Department call to counsel for the New England Deaconess Hospital, two years before, stating that it was inappropriate for Dr. Warren to support the Roberts litigation because the hospital received funds from the AEC.

On July 25, 1977, an aide to Congressman Tim Lee Carter of Kentucky contacted us to inquire about the Baneberry case. Congressman Carter was spearheading the congressional investigation of the Smoky vets, including his constituent Donald Coe. I wrote to James Santini, our Nevada congressman, to inform him that Congressman Tim Lee Carter's office had contacted us to inquire about the Baneberry case. I also related that Dr. Caldwell had told me that a Justice Department lawyer had admonished him that the CDC could not investigate the Baneberry group. Finally, I commented that I could see no distinction between the CDC's investigation of the Smoky veterans, who had filed claims for veteran's benefits, and our litigation against the government on behalf of the men exposed at Baneberry, who also were seeking compensation.[6]

On July 26, I wrote to Dr. Caldwell to memorialize what he had told me about the call from the Justice Department, to advise him of Tim Lee Carter's call to us, and to tell him I hoped "that Congress doesn't get a communication from the Justice Department that it is 'inappropriate' for them to look into this matter because of pending litigation."[7]

On August 10, 1977, the *Las Vegas Review-Journal* carried a banner story from the *Washington Post* about test Smoky and Dr. Caldwell's CDC study. The article, after referencing Cooper and Coe, noted that the CDC "recently turned up two additional ex-servicemen with leukemia who say they, too, were at Smoky."[8]

On September 2, Congressman Santini wrote us and attached a letter dated August 25, 1977, from Dr. Foege with the CDC, quashing our request to have Dr. Caldwell study the Baneberry group because it would be "inappropriate."[9]

Although Dr. Caldwell was unable to conduct a study of the Baneberry group, his study of Cooper, Coe, and the others exposed at Smoky was not squelched by the Justice Department. And Paul Cooper and the CDC study of the atomic veterans continued to receive front-page coverage in our local newspapers and likely spawned claims and lawsuits by others.

On November 30, 1977, Pat Broudy's struggle to gain benefits for the death of her husband, Major Charles A. Broudy, was on the front page of the *Las Vegas Review-Journal*. Pat filed a lawsuit in federal district court in Los Angeles alleging that her husband's death on October 27, 1977, from cancer of the lymph nodes was caused by his exposure to radiation at the Nevada Test Site and at Bikini Atoll.[10]

Paul Cooper's story was again on the front page of the *Las Vegas Review- Journal* on February 5, 1978. The article, "VA quietly awarded radiation claims," disclosed that the VA had awarded disability benefits to ten veterans exposed to radiation from atomic tests in the Pacific or at the NTS who developed leukemia or other cancers. VA representatives acknowledged that exposure to low-level radiation was not a determining factor and "not that important." It discussed Dr. Caldwell's study of the Smoky vets pointing out that eight leukemias had been found, and that the "VA Appeals Board granted him [Paul Cooper] 100 percent disability." It reported that Donald Coe's appeal was pending before the appeal board and there was a congressional investigation of the atomic veterans' claims by the House Commerce Subcommittee on Health and Environment.[11] Five days later, we learned of Paul Cooper's death from acute myeloid leukemia.[12]

The CDC study of the Smoky vets and the congressional investigations were relentless and continued despite setbacks by veterans who filed suits against the United States under the Federal Tort Claims Act for injuries they said were caused by exposure to atomic radiation. Their FTCA claims were barred by the Feres doctrine, which precluded service members who sustained injuries while on active duty to filing claims with the Department of Veterans Affairs.[13]

By September 2, 1980, Dr. Glyn Caldwell had confirmed that nine of the 3,233 men exposed to the Smoky test had contracted leukemia, three times higher than expected and statistically significant.[14] Although Dr. Caldwell was disqualified from performing the study of our Baneberry group, he did provide the name and telephone number of Dr. Alice Stewart, an epidemiologist in Great Britain.

NOTES

1. Larry Johns to Glyn Caldwell, May 4, 1977. The letter and attachments cannot be located, but is referenced in Dr. Caldwell's letter response and in the August 25, 1977 letter from the CDC to James D. Santini.

2. Glyn Caldwell to Larry Johns, May 31, 1977. Copy in author's possession. 3. DS 297.

4. *Salt Lake Tribune*, June 19, 1977, *Parade Magazine* insert. The article mentioned Paul Cooper and Donald Coe, a resident of Kentucky, and urged veterans exposed at Smoky to contact Dr. Caldwell at the CDC.

5. *Las Vegas Review-Journal*, July 17, 1977.

6. Larry Johns to James Santini, July 25, 1977. Copy in author's possession. I did not have Dr. Warren's permission to disclose the call from the Justice Department after he agreed to assist us and would not have involved him in the controversy, although we kept Dr. Warren informed of our efforts to persuade the CDC to study the Baneberry group.

7. Larry Johns to Glyn Caldwell, July 26, 1977. Copy in author's possession.

8. *Las Vegas Review-Journal*, August 10, 1977, p. 3.

9. James Santini to Larry Johns, September 2, 1977, with Dr. Foege's August 25, 1977 letter attached. Copy in author's possession.

10. *Las Vegas Review-Journal*, November 30, 1977.

11. Ibid., February 5, 1978

12. Ibid., February 10, 1978.

13. Feres v. United States, 340 U.S. 135 (1950).

14. *Las Vegas Review-Journal*, September 2, 1980.

[15]

Dr. Alice Stewart, Éminence Grise[1]

WE TELEPHONED DR. ALICE Stewart in Birmingham, England, in early September 1977, told her about the Baneberry case and that we had contacted Dr. Caldwell to study our Baneberry group, similar to his Smoky investigation. She seemed flattered that Dr. Caldwell had recommended her and asked for detailed information about the Baneberry group. We told her eighty-six men had been exposed to the radioactive cloud and two died of acute myeloid leukemia within four years. We mentioned that Dr. Shields Warren had given an opinion in support of one of our clients and thought it highly unlikely that two cases of acute myeloid leukemia would occur by chance in the group exposed.

Dr. Stewart knew of Dr. Warren's standing and role in the A-bomb studies and seemed quite surprised that we had someone of his caliber supporting our case. She was willing to review the material but was very busy. However, she said that she would be at the University of Pittsburgh in early December and suggested we meet there to go over the information. She and her colleague, Dr. George Kneale, a mathematician, were to attend a weeklong conference with Dr. Tom Mancuso. Dr. Mancuso had asked them to review an ongoing study of workers exposed to plutonium over the period from 1944 to 1974 at the AEC's Hanford Works, in Washington state. I agreed to send a letter with some of the information and the two death certificates, and meet her in Pittsburgh.

On December 4, 1977, I left Las Vegas and five hours later descended through heavy cloud cover to land in Pittsburgh around 5:00 pm. I took a cab to a motel near the university and called the number Dr. Stewart had given me. Dr. Mancuso answered, and when I asked to speak to Dr. Alice Stewart, he handed her the telephone.

Dr. Stewart said they were still at Dr. Mancuso's office working into the evening and insisted that I come right over to meet her. I grabbed my briefcase with Baneberry records and walked about four blocks to the lobby of the building that housed the Department of Epidemiology.

A tall, slender, very fit lady in her late 60s with a crop of short gray hair was waiting just inside the glass doors. After introducing herself and giving me a brisk British handshake, she said she wanted to speak with me before she took me in to meet George Kneale. He was a brilliant Oxford-trained mathematician, she explained, but a bit odd and rather asocial. She was much older than George and had somewhat taken him under her wing. Additionally, she cautioned me not to be offended if he did not talk much. On occasion, he would not speak at all.

I was apprehensive when she led me into the room and approached the desk where Dr. Kneale was seated staring down intently at a pile of documents. He looked to be in his mid-thirties and a bit out of shape. Given Dr. Stewart's comments, I was pleasantly surprised that this eccentric mathematician greeted me warmly and joined in our discussion about the Baneberry test. He asked some pointed questions about the workers and offered some statistical information about the incidence of leukemia in men of early to middle age. He also volunteered statistics about cancer incidence among the workers in the Hanford study, which they were in Pittsburgh to review with Dr. Mancuso.

When we met again the following morning, Dr. Stewart apologized that she had not thought to bring her curriculum vitae or any sort of résumé and felt she ought to introduce herself by giving me a summary of her education and work experience.

She mentioned that both of her parents were physicians who had lived into their midnineties, her mother among a small group of pioneering female physicians. Dr. Stewart got her medical degree at Cambridge in 1930 and was certified in hematology, the branch of medicine that studies blood diseases, including leukemia. During World War II she was invited to Oxford, where she served as First Assistant in Hematology. After the war, she shifted her practice to the new field of social medicine, referred to as epidemiology in the United States. She spent the next few years studying workers exposed to tetrachloride, coal miners in South Wales suffering with pneumoconiosis, and tuberculosis in workers in the shoe-making factories.

Her interest in radiation effects began in 1955. By that time, the studies of the Japanese survivors, initiated by Dr. Warren, had been published in reports by the Atomic Bomb Casualty Commission. The studies confirmed that radiation had caused an epidemic of leukemia, which peaked four to six years after the bombs.

By 1955, doctors in Britain noticed a general increase of leukemia, with the most dramatic among three-year-old children. This strange occurrence was inexplicable, since prior to that time leukemia was almost an unknown disease among them. She began collecting medical records on leukemia and cancer patients for the prior three years, 1953 through 1955. This was rather easy because medical records were well maintained in Britain following the creation of the National Health Service after the war.

When she analyzed the records, she discovered that children who had been exposed in utero to a single diagnostic x-ray were developing leukemia at a much higher rate than those whose mothers had not been x-rayed.

Dr. Stewart said she took the information to the Medical Research Council to get support and funding for a larger study, but they considered the project too ambitious and too costly. So, she decided to conduct the study on her own. By early 1956, the first results of her work were published confirming that fetal exposure to a single x-ray caused cancer and leukemia at a significantly increased rate.

This phenomenon was eminently sensible, since the cells in the developing fetus are undergoing cell division at an astronomical rate. Bone marrow cells are the most radiosensitive in an adult body and even more so in a developing fetus. The womb, which shields the fetus from external forces, cannot protect it from x-rays.

Dr. Stewart expected that her findings would be controversial, since they challenged the long-held belief that there was a threshold dose below which no harmful effects occurred. At the time, it was assumed that a single x-ray, which delivers a dose of about 25 mR gamma to the cells of the fetus, was too low to have any effect. Indeed, her findings were initially dismissed by physicians and the nuclear industry in Britain and in the United States. But she persisted, publishing, republishing, and expanding her study and responding to her critics. Her report, the *Oxford Survey of Childhood Cancer*, is now accepted by the scientific community as a classic study in the field of radiation effects.

Dr. Stewart and I then went over the information I brought regarding the odd phenomenon of the occurrence of two leukemias in the Baneberry group. But it was not sufficient for her to conduct an epidemiological study. She needed the same basic information about the eighty-six men exposed to radiation from the Baneberry vent that Dr. Caldwell had requested: name; age; sex; date of birth; current medical history, if known, or death certificate; and the radiation dose of each of the individuals who required decontamination. With that data, she could perform an epidemiological study of the Baneberry group. She told me my assignment was to demand this vital information from the government. If I needed her assistance, she would supply a statement.

A little over a month after I returned to Las Vegas, journalist Walter Pincus wrote a lengthy story, carried nationally, about Dr. Mancuso's study of the Hanford workers and his collaboration with Alice Stewart and George Kneale. Mancuso had been hired by the AEC in 1974 to refute a Washington State Public Health Service study that found an excess of cancer deaths among workers exposed to low-level radiation at the Hanford Works. When his initial findings confirmed the results of the prior study, his contract was terminated. But he persisted and with assistance from Stewart and Kneale, published the results in December 1977. They showed an excess of cancers. The article, headlined "Does low-level radiation cause cancer?" in the *Las Vegas Review-Journal*, discussed the Baneberry case and Dr. Shields Warren's anticipated testimony that low-level radiation could have caused leukemia.[2]

As mandated by Dr. Stewart, I requested the information and renewed our earlier motion to compel relying upon an affidavit from Dr. Stewart. On June 27, 1978, the court finally buckled, ordering the government to produce the name, date of birth, social security number, and radiation dose of all eighty six men exposed at Baneberry. Even so, we did not receive the information until July 27, 1978.[3]

By then, we were in the final stages of trial preparation with a pretrial order due on September 29, and a pretrial conference in November 1978. From July through early November, we could only track down fifty-six of the workers, but it was sufficient for Dr. Stewart's study.

In October, counsel exchanged witness lists and proposed issues of fact. We offered as an issue of fact: "There is no safe level of radiation exposure." This set off a firestorm. On October 20, John Thorndal and Bill Elliott objected strenuously, claiming it raised a new issue in the case.4 On October 23, we responded, pointing out that the government sought to include a finding that "any individual exposed to less than 5 Rem per year is without a remedy regardless of cause and effect."[5]

On November 9, 1978, Bill Elliott called late in the afternoon to inform us that Dorothy Roberts had contacted the DOE seeking cost data the government spent to defend her lawsuit. He was agitated and concerned "that the information might bring adverse publicity upon the government." He also told us "although Dorothy Roberts is entitled to the information," if she decides to "publicize it, the government might seek a gag order to prevent you from disclosing it."[6]

On November 10, I wrote Dorothy telling her what Mr. Elliott had told us the prior day. In the letter, I explained that I doubted that any publicity about the government's defense expenses would influence the judge and understood her frustration that the government had spent so much money trying to "defeat her claim where she can scarcely afford to eat." Dorothy was incensed to learn that the government "would fly all over the world to take the depositions of our experts, Stewart, Bertell, and Tamplin, at the taxpayers' expense," while she was "unable to send a representative." I explained that, as her attorney, I could not seek publicity or encourage her to do so, but "you have pursued this independently and may continue to do so." Finally, I told her I was not familiar with the criteria for a gag order but in my view, she was entitled to "exercise her First Amendment right regardless of this litigation."[7]

The DOE did not respond to Dorothy's oral request for information about the amount of money they had spent trying to defeat her lawsuit, and she did not pursue it. We assumed the time and expenses of the salaried Justice Department lawyers, U.S. Attorney lawyers, and DOE lawyers and their staffs was substantial but not broken down. But the legal fees and costs paid to the private law firm headed by John Thorndal over the years since the Baneberry lawsuit was filed in 1972, would be accessible, and, based upon the legal time we had spent and the costs we had paid, had to approach a half million dollars or more before we began the trial.

We did not raise the matter of the government's expenses nor did Dorothy after she called the DOE in November 1978. But Bill Elliott did on March 11, 1979, two months into the trial, when he told a reporter the government "would spend whatever it takes to win."[8]

On December 6, I sent Bill Elliott a letter regarding final trial preparation issues. In it, I referenced Elliott's request to informally discuss the Nunamaker case with Dr. Warren and explained that Dr. Warren was not disposed to informal discussions, pointing out that we "have received no opinions from your experts nor do I expect any prior to their testimony as was the case with Dr. Lushbaugh."[9] But Dr. Warren did speak with them and kept notes of the conversation.[10]

Dr. Alice Stewart was deposed in London, England, on December 5, 1978; Dr. Arthur Tamplin in Washington, D.C, on December 14, 1978; and Dr. Rosalie Bertell in Buffalo, New York, on December 15, 1978. We were unable to attend any of the depositions but knew the essence of their opinions and were confident government counsel could not persuade them to alter them, just as with Dr. Warren's deposition nearly four years earlier.

With the addition of Dr. Alice Stewart and her medical opinion and statistical analysis in support of the Roberts and Nunamaker cases, Baneberry was ready for trial. But other radiation claims, arising long after our investigation began in early 1971, attracted national attention and dwarfed our Baneberry case.

During 1978, people who lived downwind of the 1950s atmospheric tests were gathering information about the cancers and leukemias they witnessed among family members and had contacted attorneys to pursue claims against the government. Some called Alan and me, but in 1978 we were overwhelmed with Baneberry and unable to consider assisting them. In 1977, we met with MacArthur Wright, an attorney from St. George, Utah. In 1978, Dale Haralson, an attorney from Tucson, came to our office to discuss our case and told us he had been contacted to represent persons living downwind from the 1950s aboveground tests. We also spoke by telephone with Stewart Udall, Secretary of the Interior under presidents Kennedy and Johnson and now a Phoenix attorney. He had met many southern Utah residents who wanted him to file claims.

In late 1978, as we prepared for the Baneberry trial, stories about cancers and leukemias among the downwinders had gained national attention and were covered in Las Vegas. On November 28, the *Las Vegas Review-Journal* ran a banner headline, "Utah fallout probe ordered by Carter."[11] On December 1, the headline in the *Las Vegas Sun* read, "Utah Governor Seeks AEC files on fallout."12 On December 9, the *Las Vegas Review-Journal* said, "NTS picked prior to fallout study."[13] And the *Las Vegas Review-Journal*, December 9, declared, "Truman rushed Nevada testing."[14]

On December 17, the first of a series of five articles appeared in the Sunday *Las Vegas Sun*: "St. George and the nuclear dragon." It depicted a dragon spewing poison on the fearful residents of St. George, Utah. The first article featured several persons who died of leukemia and cancer, including a young Nevada boy, Martin "Butch" Bardoli, exposed to fallout from the 1951 and 1953 atomic blasts who died of leukemia in 1956 at the age of seven.[15]

The next four articles in the series were published between December 18 and December 21, 1978.[16] The series contrasted the AEC's reassurances that fallout from the atomic testing at NTS was harmless, with stories from families exposed to radioactive fallout who lost loved ones to leukemia and cancer. They had trusted the AEC, but now believed that it had deliberately concealed the dangers.

The December 19, 1978, article stated, "Scientists at Oak Ridge have demonstrated that a single particle of radiation can damage the nucleus of a cell." A few paragraphs later, it added, "In 1959 a Joint Committee for the AEC reported that the 'best assumption that can be made at present concerning the relationship of biological effects of radiation dose is to assume that any dose, however small, produces some biological effect and can be harmful.'"[17] The fourth installment on December 20, "Feds downplayed radiation danger," discussed the public relations efforts of the AEC to "keep the public on their side."

All this publicity was a prelude to an article that appeared in the *Las Vegas Sun* on December 22: "Udall files 100 nuclear test claims." These were the first claims filed on behalf of the downwinders against the Department of Energy under the FTCA. The team of lawyers pursuing the claims was Stewart Udall, Dale Haralson, and MacArthur Wright.

On December 28, Nevada governor Mike O'Callaghan joined Utah governor Scott Matheson "ordering an examination of the effects of atmospheric testing at the Nevada Test Site during the 1950s and 1960s."[18] On February 15, 1979, newly elected Nevada governor Robert List joined former Nevada governors, Charles Russell, Grant Sawyer, and Paul Laxalt in calling for the probe.[19] On January 9, 1979, the *Las Vegas Review–Journal* reported: "Fallout leukemia link report found." It disclosed that a 1965 report by U.S. Public Health officer Dr. Weiss had been shelved by the AEC. Dr. Weiss had reported twenty-eight leukemia deaths in one year in southern Utah, and that there was only "a 2 percent chance that so many leukemias would be recorded in southern Utah in one year among a population of 21,000."[20]

Based upon the national interest in the plight of the downwinders and calls from the president, governors of Utah and Nevada, and representatives of downwinders in Congress, including our Nevada congressman James Santini, the Committee on Interstate and Foreign Commerce and its Subcommittee on Oversight and Investigations, began collecting evidence to investigate the issue.[21]

As we were preparing for trial, the legal team headed by Gerry Spence, nationally acclaimed trial attorney, was preparing *Silkwood v. Kerr-McGee* for trial before a jury in Oklahoma City, Oklahoma. The Silkwood trial opened on March 8, 1979,22 and resulted in an $11.5 million jury verdict in favor of Karen Silkwood's heirs on May 18, 1979.[23]

NOTES

1. Dr. Stewart was quite a cynic. I nicknamed her *éminence grise*, a reference to Voltaire.

2. *Las Vegas Review-Journal*, January 18, 1978.

3. DS 351. In that order, the judge consolidated for trial the Roberts and Nunamaker cases.

4. John Thorndal to Larry Johns, October 20, 1978. Copy in author's possession.

5. Larry Johns to John Thorndal, October 23, 1978. Copy in author's possession. In the letter, we explained that we had no intention of agreeing to the government's position and would call Drs. Warren, Stewart, Tamplin, and Bertell to challenge it.

6. Larry Johns to Dorothy Roberts, November 10, 1978. Copy in author's possession. Elliott's statements are reported in the letter sent to Dorothy Roberts.

7. Ibid, November 10, 1978.

8. *Los Angeles Herald Examiner*, March 11, 1979.

9. Larry Johns to Bill Elliott, December 6, 1978. Copy in author's possession.

10. Following Dr. Warren's death in 1980, his secretary called to ask if I would like his personal files on the Baneberry case. They were sent to me and included notes of that conversation. Copy in author's possession.

11. *Las Vegas Review-Journal*, November 28, 1978.

12. *Las Vegas Sun*, December 1, 1978.

13. *Las Vegas Review-Journal, Trailblazer Edition*, December 9, 1978.

14. *Las Vegas Review-Journal, Final Edition*, December 9, 1978.

15. *Las Vegas Sun*, December 17, 1978.

16. Ibid., December 18–21, 1978.

17. Ibid., December 19, 1978.

18. *Las Vegas Review-Journal*, December 28, 1978.

19. *Las Vegas Sun*, February 15, 1979; *Las Vegas Valley Times*, February 15, 1979.

20. *Las Vegas Review-Journal*, January 9, 1979.

21. *Las Vegas Sun*, February 27, 1979. This article reported the official launch of the investigation and noted that Nevada congressman James Santini had called for the probe "to get the facts on the table and find out where the truth lies." In March 1979, newly elected Nevada governor List joined Utah governor Matheson in pursuing the probe (*Las Vegas Review-Journal*, March 10, 1979). On March 22, 1979, Governor List appointed a panel to study "The effects of aboveground nuke tests" (*Las Vegas Sun*, March 22, 1979). The results of the Subcommittee's investigation were published in the *Forgotten Guinea Pigs Report*, August 1980. It called for a legislative solution to assess radiation claims and provide compensation, citing several reasons: "(1) the existing legal remedy under the FTCA offers no degree of certainty or predictability regarding questions of causation which are unique to radiation claims; (2) nuclear radiation victims should not bear any further burden, particularly in terms of time and expense . . .; (3) the government must accept responsibility, whether legal or moral, for the injuries sustained by individuals as a result of the government's operation of the nuclear weapons testing program; and (4) a legislative remedy would provide the most adequate and expeditious means by which the government can accept such responsibility."

22. *Las Vegas Sun*, March 8, 1979: "Nuclear Facility Negligence Trial Opens."

23. *Las Vegas Sun*, May 18, 1979; *Las Vegas Review–Journal*, May 18, 1979.

Downtown Las Vegas before 1950, looking east down Fremont Street, with Union Pacific Depot in foreground and Pioneer Club. Photo courtesy of the Union Pacific Railroad Museum.

Downtown Las Vegas showing A-bomb cloud, looking north with Pioneer Club, Vegas Vic, and the Las Vegas Club. The A-bomb cloud is from test "Dog" detonated at NTS on November 1, 1951. Photo courtesy of the Las Vegas Convention and Visitors Authority.

Desert Rock atomic veterans at test "Dog" detonated at NTS on November 1, 1951. Photo courtesy of National Nuclear Security Administration Nevada Field Office, Nuclear Testing Archive.

The Baneberry vent. We viewed films of the venting in 1975, of which this is a single frame. Our viewing was under a protective order, and we were directed not to copy the films or disclose any information about them. The photo was released to the press and published in newspapers on October 6, 1977. Photo courtesy of National Nuclear Security Administration Nevada Field Office.

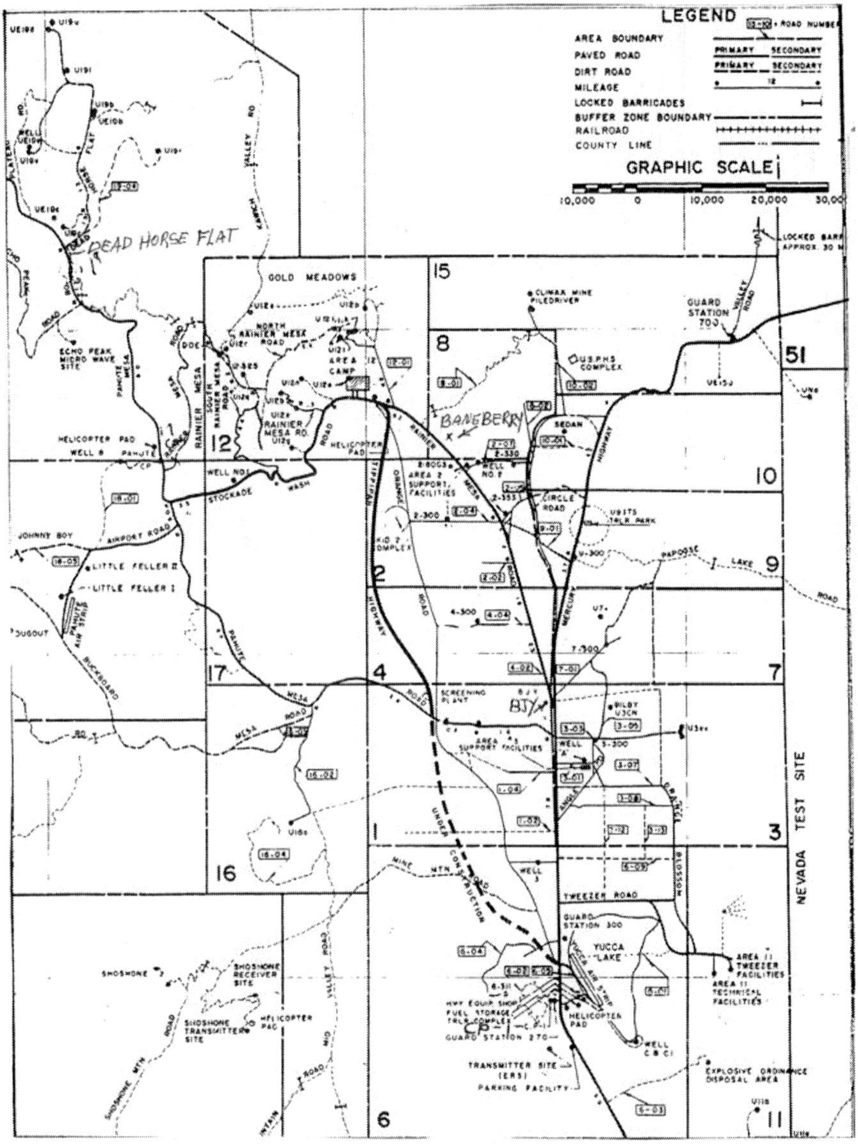

Map of Nevada Test Site. Courtesy of the author.

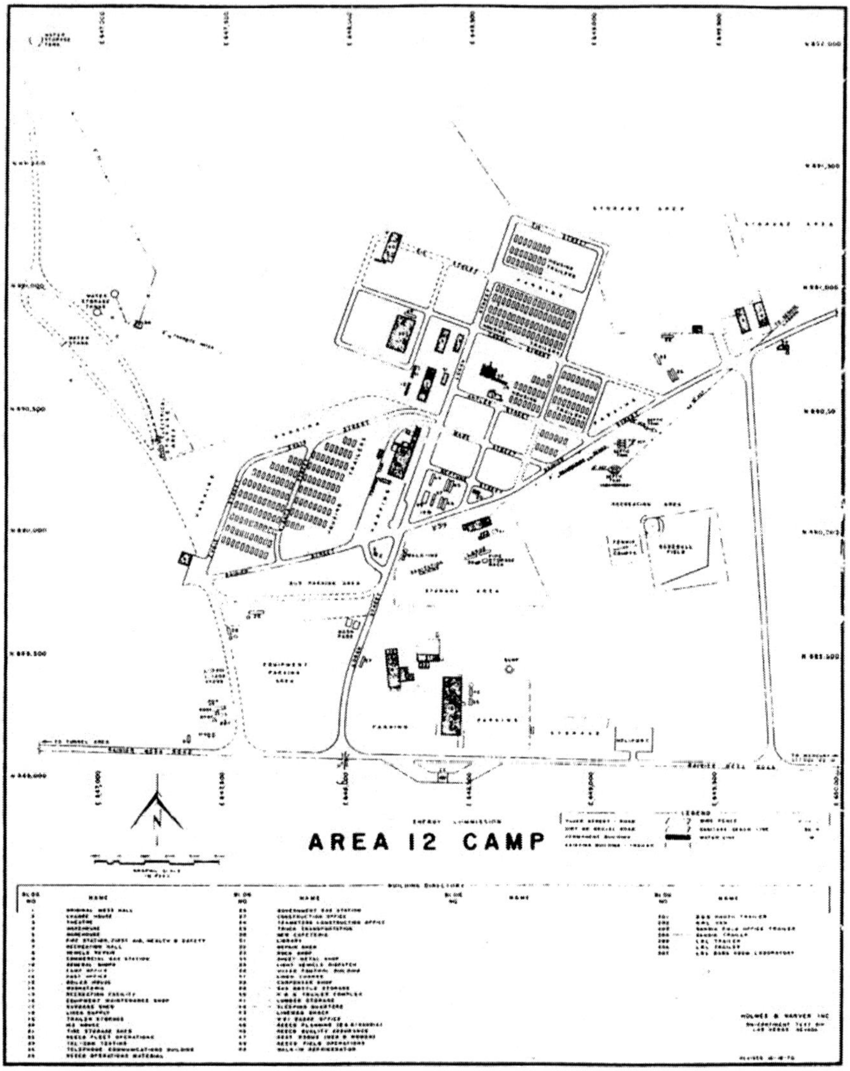

Map of Area 12 Camp. Courtesy of the author.

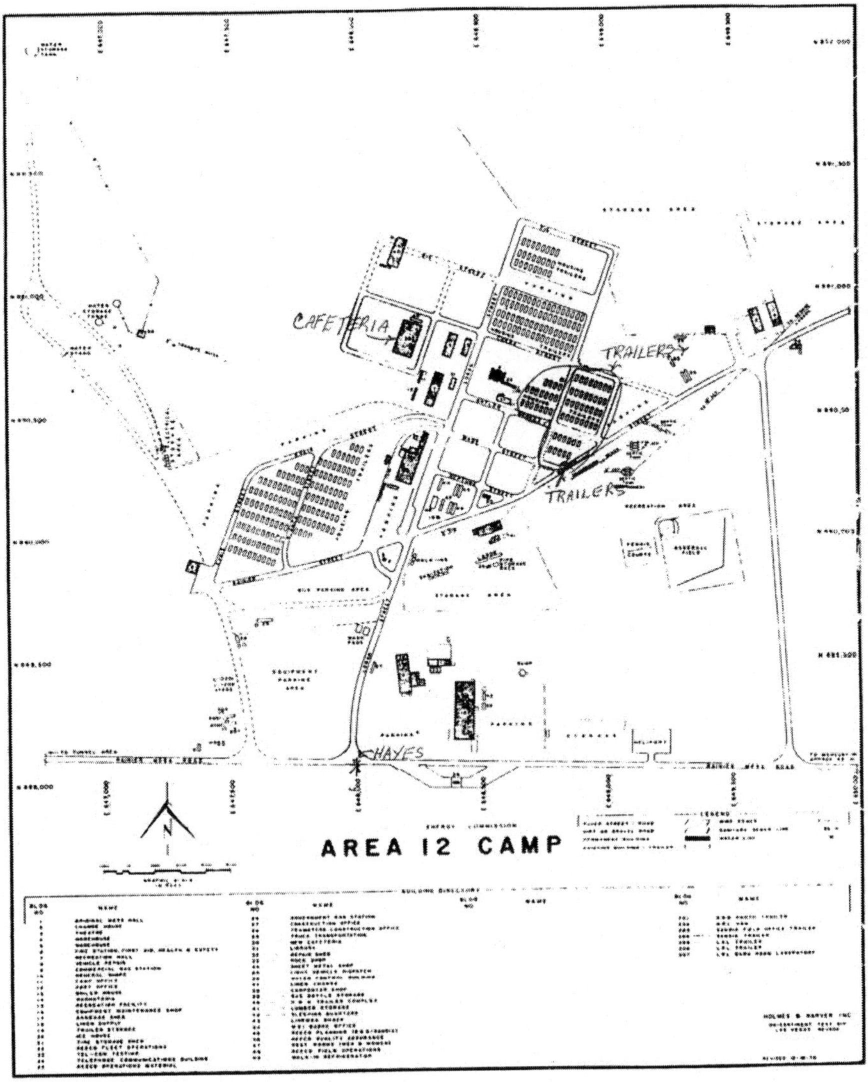

Trial exhibit 21. Map of Area 12 Camp with notations. Courtesy of the author.

Trial exhibit E-11: Baneberry surface cloud of radioactive dust in the basin just below Area 12 Camp at about 7:50 am. Courtesy of the author.

Louise Nunamaker, Dorothy Roberts, and Alan Johns standing in front of the elevator on January 16, 1979. Courtesy of Randy Tunnell, photographer.

Dr. Alice Stewart and Larry Johns. Courtesy of the author.

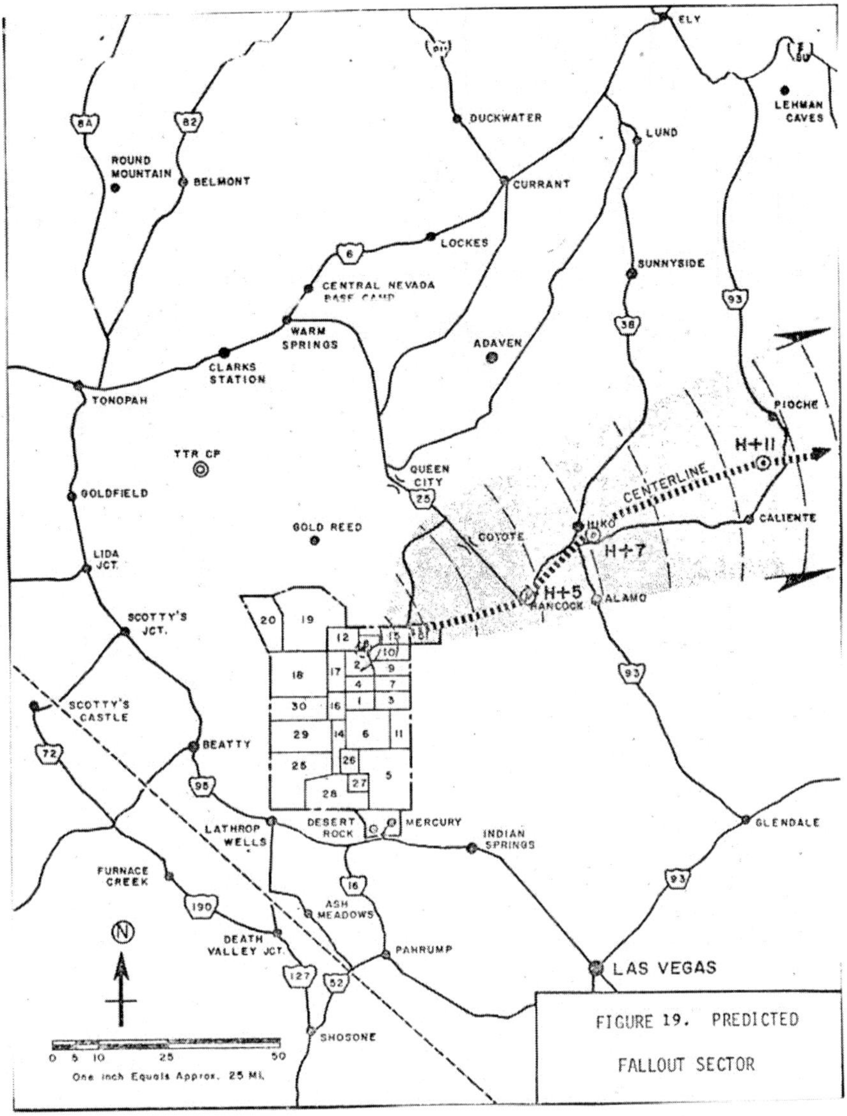

Trail exhibit 62. Map of entire Nevada Testing Site, the location of the Baneberry site, and the predicted path of fallout. Courtesy of the author.

New York Times photo of Alan and Larry Johns, December 12, 1989, after we had been involved in the Baneberry case for nearly nineteen years. Courtesy of the author.

Harley Roberts. Government counsel objected to the introduction of this photo, which Dorothy brought to court. Courtesy of the author.

William Nunamaker. Courtesy of the author.

[16]

Was It Really an Accident?

ON JANUARY 15, 1979, we made our final preparations, gathered our exhibits, and spent the day reviewing for the trial set to begin the next morning. That night, a rare snowfall covered the Las Vegas Valley, reminiscent of the snowfall that had blanketed the Test Site the night before the Baneberry test nine years earlier.

At 9:15 am on January 16, Dorothy, Louise, Alan, and I were driven from our office four blocks up the street to the back entrance of the federal courthouse. We took the elevator up to the third floor and entered the large courtroom of federal Judge Roger D. Foley. The Judge was from an established and influential Democratic family. He followed his father Roger T. Foley, who was appointed to the federal bench in Nevada and was on senior status when President Kennedy nominated Foley's son for the position in 1962. Roger D. Foley was elected district attorney for Clark County in the early 1950s and then was Nevada attorney general for three years prior to his appointment to the federal bench.

As Judge Foley ascended the bench, his slight build and frail appearance made him appear much older than his sixty-two years. After announcing the case, he asked if the plaintiffs were ready to proceed. Alan stood up and formally introduced Dorothy Roberts and Louise Nunamaker to the judge. He then stepped to the podium to give the opening statement.

"We are going to prove that the defendant, the United States Government, through agents or instrumentalities that are directly responsible to it or in many instances owe their entire existence to the federal government, was guilty of not one, two, three, or four, but in fact in this particular case, at least twenty separate acts of negligence, individually or together—interrelated—that contributed to the exposure and ultimate deaths of these individuals."

The judge seemed shocked as he interjected, "Twenty acts of negligence by the United States?"[1]

Alan appeared unfazed by the court's seeming incredulity that the United States could commit so many negligent acts in one case and went on to chronicle the twenty links in the chain of negligence. He started with decisions regarding placement of the device in a clay formation the AEC knew was water saturated and would cause the device to behave as if it were much more powerful, buried closer to the surface, and likely to vent. The AEC knew, or should have known, that there were fault lines adjacent to the detonation point. This weakness in the substrata contributed to the venting of the explosion.

Alan pointed out that since the government had steadfastly refused to disclose the purpose of the test, it might have planned for a vent. The judge was surprised by this remark and admitted he had not considered that possibility. Alan followed up the judge's comment, acknowledging that unless all the still-classified material was produced, we could not prove that it was deliberately vented. But it was not necessary to show deliberate conduct for us to prevail. All we needed to show was negligent conduct on the part of the government.

This led to a discussion of the curious name for the test. Alan pointed out that the root word of Baneberry is *bane*, which is universally defined as a cause of death or ruin, or a deadly poison. Whether by accident or design, Baneberry would be forever associated with the release of a poisonous cloud of radiation and linked to the deaths of Harley Roberts and William Nunamaker.

Alan then outlined another series of negligent acts that occurred during the drilling of the Baneberry emplacement hole. The drill hole caved in frequently, because workers were drilling through a montmorillonite clay deposit. They tried to rectify this weakness by pumping enormous amounts of cement into the hole to stabilize it and then redrill through the concrete. There were further problems. Over a hundred thousand gallons of water were used to drill the hole, which added more water to the already saturated montmorillonite clay medium. The drilling problems, caving, cementing, and redrilling to create a stable hole, were well known to everyone at the site. Workers referred to Baneberry as a "bad hole." All the drilling complications caused several delays beyond the initial test date. Ultimately, to avoid further postponement, the AEC decided to shave seventy feet off the planned depth of the shaft and scheduled the test for Friday, December 18, 1970, the last test of the year.

The judge interrupted and asked Alan whether it was his position that the government should have abandoned the hole and started drilling somewhere else. Alan stated emphatically that it was our position that the hole should never have been drilled in a water-saturated clay medium near a fault in the first place. But given all the drilling problems, he ended, "Yes, your honor, prudence dictated that they should have abandoned the hole and started over."

Judge Foley was curious that the shot was detonated at a shallower depth than originally planned. He asked if it was our position that detonating at a shallower depth caused the test to vent. Alan acknowledged that we could not prove that this factor by itself caused the vent. But it was certainly another example of conduct that might have been a link in the chain of negligent acts.

After outlining the negligence related to drilling the Baneberry shaft, Alan shifted to a discussion of wind conditions on the morning of December 18, 1970. He explained that the test manager and his panel knew or should have known that wind direction and speed were critical factors in determining whether to proceed. The test manager was negligent in proceeding with the test that morning, with the wind direction at around 7:30 am shifting and unpredictable. The judge understood the importance of planning tests when wind direction is steady, stating that he himself had witnessed an aboveground test at News Nob in the early 1950s and was aware that such tests were usually detonated when it was known that winds would carry the mushroom cloud easterly into Utah, rather than south into Las Vegas.

The judge asked Alan how many tests had vented since underground testing had begun. Alan stated we knew of around twenty-seven. I could not help noticing that this disclosure caused a stir at the government lawyers' table and among AEC representatives seated in the first few rows behind them. Some raced out of the courtroom to the public phones in the hall to confirm or dispute this number. But when they returned to the courtroom, none stepped up to question the number. Alan ignored the disturbance, pointing out that such a large number of vents should have caused the AEC to take the possibility of a Baneberry vent seriously and to plan accordingly.

Alan pursued the point, explaining that the government should have known that if the test vented, it imperiled the Area 12 base camp, which was only a little over three miles from the detonation point. The government, he continued, was clearly negligent in failing to evacuate the 900 workers in Area 12 prior to the shot as they had done previously for shots that were farther away from Area 12 than Baneberry. The AEC was also negligent in failing to abide by its own rules that required a written evacuation plan for Area 12 in an emergency exactly as in Baneberry. In fact, there was no plan at the time of Baneberry.

After Baneberry vented, the AEC was negligent in failing to order the immediate evacuation of Area 12. Instead, the test manager waited over thirty minutes to give the order. As Alan explained, the delay was inexcusable, because eyewitnesses from all over the Test Site reported to the control center that the cloud was moving toward Area 12 Camp within ten to fifteen minutes after it vented.

When the order to evacuate finally came, Alan told the court, it was implemented in a manner fraught with a series of negligent acts. Rad-Safe monitors, trained and properly equipped to enter the radiation zone, should have been ordered to conduct the evacuation. Harley Roberts and the other guards had neither the training nor the equipment to manage an evacuation safely and should not have been ordered to conduct it. They had no training in radiation safety and were provided no protective equipment or respirators to minimize exposure to the radioactive cloud.

Alan emphasized numerous negligent acts that were specific to Harley Roberts, which substantially increased the extent of his radiation exposure. After Roberts completed his duties in evacuating workers from Area 12 Camp, a Rad-Safe monitor took his readings, called them in to headquarters, and told them Roberts needed to be sent in for decontamination immediately. Instead of ensuring Roberts was decontaminated, he was sent to a remote outpost at Dead Horse Flats and left there all day, accumulating additional radiation from his contaminated clothing and vehicle.

Negligent acts regarding William Nunamaker included the decision to allow him and the entire day crew to be sent up to T Tunnel for the 8:00 am shift change, after Baneberry vented and when it was obviously heading straight toward Area 12. Had the order to evacuate Area 12 been given as soon as Baneberry vented, Nunamaker would have been out of the Area 12 Camp before the radioactive cloud arrived.

In summing up the long list of such acts, Alan stated that negligence or incompetence on the part of the government existed before, during, and after the Baneberry event. In fact, he noted, it was hard to find anything that was done right. Baneberry was a classic example of Murphy's Law, or the law of interminable bungling.

Further negligent conduct included the failure of the government to accurately measure and determine the precise amount of radiation Roberts and all others received at Baneberry. This violation of duty made it more difficult for medical experts to assess the cause of both Roberts's and Nunamaker's leukemias.

Alan pointed out that neither Roberts nor Nunamaker should have been exposed to any radiation at Baneberry. "Radiation isn't just a harmless necessity," he explained. When inhaled or absorbed into the body, it can alter cells. In this case, it altered the bone marrow stem cells, which are the most susceptible cells to radiation damage in the body. These altered bone marrow cells went on to cause acute myeloid leukemia and the deaths of both Roberts and Nunamaker.

When Alan restated that any amount of radiation can be harmful, which is why radiation exposure should be kept as low as possible, the judge asked if it was his position that there is no such thing as a safe level. The judge brought up this point, noting that he had skin cancer some years ago and was treated with radiation therapy following surgery, a practice he said he did not think was current.

Alan answered by restating that radiation penetrates and alters cells. In Harley Roberts's case, Dr. Shields Warren, whose career was devoted to the history of radiation medicine and radiation pathology, would explain to the court how radiation at Baneberry caused Roberts's leukemia. Alan then identified Dr. Alice Stewart, the British physician and epidemiologist, as our first witness. She would testify that both leukemias were the result of radiation the two men received at Baneberry. He identified two other experts who would discuss the harmful effects of radiation and add support to our case. Dr. Arthur Tamplin, a biophysicist, would discuss his studies of radiation effects. Dr. Rosalie Bertell, a biostatistician, would discuss her involvement in studying the effects of radiation and that it had been shown to cause leukemia and cancer.

Before sitting down, Alan informed the court that Dorothy Roberts was a diabetic and asked the court's permission for her to be excused at around 11:30 am each morning to give herself an injection in the restroom.

Bill Elliot, lead counsel for the government, then rose and walked ponderously up to the podium. He wore a dark blue suit that fit tightly around his shoulders and barely buttoned at the front over his large frame. He exuded confidence, almost contempt, as he tried to counter Alan's catalogue of multiple acts of negligence.

Setting the tone for the AEC's ultimate defense of the negligence case against it, he said, "The context in this case is an accident occurring in an experiment with nuclear energy, which was conducted in the national defense." We scribbled the gist of the comment on our note pads, reflecting that it was AEC code for their standard position: the AEC is above reproach; our conduct cannot be questioned.

Elliot then discussed geology, sticking firmly to discredited statements in the May 1971 press release that asserted that the geology of the Baneberry site was unknown and poorly understood when the site was selected. In a brash but not unexpected move, he admonished the judge that he must be careful not to exceed his authority to review the AEC's conduct. "The Court clearly may not, and indeed must not, through an act of hindsight, superimpose the inventions or knowledge of the present on conduct occurring in the past," he said, and demanded that the court "create a time warp which will allow it to go back in time and place itself in a position of knowing nothing which occurred after December 18, 1970. Only in that way," he warned Judge Foley, "can a judgment be made of whether the Defendant acted in a non-negligent manner."

The admonition was prelude to introducing the two men directly responsible for not knowing or understanding what the other was doing. One would contend he did not realize the implications of detonating the device in the Baneberry geological formation, even though they fit his own specific criteria and objectives. The other would claim he did not study or understand the geology of the Baneberry site when he selected it to meet the specifications for the test laid out by his counterpart. It was, we thought, a masterful display of finger pointing by which both sought to escape responsibility.

The first government expert to be called was Phillip Coyle, Test Director for Baneberry. Defense counsel assured the court that Mr. Coyle would explain the scientific criteria for the test, or "experiment," as he called it. The Test Director was looking for a site that would produce a seismic velocity, which we understood to mean that the device would transmit sound waves through the subsurface strata at the requisite speed.

The second man, Richard McArthur, was the geologist who searched the Test Site and located the Baneberry site. It was his job to select a geological formation that would guarantee the seismic velocity criteria required by Test Director Coyle.

Judge Foley clearly understood this important issue. He bluntly asked Bill Elliott whether the water content in the clay medium and the presence of the fault were known prior to the detonation. This prompted Elliott to try to redefine "known" to mean "fully understood." But this ruse was unsatisfactory. When pressed further about the Baneberry fault, Elliott had to admit that a fault was "inferred" to be present but claimed that it was inferred to be farther away from the detonation point than it actually was.

Elliott conceded what Alan had stated in his opening: the venting was caused by the combination of these two geological conditions. But he also felt compelled to comment on Alan's statement that there had been twenty-seven vents prior to Baneberry. He conceded he could not dispute it but tried to downplay the number by describing the different types of vents and the various devices used to monitor radiation releases.

He then concluded his opening statement with a general discussion of radiation, asserting that neither of these two leukemias was caused by radiation from Baneberry and identified some of the medical experts who would testify for the defendant. Anticipating Dr. Warren's testimony about the C-7 deletion and its significance in the Roberts case, he perfunctorily stated that the defendant would call Dr. Janet Rowley, a cytogeneticist, who would testify that radiation from Baneberry did not cause Roberts' C-7 chromosome deletion or his leukemia.

When Bill Elliott finished, the judge asked us to call our first witness. Dr. Alice Stewart took the stand and the oath. She stated her current position was Senior Research Fellow in the Department of Social Medicine and sub department of Cancer Epidemiology at Birmingham University in England. She explained that she came to Birmingham four years earlier from Oxford, where she had served many years as head of the Department of Social Medicine.

After outlining her education, training, and expertise, she offered her opinion that both Harley Roberts and William Nunamaker died from acute myeloid leukemia and that the most likely cause was their exposure to radiation at Baneberry. Then she began to explain the bases for her opinion.

First, the bone marrow is the most radiosensitive tissue in the human body and myeloid leukemia is a cancer of the bone marrow. This is generally known and has been conclusively established in numerous studies, including the atomic bomb survivor studies and her Oxford survey of childhood leukemia.

Second, persons fifty years of age and older are more sensitive to damage from radiation than younger people. This susceptibility is part of the aging process. Both Harley Roberts and William Nunamaker were over fifty at the time of Baneberry. Roberts turned fifty in 1970 and Nunamaker was fifty-seven.

Third, both men had chromosome abnormalities, and everybody who had studied radiation effects agreed that the immediate effect of radiation exposure is chromosome damage. Roberts's chromosome abnormality, a deletion of C-7, was detected about eighteen months after Baneberry. Nunamaker's chromosome abnormality, chromosome breakage, was detected when he was hospitalized in September 1974.

Fourth, the latency period, the length of time from their exposure to radiation on December 18, 1970, to the diagnosis of their acute myeloid leukemias, was quite compatible with the latency period in numerous studies. Those studies included the Japanese atomic bomb survivors and Dr. Stewart's study of children who were exposed to x-rays in the womb. Following their common exposure to radiation on December 18, 1970, Roberts's latency period was three years and three months and Nunamaker's three years and nine months.

Finally, all parties agreed that both men were exposed to radiation at Baneberry, although there was debate about the full extent of their specific radiation doses. Dr. Stewart noted that her fetal studies confirmed that a single x-ray was sufficient to alter the highly sensitive bone marrow cells and thus the doses Roberts and Nunamaker received were sufficient to initiate the leukemic process.

After she had finished outlining all the clinical bases for her opinion, she discussed epidemiology. She explained that epidemiology is the branch of medicine that studies an increased incidence of a disease—an epidemic—over the number of cases that would have been expected. Epidemiological studies have produced the evidence that now forms a basis for analyzing the causes of disease in general. The epidemiological studies of persons exposed to radiation, such as the A-bomb survivors, established that radiation caused an excess of leukemia and cancer, although there was dispute about the level of radiation required to produce that excess. The A-bomb survivor studies, her Oxford Survey, and others confirmed that leukemia is the first cancer that will show up in a group of persons exposed to radiation.

Dr. Stewart performed an epidemiological study of the eighty-six men at Baneberry who were exposed to radiation doses considered to be high enough to require decontamination procedures. Relying upon the information provided by the government, she had traced fifty-nine of the eighty-six workers.

Based upon her qualifications as one of the leading epidemiologists in the world, she presented statistical evidence that the odds of two persons in that group dying of leukemia during the eight-year period from 1971 through 1978 was three in 100,000. Statistically, there should have been only .023 leukemias in that group over that period. The statistics showed that these two leukemias could not have been a chance occurrence. The most probable explanation for this epidemic, or increased incidence of leukemia, was the radiation from Baneberry.

When Dr. Stewart ended her direct testimony late that afternoon, we had presented clinical and statistical evidence that Roberts's and Nunamaker's leukemias were caused by their exposure to radiation from the Baneberry vent cloud.

The court recessed until the next morning. Dorothy and Louise sat through Dr. Stewart's testimony and followed her explanations closely. After court, we all returned to the office. Dorothy and Louise both knew they were at the beginning of a long ordeal. But Dr. Stewart's compassion and concern was evident, and meeting and thanking her for her help and support boosted their spirits more than anything Alan or I could possibly have done.

NOTES

1. *Baneberry Collection*, TR.

[17]

Murphy's Law

THE SECOND DAY OF trial began with government counsel's cross-examination of Dr. Stewart. With the tenacity of an English bulldog, she stuck to her clinical opinion that both leukemias were the result of Baneberry. In her view, there was simply no other explanation for the occurrence of these two unique leukemias, a type known for decades to be radiation caused. But she did concede, reluctantly, that if one of the two leukemias did occur purely by chance, she would be forced to acknowledge that Mr. Nunamaker's leukemia would likely be the chance occurrence, since he received a smaller dose of radiation than Roberts. While it arguably hurt the Nunamaker case, it seemed to strengthen the likelihood that Roberts's leukemia was caused by Baneberry.

When Dr. Stewart was excused, we called Frank Cluff, the test manager for Baneberry. In the opening statement, Alan had confidently criticized many of Cluff 's acts. My job was to ask questions that would show the decisions he made the night before the test and on the day of Baneberry were not prudent, thus needlessly exposing both of our clients to radiation.

I began my questioning by asking about his education and background. He had a master's degree in meteorology from the University of Utah and after college worked for what was then called the U.S. Weather Bureau. Because of his work, he knew meteorologists involved with the Nevada tests who were responsible for mapping the fallout patterns from the aboveground bomb tests. In 1957, he went to work for the AEC and joined a group that predicted the fallout trajectories. He explained that the objective throughout the 1950s was to ensure that the radioactive fallout passed easterly into southern Utah and away from populated areas such as Las Vegas or California.

Mr. Cluff retired a few years after Baneberry and had not reviewed any of the documents or exhibits in preparation for his trial testimony. Since he had no background in geology or physics and thus the complex scientific issues underlying to the site selection and reasons for the vent, I did not waste time asking him about them.

As test manager, Cluff was responsible for the safe conduct of the Baneberry test and specifically to assure the safety of the Test Site workforce and the off-site civilian population as well. To show that the decisions he made after Baneberry vented were unsupported, I showed Mr. Cluff the Test Manager's Operation Plan for Baneberry, which he admitted was the blueprint for the test.[1] It included detailed plans for the preshot evacuation or "sweeping" all personnel who were within the designated test area. At meetings the day before and early on the morning of the test, there had been discussions regarding which areas should be swept. Mr. Cluff acknowledged that the ultimate decision was his.

I asked Cluff if he thought it was prudent to leave Area 12 open when there were nearly a thousand workers just a little over three miles from the Baneberry test. As the basis for his decision to leave the workers near the test, he relied on preshot readings from weather stations around the Test Site taken over a twelve-hour period ending around 5:15 am the morning of the test. Those readings predicted decreasing surface wind speeds that would be very light or nearly calm by around 7:30. I asked him whether readings hours before were reliable in predicting surface wind direction at the time of the test. I was surprised when he admitted that they were not and that the last forecast a few minutes prior to the test predicted a wind change at shot time that would carry any fallout southwest of surface ground zero. This shift in the surface wind trajectory would move the radioactive cloud into the basin just south of Area 12 Camp instead of northwest, away from the camp, as the earlier predictions had indicated.

When I asked about surface wind readings after the venting, his testimony was even more surprising. By 7:38 am, just five minutes after the venting, the weather station nearest ground zero reported southwesterly surface winds, exactly as the last reading prior to the shot predicted. Two minutes after that reading, a large section of the cloud collapsed to the desert floor south of Area 12 Camp and began swirling around. By 7:47 am, surface wind readings were blowing due west toward Area 12 Camp. Readings from this same station at 7:52, 7:57, and 8:01 am confirmed that the surface winds were now blowing directly toward Area 12 Camp.

When I finished my questioning about the wind direction, everyone in the courtroom knew that Mr. Cluff had ignored the surface wind predictions just prior to the test and inexplicably refused to accept postshot readings confirming those predictions. Given those readings, there was simply no reason for Mr. Cluff to wait until 8:05 am to order the evacuation of Area 12. Or was there?

We presented evidence explaining the dilemma he faced after the shot vented: his own written Test Manager's Plan, AEC Policies and Procedures,[2] and a written requirement that there be an Emergency Evacuation Plan for Area 12 Camp and a designated Area 12 Camp coordinator to carry it out.[3] When confronted with these documents that governed the emergency presented by the Baneberry vent, Mr. Cluff appeared flummoxed. All he could do was accept responsibility for the failure to implement any of the required procedures. For example, when I asked him to identify the designated Area 12 Camp coordinator on the day of Baneberry, he shrugged, responding that he assumed there was such a person but had no idea who that person was. When asked to identify the organization charged with responsibility for the evacuation, all he could say was that he "was not sure of the organization that would aid [in the evacuation] but I keep thinking it was part of the Teamsters."

Cluff 's ignorance of the emergency evacuation policies was even more surprising because Area 12 Camp was the largest forward area facility on the Test Site. And judging by the feeble way he ended his responses, he must have known that he had failed to carry out his duties as Test Manager. The most he could offer was a vague recollection of an evacuation plan.

As I reached the end of my examination, I sensed by Mr. Cluff 's frustration that he thought he could excuse his lapse of memory by relying upon the passage of time, his retirement since the event, and his age. But there was also, I suspected, some resentment on his part that he had been made the scapegoat for the entire Baneberry test, designated to take full responsibility for the venting and the lawsuit that arose out of it.

Government counsel tried to rehabilitate Mr. Cluff. They stressed his credentials as a meteorologist and discussed the years he worked in the field. From our perspective, they failed. Virtually every decision he made before and after the venting was either wrong or too late to avoid the exposure of eighty-six persons to radiation from the vent cloud. And he failed spectacularly in the field where he had the most expertise—wind conditions at the Nevada Test Site.

When Cluff stepped down, we called witnesses to show that we had established, out of his mouth, the elements of negligence. They were called to highlight Cluff 's negligence and discredit his statements. Among them was Chan Griffin, the top AEC security officer at Mr. Cluff 's side on the day of Baneberry. He testified unhesitatingly that there was no evacuation plan for Area 12 Camp on the morning of the Baneberry Test.

The Test Manager's Plan for Baneberry required REECo to have teams of monitors standing by at thirty minutes before shot time to conduct an emergency evacuation. But there were no teams of monitors. Tom Hayes was the only REECo Rad-Safe monitor anywhere near Area 12 Camp. He stood near his truck, a quarter mile east of the entrance to Area 12 Camp and three miles from the Baneberry site, at the same location as security guards Yager and Holly.

Hayes recounted his activities after the vent. He called the control point at 8:00 am, as the grayish-tan radioactive cloud caused his Geiger counter to jump to 50 mR and then watched it engulf the Area 12 Camp. Other than RadSafe monitor Perry, who, at Hayes's request, came by his station at 9:00 am to double-check Hayes's readings, no other Rad-Safe monitor was in the radiation cloud that morning.[4] And none of the Rad-Safe monitors assisted in the evacuation of Area 12 Camp. When Hayes was asked who had responsibility for conducting the emergency evacuation of Area 12 Camp on the morning of Baneberry, he said he "didn't know and wouldn't hazard a guess."

To leave no doubt that Cluff and his panel were negligent in failing to order an immediate evacuation of Area 12 Camp, we called Holly and Yager, who saw the swirling surface cloud coming up the hill toward them and called to ask permission to move their station. Bob Yager explained why he knew they would be engulfed by the cloud: as the sun began to warm the desert test basin, the surface winds were going to head uphill "like the dickens."

We called Rad-Safe monitor Troy Ellis, who had led a caravan of thirty five to forty-five cars and three buses into Area 12 that morning. At 7:45 am, he called to warn that the cloud was approaching the camp and tried to block ingress. But he was ignored, and hundreds of workers flooded into the camp, only to be ordered out later.

To show that REECo, not the security force, was required to evacuate persons in a radiation zone, we called Jack Cupples. He had worked security for the AEC beginning in 1948 at Los Alamos, New Mexico, and came to work as a security guard for Wackenhut Services at the Nevada Test Site in 1965. In all that time, he had never received any training in radiation or radiation safety. He was astounded to learn that Area 12 Camp would be left open for the Baneberry test, because it had been evacuated for four previous tests that week, each farther from the camp than Baneberry. He told the judge he was positive Baneberry was the closest shot there had ever been to human beings or any personnel at all.

When asked if he had ever been ordered into a radiation zone before, Cupples was adamant that in all the years he had worked security for the AEC he had never been asked to enter a contaminated area. That was not part of their job.

Over the next few days, we called other witnesses who had warned their supervisors at the control point that Area 12 was in danger. By the end of the first week of the trial, we had established that the test manager had failed to contain Baneberry, failed to evacuate Area 12 Camp prior to the test, and failed to order the evacuation immediately after the venting, leaving 900 workers in Area 12 trapped by the vent cloud. We had established that fourteen untrained and unequipped Wackenhut security guards were ordered to enter Area 12 to get the workers out. It was time to call Sergeant Ernie Dyer, the man in charge of the evacuation and brother-in-law of Harley Roberts.

We knew Ernie was the one witness who could put the entire day of Baneberry in perspective to reinforce the multiple acts of government negligence previous witnesses had already shown. He had lived the Baneberry nightmare from the time he reported to work at 6:00 pm on December 17 until late the following day. He had tried to locate Harley throughout the day of the vent and then helped Harley and Dorothy as Harley slowly died.

Dyer testified that he joined the guard force in 1961 and had a one-week training course. It did not include any instruction in radiation or radiation safety. If radiation was present in any area, their job was to keep people out of harm's way. They were posted outside the radiation zone and allowed only those persons trained in radiation safety and fully equipped with protective gear to enter. There were hundreds of REECo Rad-Safe monitors at the Test Site who were qualified, equipped, and trained to enter radiation zones as part of their duties.

Dyer also related his futile efforts to get Area 12 Camp evacuated before the shot and efforts to post a force of security guards near Area 12 Camp if Baneberry vented.

NOTES

1. *Baneberry Collection*, EX 9.
2. Ibid., EX 5.
3. Ibid., EX 6.
4. Ibid., EX 91. Perry's brief trip to Hayes's station, where he recorded radiation readings of 1,500 mR gamma, resulted in his contamination. See EX 91, list of 86 men decontaminated at CP-2.

[18]

To the Rescue

WHEN MR. CLUFF GAVE the order to evacuate Area 12 at 8:05 am, he did not know what radiation levels the Wackenhut security guards would encounter when they reached Area 12 Camp to begin the evacuation. But although he knew the security guards had no protective equipment or respirators, he took no steps to muster Rad-Safe monitors to accompany them into the Area 12 Camp for readings to be taken and reported to him.

Given Cluff 's uncertainty about the radiation levels at the camp, Dyer and his men could not know the peril they faced. They figured the Baneberry cloud must be dangerous. Otherwise, he and his men would not have been ordered to circle around the cloud to try to get to the camp ahead of it. But the Baneberry cloud would not be outflanked. It climbed up the hill and waited at the entrance to greet Dyer and his men when they arrived.

Dyer gave a complete picture of the evacuation that had become his responsibility. His testimony highlighted the irony that Dyer, who had spent all night trying to talk sense into the big shots at the control point, turned out to be the man Cluff placed in command of the evacuation. After testifying about his night-shift efforts to get clearance to sweep Area 12, Dyer talked about his vigil as he waited for the countdown and then watched Baneberry blow a hole in the test manager's assumption it would stay underground.

Within a minute after the order to evacuate was relayed from AEC security Chief Chan Griffin to WSI Captain Tackett and then to Dyer, he began mustering the guards to evacuate all personnel in Area 12. He got on the radio and gathered a force of eight whose pickup trucks fell in behind him and climbed up onto the Pahute Mesa Ridge. Traveling at speeds up to seventy miles per hour over icy roads, Dyer thought about his efforts to get Area 12 swept the night before the test. He was still angry, but too tired to complain. Besides, every minute counted now.

As Dyer drew within ten miles west of the camp, evacuees passed him heading west. Dyer would later learn these early evacuees were on the move due to the foresight of the Area 12 cafeteria chef, who closed the cash registers, ordered everyone out, told them to leave the camp, and locked the door.

At 8:25 am, Dyer reached the blockade where monitor Hayes and security guards Yager and Holly were posted. As he turned left on Logan Road and drove a quarter mile to set up his station near the Area 12 cafeteria, the cloud was blanketing the entire camp. He parked his vehicle and sized up the situation. He ordered the guards to fan out to cover the one-square-mile Area 12 Camp. Harley Roberts was sent to clear the trailers in the easternmost sector, farthest from the Area 12 cafeteria.

Dyer described his confrontation with the firemen at the fire station and the ten-minute delay before the siren was turned on. He testified that Roberts was the last of his guards to report back and recounted his second confrontation at the fire station. Dyer was that last man out of the evacuated camp and when he met Hayes at his post outside the camp, ordered him out and then took his place at the end of several hundred cars heading west.

According to Dyer, it took less than an hour for the guards to evacuate over 900 people from Area 12 Camp and the tunnel complexes in Area 12. Dyer and all the witnesses confirmed that there were no Rad-Safe monitors anywhere in the entire Area 12 Camp.

After Dyer described the evacuation, he discussed his efforts to locate Harley Roberts and made a point of the fact that Captain Tackett, who gave him the order to evacuate, was the focus of his repeated demands that Roberts be located and sent in for decontamination.

Dyer and other guards testified about the cold showers at CP-2. But Dyer was far more concerned about his brother-in-law and the failure of Tackett and the AEC security chief to find him. Nine years after the event, Dyer's anger had not subsided. He refused to accept their excuses and considered their unconcern regarding Roberts the worst blunder of the day. Dyer felt personally responsible for Roberts and wondered whether the failure to locate and decontaminate him contributed to his death.

Harley was not present to testify about his activities that day, but Alan and I read his deposition into the record. I played Harley and Alan played the government lawyer who examined him at the AEC building five years earlier. Reading the words Harley spoke was a poor substitute for the sound of his voice, the expression on his face, and the feelings he expressed on February 20, 1974. We remembered how pale his face had been that day.

In the deposition, Harley described the incident on Stockade Wash Road where the monitor took measurements and told him he was "hot as hell." He remembered arriving at 17 Camp, telling the captain he was contaminated and how the captain came out of the command post and selected him to go up to Dead Horse Flats. He talked about the readings taken by Rad-Safe monitor Virgil at Dead Horse Flats after they set up the blockade and Bill Earnest's measurements taken late in the afternoon. Finally, he described the decontamination procedures and showers he had to take at the CP-2 decon facility and at Mercury Medical later that night and the gloves he was told to wear to bed because his hands were still reading 25 mR.

Bill Nunamaker died over a year before we first met Louise. He could not testify about his activities and never filled out a report as Harley and the guards had done. Only one witness recalled seeing Bill Nunamaker that morning. We called Walter Adkins, the bus driver. He transported Nunamaker and others up to T Tunnel for the 8:00 am shift change and stood by because it was obvious the radiation cloud was heading up canyon toward the tunnel.

When the evacuation order came, Nunamaker and others jumped back into Adkins's bus and rode down canyon directly into the Baneberry cloud. Adkins described how some of the workers stuffed paper into the cracks around the windows to keep the radioactive dust from seeping in. He said when they arrived in Area 12 Camp the guards were starting the evacuation. He did not see Nunamaker after he got off the bus there. Adkins was covered with radioactive fallout and had to take showers at CP-2 to clean it off.

On the day of Baneberry, Dyer and his men knew little about radiation or the amount they received while in the cloud. But they knew they were exposed to enough radiation to require showers and decontamination at CP-2 and the medical facility at Mercury. And they figured their radiation doses were of concern to the AEC or they would not have been bused to the Public Health facility in Las Vegas for further tests.

They also knew that Harley Roberts had been in the same radioactive cloud, was not decontaminated until later that day, and had died of leukemia. They were strong men and none wanted to appear unduly concerned that they would develop cancer, but they realized they could develop cancer in the future.

[19]

The Fault is in Ourselves

ARMED WITH THE USGS report, NVO-95, the opinions of our two geologists, and admissions by government experts, we put on our case to show that the AEC knew or should have known that there was a high probability that Baneberry would vent.

In his opening statement, Alan had planted the seeds of doubt, implying that the AEC may have planned for Baneberry to vent. We knew we could not get the government to admit it, but we intended to show that the AEC's decision to proceed with Baneberry was a reckless display of incompetence, since the scientific evidence pointed to a high probability it would vent.

We intended to prove that the *Baneberry Summary Report* distributed to a trusting populace at a press conference in Las Vegas in May 1971 was filled with statements the AEC knew at the time were false or at best grossly misleading. We called our two geology experts, Drs. Angino and Halepaska, to prove our position.

Dr. Angino was called to establish that the sixteen-page, May 1971, *Baneberry Summary Report* contained statements about the geology of the Baneberry site that were not supported by evidence in the possession of the AEC at the time the report was issued.[1] Referring to the January 1971 USGS report, Dr. Angino pointed out that the geologists who investigated the cause of the Baneberry vent reviewed the geological information available prior to and during the drilling of the 980-foot shaft into which the device was placed.[2] It was clear that the nuclear device was placed in a 98 percent water-saturated montmorillonite clay deposit extending about 200 feet above the shot point. This evidence established that the statement in the *Baneberry Summary Report* that the "primary cause of the vent was an unexpected and abnormally high water content in the medium surrounding the detonation point" was not true.

Based upon the USGS report, Dr. Angino testified that it was known, or should have been known, that there was a fault close to the shot point. The

USGS report included a drawing of the fault, named the Baneberry Fault, to illustrate its location 130 feet from the shot point. Dr. Angino reviewed the same material the USGS relied upon and concluded the fault was there prior to the shot, and its presence would have been known to those who selected the Baneberry site.

Dr. Halepaska was specially trained in groundwater hydrology and had drilled several hundred holes in montmorillonite clay. Having served as chief of the groundwater section of the Kansas Geological Survey at the time it investigated and recommended against the burial of high-level nuclear waste in Kansas, he was uniquely qualified to support the conclusion of both the USGS and Dr. Angino that the Baneberry device was detonated in a water saturated montmorillonite clay medium. He based his opinion on drill logs during the drilling of the hole. It was his opinion that those who drilled the hole must have known this. Dr. Angino also confirmed that all the geological data showed that a fault was present adjacent to the Baneberry shot point.

The cause of the vent was clear, and it was also clear that on May 14, 1971, the AEC had handed out the *Baneberry Summary Report* and issued a press release containing information they knew was false, then compounded their duplicity by trying to avoid disclosure of NVO-95 and the USGS report.

Although the twin falsehoods about the geology of the site were exposed, the AEC still hoped it could exonerate itself by claiming no one could have anticipated the increased force, or enhanced coupling, of the ten-kiloton device. To knock out this last defense, we called two scientists.

First, Dr. Robert Brownlee, a member of Frank Cluff's Test Evaluation Panel that reviewed the geologic information before Baneberry and approved the test. Dr. Brownlee also sat on the five-member panel that authored NVO-95. In testimony, he answered my question about the effects of detonation in a water-saturated medium.

> A: [Dr. Robert Brownlee] I think it is fair to say that those of us who have been involved with containment for many years have always recognized that a medium which is saturated with water behaves quite differently in a nuclear explosion to a medium which is very porous, where the pores are filled with air.
>
> I first did calculations on the subject of water coupling for nuclear events in 1956, so it is something that . . .
>
> Q: [Larry Johns] Is there any kind of ratio or formula or whatever— in other words, let me suggest to you that—I have heard it increases the coupling anywhere from two to five times in a [water] saturated medium. Do you agree with those general figures?

> A: Yes, and I think that covers most of the range; actually, I don't know why you stopped with two. It can couple depending upon the circumstances from one, which means no coupling right on up to fifty [times due to the water-saturated medium]. We will be conservative.

Second, Dr. Wendell Weart, Dr. Brownlee's colleague on the NVO-95 panel but not involved in the Baneberry site selection, confirmed that detonating in a water-saturated medium would substantially enhance the force of the device. In fact, he stated that had he been consulted prior to the shot, he would not have endorsed detonation.

Through the evidence at trial, we had exposed the AEC's deception in publishing its May 1971 *Baneberry Summary Report* and its efforts to cover up that deception by invoking national security. Had a jury of ordinary citizens listened to this evidence, we thought they would have been as shocked and disillusioned as Alan and I to learn the truth about the Baneberry venting. It might have so tarnished the AEC's image in the eyes of jurors that they would be skeptical of the AEC witnesses called to discuss our clients' radiation doses and to offer opinions as to whether those doses caused their leukemias.

The judge must have understood the significance of what we had shown, but we had no way of knowing whether it would raise questions for him regarding the veracity of the government witnesses who would come to testify for the defense.

NOTES

1. *Baneberry Collection*, EX 66.
2. Ibid., EX 37.

[20]

No Harm, No Foul

ONCE WE HAD ESTABLISHED the government's negligence in exposing Roberts and Nunamaker to radiation, we then sought to show how that negligence also caused their leukemias. Dr. Alice Stewart had carefully reviewed the medical records and work histories of each man prior to Baneberry and found nothing other than radiation at Baneberry to account for their leukemias.

Medical records and work histories are cold and impersonal. We wanted to present evidence supporting Dr. Stewart's assessment to show them as strong, healthy, hardworking husbands and fathers before Baneberry.

Our first witness was Harley Roberts himself. He answered questions from government lawyers about previous employment and denied that he had been exposed to pesticides or any other toxic substances prior to Baneberry. Dorothy Roberts listened stoically to Harley's words, and though someone else read them, she heard his voice and understood his thoughts and feelings as only she could. She sat motionless as she heard Harley describe his activities on the day of Baneberry. But when he began to describe their life back in Indiana, his jobs as insurance agent, filling station operator, and route man and their weekend camping and fishing with son Randy, it brought back all the happy memories of life before they came to the Test Site. When he began to describe his failing health and hospitalizations after Baneberry and then told the government lawyer he knew he did not have much time left, Dorothy relived a flood of painful memories of his last agonizing months. She bowed her head and wept quietly.

The negligence phase of the trial was cold, scientific, and impersonal. But the lives of these two men, their suffering, and their deaths were deeply personal. Harley could speak through his deposition, but Bill Nunamaker could not. The only way we could bring them back to life to speak about their lives was through the testimony of their wives, families, coworkers, and friends.

We wanted to show that Harley and Bill, dedicated family men, were needlessly exposed to radiation at Baneberry and had suffered and died as a result. But as we began to present evidence to show the consequences of the government's negligence upon our clients, we would have preferred having a jury decide the case, denied us in this FTCA action.

It became clear the strategy of the government lawyers was to depersonalize and dehumanize Harley and Bill and to make the trial an abstract discussion of radiation and leukemia. Any testimony about the lives and agonizing deaths of Harley Roberts and William Nunamaker was, to the government, an uncomfortable reminder of the human consequence of their blunders.

We knew the AEC had carefully planned to minimize the amount of its radiation exposures and then claim that Baneberry could not have caused harm to anyone. Baneberry would be portrayed as just another day at the Test Site. Yes, the venting and the radiation cloud were the result of an unfortunate miscalculation and, yes, all the decontamination measures gave the appearance that the workers were in danger. But no, the radiation caused no harm. It was a classic "no harm, no foul" defense.

Dorothy Roberts and Louise Nunamaker saw the trial through a different lens. Day after day they listened to testimony about complex scientific issues and activities at the Test Site on the day of Baneberry. For them, the trial was not an exercise in geology, wind direction, radiation exposure, nor was it about someone else's illness. It was about the men who had shared their lives and the loneliness their deaths had brought.

Dorothy Roberts testified next. After introducing her, I showed her an eight-by-ten photograph of her husband and asked her to identify it. Government counsel objected. "It doesn't matter whether an individual is handsome or not handsome or what he looks like. It is simply irrelevant." When the government lawyer cut her off with his objection, Dorothy looked perplexed and hurt, trying to understand why a photograph of her husband, who had lived through Baneberry, testified about it in a deposition read in court and, in her mind, died from Baneberry, was irrelevant to the case and of no consequence to the government.

The court asked the purpose of the photo, and I explained it was simply to identify Harley Roberts. I was surprised the judge had asked the purpose of offering the photo, since a photograph of the deceased is routinely admitted into evidence in a wrongful death case and this trial was all about the death of Harley Roberts. The judge overruled the objection. But the objection by counsel and the judge's question were troubling.

Had the case been tried before a jury, we thought the men and women in the jury box would have wanted to see a photograph of Harley Roberts to put a face to the man whose testimony was read in court. They would have wanted to see the central figure on the day of Baneberry, whose death was the reason they had been called to jury duty. Had government counsel raised the same objection in their presence, we suspected the jurors might have been as shocked as we were, wondering why the government did not want them to see the treasured photo of Harley Roberts, which his widow had brought to court.

Dorothy then gave her description of their life together. She met Harley before the war in 1941. He was inducted into the Army after Pearl Harbor. At boot camp, the top bunk fell and hit him, and it was discovered he had no sense of smell. He was given a medical discharge and went to work at a defense plant in Detroit, where she was also working. They were married on October 21, 1944. Harley was working as a deliveryman for a creamery when she met him in 1941 and returned to that job when they married in late 1944. He owned a filling station for a short time, delivered pop for RC Cola over the years, and had an insurance agency before they moved to Las Vegas in early 1966. She discovered she had diabetes when she miscarried her first child and had been self-administering insulin injections ever since. She and Harley had only one surviving child, a son, James Randall Roberts, born in 1949. She miscarried a little girl several years later.

She spoke with pride about Harley's physical condition before Baneberry. He was healthy and very active. He played basketball on town teams in Bicknell, Indiana. He won many golf trophies. She played golf herself, and she and Harley frequently played together back in Indiana. Harley liked to take his family camping, fishing, and boating. After they moved to Las Vegas, Harley played basketball at the YMCA with their son Randy and golfed with friends nearly every weekend on his days off. The fishing was not as good as in Indiana, but they went out to Lake Mead camping twice a month when the weather allowed.

During the years they lived in Bicknell, Harley never had a doctor. He had minor surgery in the early 1950s at a hospital in nearby Vincennes for a hydrocele, a swelling in his scrotum. A year or so after they moved to Las Vegas, Harley began complaining about his sinuses. He went with Dorothy to see the doctor who was treating her diabetes. The doctor told him all he could do for his sinus problem was wash out his nasal passages with salt water.

Dorothy heard about the Baneberry blowout from a neighbor late in the afternoon. She did not see Harley until the following day. When he came home around noon, all he said was "I guess you heard about the excitement we have had." He did not talk about it, because he did not want to worry her. Dorothy said she never knew he had leukemia. Harley never told her and neither did anyone else. Even though he was in the hospital several times and was at Loma Linda for five weeks before he died, she never believed he was going to die. She was asleep on a sofa outside the cancer ward when her son, Randy, knelt and whispered to her, "Mom, he's gone."

When I asked Dorothy to describe how Harley's illness and death had affected her, the government lawyer objected. "Her physical condition or needs are not relevant. She could be a millionaire or could be very poor. It makes no difference." The judge appeared unconcerned and took the government's side. She was only allowed to testify that she was a brittle diabetic, the type of diabetes that is hard to control.

When I asked Dorothy about her financial condition after Harley's death, the government lawyer objected again. Dorothy's impoverished situation during Harley's long illness and following his death were of no concern to the government. The judge acknowledged that the loss of her husband's earnings was a measure of economic damages but would not allow her to go into the matter. He made it clear that he wanted us to move quickly into the figures for loss of income: tax returns, pay stubs, and employment records.

Dorothy could not provide that information. We had hired an economist to discuss the loss of income. But she could testify about the unpaid hospital bill at Loma Linda for the final six weeks of Harley's life and identified receipts for payment of Harley's funeral and burial costs in Bicknell, Indiana. They totaled around $12,000.00.

I ended by asking her if she felt her claim for $500,000, the amount stated in the federal tort claim, was reasonable. She replied, "Well, really there is no figure that would be reasonable because it wouldn't bring him back, and I have lost so much. No amount of money in the world."

After Dorothy stepped down from the witness stand, we called Dixie Dyer, Harley's younger sister. Her testimony lasted less than fifteen minutes. She was very close to both Harley and Dorothy and described her brother as very active and in excellent health before Baneberry. After Baneberry, he tired easily and needed a Bird Machine to help him breathe. A family member bought the machine because Harley could not afford it. In late 1972 or early 1973, she and Harley went out to Lake Mead to fish. She packed up the fishing gear and had to help him back to the car. It was his last fishing trip.

Dixie loaned Harley her compact car for trips to Loma Linda hospital, because his pickup truck used too much gas. When he could no longer drive himself to Loma Linda, she drove him there on a couple of occasions. After

Harley died, Dorothy was alone and dependent upon neighbors and family to take her everywhere. Dixie took Dorothy to the emergency room on a couple of occasions when she went into a diabetic coma.

As we listened to Harley's widow and sister testify, the reason the Federal Tort Claims Act protects the government from a trial by a jury became even more apparent. Without a jury, the government's legal team could avoid dealing with the human consequences of its negligent conduct. And, reluctantly, Alan and I realized we should have expected the treatment Dorothy and Louise would receive during this trial before a federal judge who seemed as willing as government counsel to avoid dealing with the messy human costs.

After Bill Elliott took over as chief counsel for the government, he jokingly or sarcastically referred to Dorothy and Louise as the Baneberry widows and the press picked up that characterization. In our minds, it was a denigrating label that stripped Dorothy and Louise of their identity as loving wives whose suffering was immense and unknowable to anyone but them.

But through the testimony of Dorothy and Dixie we had at least reinforced Dr. Stewart's opinion that there was simply nothing other than Baneberry to explain Harley's leukemia. We needed our strongest witness to persuade the judge that Baneberry caused the death of Harley Roberts and to personalize the profound effect of his death upon his widow.

[21]

Occam's Razor

DOROTHY ROBERTS KNEW HER case depended almost entirely upon the testimony of Dr. Shields Warren. She had rejected the government's settlement offer, and we agreed to try her case on the strength of Dr. Warren's opinion and to honor Harley's last request.

Dr. Stewart testified as our first witness in order to accommodate her travel plans in the United States. This was not our preference. Ideally, we would have had Dr. Stewart and Dr. Warren testify back-to-back as our two chief causation witnesses. It would have been a fascinating display with two of the world's leading figures in the field of radiation complementing each other's testimony: one male, one female; one a pioneering pathologist in the study of radiation effects; one a hematologist and pioneer in radiation epidemiology. Dr. Warren was eighty and Dr. Stewart seventy-two. Each stood at the pinnacle of outstanding medical careers.

As we worked through the negligence part of the case, we stayed in close contact with Dr. Warren. We wanted him to testify as one of our final witnesses to close our case on a strong note. By late January, he called and told us he had other commitments and had to plan his testimony in Las Vegas accordingly. He could block a couple of days during the week of February 5 to fly to Las Vegas.

By court order, we were required to disclose to government counsel a list of witnesses we intended to call at least forty-eight hours in advance of their testimony. On Friday afternoon, February 3, 1978, we disclosed that Dr. Warren would testify the following Tuesday and made travel arrangements for his arrival Monday afternoon.

On Monday morning at around 7:00 am, Dr. Warren called the office. He was agitated. He said Robley Evans, the government's radiation dose expert, had called him at his home Sunday evening. Evans said he had been told Warren would be coming to testify on Tuesday. Evans seemed surprised and was calling to confirm that Warren was going to testify and that he had not changed his opinion supporting the Roberts case. Warren was taken aback by the call. It reminded him of the Justice Department lawyer's effort to pressure him into withdrawing his support of the Roberts case and again Dr. Evans's call prior to his deposition in 1975. We could tell he was displeased. He said he told Dr. Evans that he had not changed his opinion in the Roberts case and had indeed arranged to fly to Las Vegas.

This call by Dr. Evans was a chilling reminder of the government's highhanded tactics. But we also realized that the government was worried about Dr. Warren's opinion.

Dr. Warren arrived the day before he was scheduled to testify. We met briefly after court, but there was no need to go over his opinion. He had testified in court many times.

He took the oath at around 9:30 am on February 7, 1979, and identified his curriculum vitae, which included his education, his life work, all his honorary degrees and awards, and listed over 450 scientific papers authored over fifty-five years of medical practice. We could have spent half a day chronicling his work in the field of radiation effects. We needed to establish his preeminent position as the leading radiation pathologist in the world.

After earning his MD degree from Harvard Medical School in 1923, he served a two-year residency in pathology at Boston City Hospital and then became an instructor in pathology at Harvard. Except for an interruption while on active duty with the Navy during World War II, he taught pathology at Harvard continuously until 1967, when he became professor emeritus. He explained that his office was in the Shields Warren Radiation Laboratory at the New England Deaconess Hospital in Boston. The lab named in his honor was the headquarters and primary research unit for the Department of Radiology for Harvard Medical School.

He held certifications in anatomical, clinical, and forensic pathology, the last a special qualification awarded to pathologists who offer opinions in court cases or worker's compensation hearings about the cause of disease and death, just as he was doing in the Baneberry matter.

Radiation pathology is a subspecialty. His interest in radiation effects began during his residence training in 1923 when he performed autopsies on patients treated with radiation to study the cause of death. At that time, there were only a few pathologists in the world studying radiation effects. A leading medical researcher in this new field, he published his findings and documented virtually all known effects of radiation on all systems of the body in 1940 in the Archives of Pathology—before the Manhattan Project began development of the atomic bomb.

With the dropping of the A-bombs in August 1945, radiation effects on humans became a matter of tremendous importance. Dr. Warren, serving as Commander in the Navy Medical Corps, was selected by the Department of the Navy to lead a team of naval doctors to study the effects of radiation on blast survivors. His team waited at Okinawa for the signing of the treaty aboard the USS Missouri then flew immediately to Sasebo, the port city where the survivors of Nagasaki were being treated in hospitals, just over a month after the blast.

Dr. Warren and his team of physicians were not allowed to treat the Japanese victims, but they assisted and offered advice to their Japanese colleagues. He kept careful records and set up the standards used to study the short-term and long-term effects of radiation. His study, begun in 1945, was carried on until assigned by the National Academy of Sciences (NAS) to the Atomic Bomb Casualty Commission (ABCC) formed in 1950. Dr. Warren was appointed the first director of Biology and Medicine for the AEC when President Truman formed it in 1947. In his position, as medical director and as a member of the NAS committee involved in setting up the ABCC, he supervised the transfer of the data and information. It was also his responsibility to see that the AEC properly funded the project.

Dr. Warren began his study of the effects of radiation on chromosomes in the early 1930s. The first detailed work with chromosomes began with Theodor Boveri in 1905 and continued into the 1920s. It had been known since 1907, when Dr. Boveri published his first papers, that a cell in the stage of division is especially sensitive to radiation. Dr. Warren's own studies confirmed that radiation produces abnormalities that show up in the daughter cells. In the late 1920s, Dr. Hermann Muller performed his studies of the effects of radiation on fruit fly chromosomes. His work earned him a Nobel Prize.

Dr. Warren's active laboratory studies continued until he took emeritus status 1967. Over many years, he had technicians and graduate students working on chromosome studies. Those studies confirmed that radiation to the bone marrow produces chromosomal abnormalities.

Dr. Warren discussed the honors and awards he had received over his long career. At the top were the two highest honors the Defendant AEC could bestow: the Albert Einstein Medal and the Enrico Fermi Award. He considered these two awards as having the same standing in his scientific field as the Nobel Prize. He was also elected a member of the prestigious National Academy of Sciences, the only witness in the Baneberry trial upon whom that honor had been bestowed.

Dr. Warren understood the various types of radiation produced by nuclear fission and the radiation to which Harley Roberts was exposed at

Baneberry. When he was overseeing the AEC's health division from 1947 until July 1, 1952, some of the world's leading experts advised him in setting standards.

His study of the long-term effects of x-rays and gamma radiation was heightened by his concern for older physicians exposed to radiation while diagnosing or treating their patients before safety measures were introduced. Using all the information he had gathered over the years, Dr. Warren laid down the criteria for the pathologic and diagnostic effects of radiation.

Dr. Warren knew that Harley Roberts's film badge recorded external gamma of slightly more than 1 R or 1,045 mR, a dose he considered more than sufficient to cause chromosome deletion. He was also aware that Harley Roberts was in the radioactive Baneberry cloud for nearly an hour that morning, but was not decontaminated until late evening. Over strong objection from government counsel, Dr. Warren, formerly the highest health and safety official in the AEC, testified that the failure to decontaminate Roberts immediately after he was irradiated in the camp was clearly a "poor practice."

When we asked whether he had formed an opinion as to whether Harley Roberts's exposure to radiation on December 18, 1970, was sufficient to have caused the chromosome abnormality that resulted in his leukemia and subsequent death, he stated that it did cause the leukemia and supported his opinion in a series of well-reasoned segments.

First, he admitted the difficulty of determining a direct cause-and-effect between a radiation dose less than 25 R (25,000 mR), say in the range of 1 or 2 R (1,000–2,000 mR), which he felt might be the case here. Therefore, one must consider many factors.

Primary among these other factors was the certainty that a dose of 1 R (1,000 mR) or somewhat less can cause chromosomal damage. This had been demonstrated over and over. In fact, it was the general assumption of geneticists that some of the chromosome abnormalities in the human gene pool are due to accumulated natural background radiation. Humans accumulate natural background radiation over a lifetime in extremely small doses, primarily gamma rays from interstellar space.

He was emphatic that there was no known threshold dose of radiation below which *it did not* cause chromosome damage. To illustrate the point, he approached the easel and drew a graph depicting a linear hypothesis, which is generally accepted by the vast majority of the scientific community. Accordingly, as the radiation dose decreased, there would be fewer and fewer cancer cases. But until one reaches the zero point, there would be the probability of another case or two in addition to the spontaneously occurring cases.

Dr. Warren stated unequivocally that any amount of ionizing radiation had deleterious effects, which is why radiation standards required that human exposures be kept as low as possible. His testimony underlined why Frank Cluff had noted that his primary duty was to contain the device to avoid exposing personnel to radiation.

Throughout his examination, Dr. Warren stated that Roberts's gamma dose per his film badge was in the range of 1 R and that dose was probably delivered to all the cells of his body in a short period. There is a significant difference between the 1 R gamma bone marrow dose Roberts received at Baneberry over an hour, and a 1 R Gamma dose delivered over a long period from accumulated background radiation.

As he explained, "The whole reason man and other life forms have been able to survive in this environment is that they have the ability to repair a whole range of injuries. And the rate at which the injury occurs, therefore, is a very important thing."

The next area dealt with the dose of radiation to the bone marrow, where the blood-forming stem cells of the body are manufactured. Dr. Warren explained that there are two kinds of marrow: the red marrow is the blood forming marrow, while the yellow marrow is fat containing, which accounts for its color. The red marrow is located primarily in the flat bones of the ribs, sternum, pelvic girdle, skull, and vertebrae. The long bones in the legs, arms, and hands contain the yellow marrow that has nothing to do with the formation of the blood elements. In this case, gamma rays penetrated all cells of the body, including those in the red bone marrow.

To illustrate the penetrating power of external radiation to reach red bone marrow, Dr. Warren placed his hand on his own ribs and skull and with a wry smile noted that the bone marrow in the flat bones of his ribs, sternum, and skull are covered by a thin layer of skin. Based upon his anatomical illustration, and although Dr. Warren recognized that beta radiation can only penetrate about half a centimeter of human tissue, his demonstration showed that the external radiation, including a small amount of external beta radiation could reach the red bone marrow.

Finally, he maintained that the bone marrow gamma dose recorded on the film badge—1 R or a little less, in his view—did not consider the internal bone marrow dose Roberts received from inhaling radioactive iodine and other radionuclides present in the cloud that would have entered his lungs and then the blood stream. Because there were no readings taken of the radionuclides present in the Baneberry cloud in Area 12 Camp, Dr. Warren would not speculate or quantify the additional bone dose Roberts received. Instead, he accepted the bone marrow dose proffered by Evans and simply stated his opinion: "This is one of those cases involving low-level radiation which everyone assumes will occur so long as the linear theory applies and can be demonstrated by examining all of the clinical evidence."

And that is what Dr. Warren did. He explained that Roberts's leukemia was a two-step process. The external gamma rays probably reached all the cells of his body, but damaged only one of the bone marrow stem cells. In this case, the damage resulted in the loss of a chromosome in the C group, a group of six chromosomes (C-6 through C-11) that contain the genes involved in forming blood cells. The missing C chromosome, detected in July 1972, was not clearly identified as a missing C-7 chromosome until late 1973, after Dr. Caspersson developed his banding technique that made it possible to clearly distinguish each of the twenty-three pairs of chromosomes, including C-6 to C-11.

Roberts's C-7 chromosome deletion occurred instantly or with the speed of an average chemical reaction in the body. It would have been apparent in the first cell division, when one of the daughter cells was missing the C-7 chromosome. Bone marrow stem cells, which are found in the red marrow, are among the most rapidly dividing cells in the body, because they are required to produce all blood cells. By July 1972, eighteen months after Baneberry, the abnormal bone marrow cell with its missing C-7 chromosome had multiplied and overpowered the normal cells. They were detected in the bone marrow test and clearly seen under the microscope.

The C-7 deletion is a rare chromosome abnormality. When Dr. Warren came to testify, there were only thirteen reported cases in the medical literature. In all thirteen, it was seen in patients who had a blood disease that caused them to seek medical help. And in all cases, there was a clear connection between the C-7 deletion and blood abnormalities.

The second stage of Roberts's disease was the development of acute myeloid leukemia. In every case where the C-7 deletion has been detected, the patient develops acute myeloid leukemia within two years and dies within two or three months after diagnosis. Dr. Warren noted that Roberts followed this trajectory exactly.

Dr. Warren then carefully reviewed Harley Roberts's medical records before Baneberry. In the summer of 1969, a year and half before Baneberry, he had his annual physical examination, required by his employer Wackenhut. He was in good physical condition. His blood study was normal and showed no signs of any disorder.

He was exposed to radiation at Baneberry on December 18, 1970. He went to Loma Linda University in July 1972, complaining of chest congestion and fatigue. Blood tests revealed an abnormality, which caused

Dr. Kuhn, his hematologist, to study his bone marrow. The study revealed either the process of recovery from an injury to the bone marrow or the presence of a blood disorder. Dr. Kuhn was extremely alert and did additional studies, discovering that Roberts was missing a chromosome in the C group. Roberts was followed continuously as his condition progressed. He was diagnosed with leukemia at Loma Linda in February 1974, during his final hospitalization, and died there on April 17, 1974.

Dr. Warren concluded that the time from Baneberry in December 1970 to July 1972, when the C-7 deletion was detected, was a reasonable period to permit the bone marrow cells damaged by radiation at Baneberry to grow and become the predominant abnormality.

Dr. Warren discussed the latency period, the time between radiation exposure and diagnosis of leukemia, for a radiation-induced leukemia. He noted that the first case among the Japanese survivors where a probable relationship existed was about fifteen months after the explosion. The survivors were studied extensively: leukemia incidence rose in the first few years and peaked approximately five to seven years after the bombing and had been dropping off ever since. Also, there was a higher proportion of cases of acute myeloid leukemia than any other. Roberts had acute myeloid leukemia.

Dr. Warren also reviewed Harley Roberts's occupational and medical history prior to Baneberry. He indicated there was no evidence that he was exposed to any agent in his prior employment that could have caused the C-7 deletion.

When government counsel cross-examined Dr. Warren, he pointed out that Roberts had operated a filling station for about a year around 1960. Dr. Warren found nothing in that work experience that could have caused a C-7 deletion detected twelve years later.

Government counsel then asked Dr. Warren to identify any scientific studies showing that radiation in the range of 1 R had caused C-7 chromosome deletions. Dr. Warren explained that this was a very recently discovered syndrome. The researchers who reported this rare condition had not carefully studied or reported on the patients' prior exposure to radiation, so it was an open point whether radiation was the cause. Not content with this answer, counsel was determined to press the issue further and got an answer he did not want.

Dr. Warren referred to Dr. Alice Stewart's pioneering study as evidence to support his opinion. He explained that she studied a very large number of cancer cases in children exposed to radiation in the womb and that an increased number of them developed cancer and leukemia. The Court remembered Dr. Stewart's testimony and wanted to be sure Dr. Warren agreed with her findings. Dr. Warren not only endorsed her findings, he pointed out that while the practice of subjecting pregnant women to x-rays was common in the 1950s, due to Dr. Stewart's work, it was now, fortunately, very rare.

Government counsel knew that Dr. Warren had spoken on several occasions with Dr. Robley Evans who was present in the courtroom while Dr. Warren testified. Counsel asked Dr. Warren whether he agreed with Dr. Evans's calculation that Roberts's bone marrow dose was less than .5 R gamma. Dr. Warren acknowledged that he was aware that Evans had arrived at bone marrow dose less than half the gamma dose reported on Roberts's film badge but would not back down from his opinion that the dose was in the range of 1 R and sufficient to cause the C-7 chromosome deletion. He also pointed out that Dr. Evans was not a medical doctor nor had he studied radiation effects on chromosomes as he had done over his lifetime.

Before Dr. Warren ended his testimony, he made sure the judge understood his opinion that Roberts's overall bone marrow dose was not limited to the external gamma dose of around 1,045 mR on his film badge. He explained again that there was an additional bone marrow dose from inhalation that was not included in Robley Evans's calculations, since Evans only considered the radioactive iodine that concentrated in Robert's thyroid gland. To emphasize the point, Dr. Warren looked directly at the judge and said, "I might say that there will have been other substances than iodines in the cloud, of course. One has, what one might term the ashes in an atomic explosion, a quite wide range of radioactive isotopes." But Dr. Warren knew that no measurements were taken of the cloud to identify the other isotopes and went no further. He stood on his reputation and his opinion that a radiation dose of 1 R or slightly less was sufficient to cause Roberts's C-7 deletion and leukemia.

We did not ask Dr. Warren about the Nunamaker case. But the government lawyers did. During cross-examination, Dr. Warren was asked if he had formed any opinion in the Nunamaker case. We objected to the question, but the judge allowed Dr. Warren to express his opinion. We knew that he could not support Nunamaker's case. He said that he had been unable to arrive at a firm opinion in that case because he found a number of conflicting pieces of evidence.

On one hand, Nunamaker did have several chromosome abnormalities, particularly ring chromosomes found in a large number of his bone marrow stem cells in September 1974. Ring chromosomes are formed when a break occurs in one of the arms of the chromosome, which loops around and attaches to the other, forming a circle or ring. Radiation is the most widely recognized cause of ring chromosomes. This was evidence that the radiation

Nunamaker received at Baneberry could have caused the ring chromosomes identified in September 1974.

On the other hand, Nunamaker's external gamma exposure was about one tenth of the 1 R gamma dose he testified was sufficient to cause the C-7 deletion in Roberts's case. Because of these conflicting issues and Dr. Warren's reliance upon the C-7 deletion as the cause of Roberts's leukemia, he was unable to arrive at a firm opinion that Nunamaker's leukemia was caused by his exposure to Baneberry.

Court ended at around 4:45 pm. Dr. Warren, Alan, and I were driven back to the office. Dorothy rode with Louise and arrived a few minutes after us. When Louise came through the back door, she was understandably upset with Dr. Warren and confronted him. Angry and tearful, she could not understand why he had not testified for her, even though she knew he had not been able to support her case. Dr. Warren was as gracious as possible under the circumstances. He told her he was sorry he could not give a firm opinion in her favor.

Dorothy watched with embarrassment. She had wanted to talk to Dr. Warren after court and express her gratitude, but under the circumstances could not. She asked us discretely for Dr. Warren's address so she could send him a letter. We never saw her letter, but Dr. Warren told us it was a very nice letter of appreciation. Dr. Warren left immediately and was driven to the Golden Nugget and later that evening took a cab to the airport to catch a red-eye back to Boston for an early morning board meeting.

After he left, we tried to calm Louise, explaining that her case was supported by Dr. Alice Stewart and her family physician, Dr. Russell Miller, who had also agreed to testify. We also told her that Dr. Arthur Tamplin and Dr. Rosalie Bertell had called the office and were ready to testify the following day. Each would support both cases. This seemed to placate her.

Before Alan and I went home, we called Dr. Tamplin and Dr. Bertell and arranged to meet them early the following morning to coordinate their trial testimony. We expected their testimony would help the judge understand that low-level radiation was harmful, as Drs. Warren and Stewart had already stated, but we knew that in the person of Dr. Shields Warren we had brought into a Nevada courtroom an unparalleled medical doctor and scientist in the field of radiation effects who was feared by the AEC, its team of lawyers, and the experts we knew they would call to challenge him.

It was obvious to us that the judge was impressed by Dr. Warren and the logic he applied to set forth each premise of the syllogism upon which his opinion was based. We could not imagine how any objective person could fail to find in favor of Dorothy Roberts. Dr. Warren's testimony was particularly satisfying to us, knowing that he had withstood a justice department lawyer who tried to disqualify him and had not backed down when Robley Evans subtly tried to dissuade him from testifying. The government's tactics were, in Dr. Warren's view, "dirty pool," but he was a man of impeccable integrity. He would not have allowed us to bring up those matters, and we dared not do so.

[22]

Nickeling and Diming Them to Death

DR. WARREN'S TESTIMONY WAS the high point of our case. While he was concluding his testimony, our next two experts had flown in and were waiting to testify the next day.

Dr. Arthur Tamplin earned his PhD in biophysics at UC Berkeley and worked at LLL from 1963 until the early 1970s. He was there at the time the LLL scientists planned and fired the Baneberry test. Dr. Tamplin was a charter member and group leader of LLL's biomedical division, working under Dr. John Gofman, the lab's director of Biology and Medicine.

Dr. Tamplin's group was commissioned by the AEC to determine the amount of radiation released into the atmosphere and the types of radiation and doses received by people living downwind from tests at the Nevada Test Site between January 27, 1951, and October 31, 1958, when the test moratorium went into effect. The purpose of the study was to assess the long-term health effects on people exposed to radiation from the tests. It included other studies, classified, suggesting that radioactive iodine from those tests had caused injury to children in southern Utah.

Tamplin's group completed their analysis and concluded that the radiation doses were much higher than earlier crude estimates, particularly to the thyroid glands of the exposed children. Thus, the biological effects on the downwind population were much more serious than the AEC had expected. The findings were not well received, because they challenged the AEC's position that no harm from atmospheric testing had befallen downwind populations.

The AEC withdrew funding for Dr. Tamplin's studies soon after the AEC learned the results. But in 1977, Dr. Tamplin published the results in an article entitled "The Biological Effects of Radiation: Ten Times Worse than Estimated." Referencing his own studies and those of numerous other scientists, Dr. Tamplin showed that radiation doses at levels previously thought to be harmless had, in fact, caused cancers among the downwind population.

Dr. Tamplin educated the judge about the types of radiation produced by an atomic blast and described how they affect the tissues and cells of the human body, including damage to human chromosomes. Dr. Tamplin corroborated Dr. Warren's statement that there was no threshold dose below which radiation had no harmful effects and embraced the linear theory Dr. Warren graphed, which posited that radiation affects human tissue at doses all the way down to zero. To support Louise Nunamaker's case, he stated that the biological data would indicate that a dose as low as .1 R is enough to cause leukemia.

Rosalie Bertell, PhD, followed Dr. Tamplin. Her doctorate in mathematics was earned under a special biometry program established by the National Institutes of Health to train mathematicians in the study of biology and medicine. She continued her training under a postdoctoral grant from Roswell Park Memorial Institute, the world's first cancer research institute.

At Roswell Park, Dr. Bertell was deeply involved in a study of 16 million people in the states of New York, Minnesota, and Maryland. Every confirmed leukemia case in that population base was included in the study, which became known as the Tri-State Survey. Extensive interviews of the leukemia patients and reviews of their medical records were carried out, based upon guidelines established after Dr. Bertell and others met with Dr. Alice Stewart. They consulted Dr. Stewart because her Oxford Survey was recognized as the gold standard for an epidemiological study of this nature.

Over 3,000 leukemia cases were identified in the Tri-State Survey, broken down into five distinct categories, one of which was acute myeloid leukemia, the type from which both Roberts and Nunamaker died. Dr. Bertell testified that the findings of the survey confirmed Dr. Warren's statement that a linear "no threshold" relationship exists between myeloid leukemia and radiation down to the lowest reported amount of exposure. The "increase [was] across the board" and "this was true at the smallest dose they could measure, which was about 5 millirad [5 mR]."

Dr. Bertell, a mathematician and epidemiologist, calculated the probability that acute myeloid leukemias in Roberts and Nunamaker occurred purely by chance. Her independent tabulation agreed with Dr. Alice Stewart's, showing that the odds of two leukemias occurring purely by chance among the group of eighty-six men exposed to radiation at Baneberry were 3 in 10,000.

Neither Dr. Tamplin nor Dr. Bertell was a medical doctor and neither was allowed to offer a medical opinion that the Roberts or Nunamaker leukemias were caused by Baneberry. But they had confirmed Dr. Warren's testimony that there was no safe or threshold dose.

We had promised Louise Nunamaker that Dr. Russell Miller would testify in support of her case. Dr. Miller had practiced medicine in Las Vegas for many years and treated Bill Nunamaker until his death in December 1974. He consulted specialists to diagnose and treat Bill's leukemia and ordered an autopsy to confirm that he died of the disease. Based upon the autopsy, Dr. Miller confirmed that Nunamaker's final diagnosis fell under the general category of acute myeloid leukemia, although referred to as acute myelomonocytic leukemia, Naegeli type.

Dr. Miller testified to a reasonable degree of medical certainty that Bill Nunamaker's leukemia was caused by his radiation exposure at Baneberry. He stuck to his opinion despite efforts by government counsel to diminish his qualifications. "I can only tell you what has been published about the causes of leukemia. It is agreed that radiation causes leukemia," he stated. Dr. Miller also reviewed Nunamaker's work history prior to his employment at the Test Site and stated that he was unaware that Nunamaker was exposed to any agent, other than the radiation at Baneberry that could have caused his disease.

Dr. Miller lacked the standing of Dr. Warren, but Louise Nunamaker was pleased and relieved that he came to court. She beamed throughout his testimony.

After Dr. Miller finished, Louise took the stand. She was much more emotional than Dorothy and broke down frequently as she described her husband and their life together. She identified a picture of Bill in his Test Site work clothes and hardhat. It captured Louise's image of her husband. He was a big, almost bearlike figure, a man in charge, who protected the wife who adored him and worked hard to raise their four children.

We suspected the judge was no more interested in hearing about Louise's and Bill's life together than during Dorothy Roberts's testimony about Harley. But Louise was determined to tell her story and looked over frequently at the judge who responded with restrained courtesy. Bill was in the Navy during World War II, she told him with obvious pride. They met in 1943 and married as soon as the war ended. Bill was qualified to work in various kinds of construction and had worked all over the Pacific Northwest with his family in tow. They came to Las Vegas, where Bill took a job at the Test Site. Very experienced and liked by everyone, he was promoted to foreman and ran a shop in the tunnels.

Louise remembered the Baneberry blowout. She wanted the judge to know that when her husband walked through the door that evening wearing a paper coverall and booties, he told her, "I was right in the middle of it."

When we asked about Bill's health before Baneberry, Louise described how strong and healthy the man in the photo was before his radiation exposure.

After Baneberry, Bill went right on working as hard as ever. Then he just fell apart. He went to Dr. Miller in September 1974 and entered the hospital for tests. Louise struggled through multiple crying spells, as she described the last few months of his life. It was "terrible, just terrible." She was in a state of shock when he died and did not think she'd ever recover. They were so happy until he got sick. When asked the basis for her $500,000 damage claim, she responded as Dorothy had. Nothing could ever bring him back.

When the government lawyers cross-examined Louise, they were careful to avoid questions that might evoke the emotions she had expressed about her life with Bill and her loss. Instead, they wanted to emphasize that Bill Nunamaker was an older worker. He was fifty-seven when he was exposed at Baneberry and sixty-one when he died in December 1974. They sought to emphasize that he was near the end of his working years when he passed away. To bring home the point, they asked Louise her age. She squirmed in the witness chair and seemed genuinely offended. She commented that she thought it was improper to ask a lady her age, then coyly looked over at the judge and said that if she was required to answer she would whisper the number to him. The judge acquiesced and she stood and leaned over the bench and told him. The government knew her age and that she was nearly two years older than Bill when they married. Louise was sixty-eight in February 1979 when she testified, but the record does not show it.

After Louise finished, we called family members to testify how close Bill and Louise were and how happy they had been until Bill developed leukemia. Their testimony was brief. We knew the judge wanted us to present the economic information about the income the two widows had lost when their husbands died.

Our final witness was Clarence Ray, an associate professor of economics at the University of Nevada, Las Vegas. He had calculated the economic loss from the men's deaths. It was a simple arithmetic calculation set out on two separate sheets. The calculation for Roberts included several assumptions. First, it assumed that if Roberts, age fifty-four at the time of his death, had worked until 1985 and age sixty-five, he would have earned $260,000. Second, it assumed that if he worked to age seventy, the economic loss was $367,000. Each calculation included interest that would accrue on income over the years.

Dr. Ray calculated Bill Nunamaker's loss using similar assumptions. First, it assumed that if Nunamaker, age sixty-one at the time of his death, had worked until sixty-five, he would have earned $98,000; and if he worked to age seventy, he would have earned $248,000. His figures also included interest that would accrue on income over the years.

The government lawyer began his cross-examination suggesting that the men might have retired before age sixty-five or could have been laid off or disabled and asked if he had considered that possibility. Dr. Ray indicated that he had not and their deaths in 1974 prevented our knowing whether they would have retired early. The government lawyer then challenged Dr. Ray's inclusion of subsistence pay each man had earned in his tabulation of annual income and insisted that Dr. Ray set up another column on the far right of his calculation sheet to reflect amounts counsel insisted should be deducted from Dr. Ray's figures.

In Dorothy Roberts's case, in addition to deducting subsistence pay reported on Harley's pay stubs, the government lawyer pointed out that she had received the proceeds of a $10,000 insurance policy. This should not be included, he insisted, since Harley's employer, Wackenhut, had paid the premiums for the policy and the AEC reimbursed Wackenhut for the premiums under its contract. Dorothy looked stunned.

There were other deductions government counsel insisted Dr. Ray include. But the final insult was when he demanded that Harley's annual income be reduced by 40 percent per year after his death, since he was dead and would not have consumed that amount of his annual income. Dr. Ray objected. He explained that even if he accepted the proposition that some amount should be deducted, the figure could not be more than 20 percent, since the standard expenses of any household include fixed items such as a mortgage, utilities, taxes, and others, and the widow ought to be allowed to remain in the family home.

As the lawyer added more and more deductions, the total income loss was chopped down substantially. After going over Harley's economic loss with Dr. Ray, the government lawyer went through the same procedure with Bill Nunamaker. As he was whittling away, I leaned over and whispered in Alan's ear that I was afraid when all the deductions were made, Dorothy and Louise might end up owing the government money for their husband's deaths.

The nit-picking on the part of the government was not lost on Dorothy Roberts. It affected her much more than Louise, because she had been left with so little when Harley died. She had listened patiently as Dr. Ray was directed to deduct amounts in the separate column. But when 40 percent of Harley's annual income and his subsistence pay were deducted for each year, the tactics seemed to her stingy and coldhearted. She had struggled through the last year of Harley's life, and when he died was forced to sell the house, the car, and virtually everything Harley had worked for his entire life. They had lived very modestly on his Test Site salary, putting away enough for retirement. After Harley's death, she returned to Indiana, intending to stay there.

Now the government lawyer demanded that she live on half of Harley's income and deduct the $10,000 life insurance money she used to bury Harley and buy a small house trailer so she could move back to Las Vegas to be near her son. She had gone from a nice home to a trailer, no car, and scarcely enough money to allow her to eat and pay for the diabetes treatment. Having downgraded her lifestyle well below the poverty level, she was dependent upon the charity of friends and family and even had to get Louise to pick her up each day to bring her to court. She had borne her humiliating circumstances with dignity, carried on the lawsuit for the past five years, and now was stunned that the government begrudged what she thought was fair.

Dorothy could not express her feelings in court as she listened to Dr. Ray and the government lawyer bicker about her. But after court ended that afternoon and we returned to the office, Dorothy, who rarely commented about the testimony and evidence, let loose emotions bottled up for years. She wanted us to know how disgusted she was about the way her government had treated Harley the day of Baneberry and how degraded she felt when the government lawyer sliced away at the numbers, as if Harley were nothing to the AEC and his life had no value.

After venting her emotions for several minutes, she said with contempt that she was surprised they did not demand that Dr. Ray deduct the amount she owed the IRS for the travel pay deduction Harley had taken on their tax returns. The IRS had been thwarted and embarrassed, she said, when they tried to take her trailer to pay the amount owed. But the way the lawyer was going, she kept expecting him to try to pry the money out of her one way or the other.

When Dorothy finished, Louise chimed in. She said she could not help feeling that that the government lawyer's whole purpose in attacking Dr. Ray was to make them look like a couple of greedy widows trying to get rich off the deaths of their husbands. She was hurt by the suggestion, pointing out that she had never talked to Dr. Ray and had not seen the numbers he offered until he came to court. To Dorothy and Louise, the government had spent far more money defending the case than the amounts they felt would be fair for the loss of their husbands.

After Dr. Ray gave the judge the numbers he had been seeking, we rested our case. Government counsel immediately raced to the podium and moved to dismiss our case, arguing that we had not established negligence on the part of the government or that radiation from Baneberry caused their deaths. The judge listened patiently but summarily denied the motion and recessed for the day. The government lawyer seemed surprised, as if he could not believe what he was hearing. Your honor, he protested, and continued arguing even as the judge stepped down from the bench to exit the courtroom. Both Alan and I were a bit amused, but were also struck by the thought that the government's lawyer acted as though he believed, or had been led to believe, the judge would dismiss the case and the government would not have to mount a defense.

When we left the courtroom that afternoon, we were elated that the government would have to participate in the trial. But when we returned to the office and listened to Dorothy and Louise describe how humiliated they felt by the government's attack upon Dr. Ray, we realized all over again that the government's plan was to depersonalize and dehumanize the two men who died and minimize and denigrate the widows' losses. The deaths of their husbands had deeply affected Dorothy and Louise and we thought would have impressed a jury as well. But now we were concerned that the government's strategy might have resonated with our federal judge.

[23]

Give 'Em the Old Razzle-Dazzle

IN MID-FEBRUARY, THE AEC began its defense. Since we had shown multiple acts of negligence on the part of the government, and Mr. Cluff had all but conceded that he violated his duty to avoid exposing our clients to radiation, we thought the government might abandon its defense of the negligence claim. But it did not give up gracefully. Instead, it tried to rehabilitate Mr. Cluff and even tried to justify its selection of the Baneberry site for the test. Neither, in our view, was successful.

To justify Test Manager Cluff 's decision to leave Area 12 open for the Baneberry test and explain his inordinate delay in ordering the evacuation of Area 12, the government called a highly qualified meteorologist. Maps showing the location of all wind instruments operational on the day of Baneberry were spread out before him. He reviewed pages and pages of readings from each instrument at locations all over the Test Site.

Our heads were spinning as he went through the information and we wondered whether the judge could make sense of the data. If the purpose of calling the meteorologist was to show that the Nevada Test Site was one of the most carefully monitored places on earth, the government succeeded. The expert gave an elaborate explanation, meticulously pointing out how each of the stations had to be reviewed serially and at intervals to make projections of wind velocity and direction.

After he had lectured the court for the better part of an hour, it became apparent that his objective was to show that weathermen have one of the most difficult jobs any scientist could possibly have and that the court should feel sorry for Mr. Cluff and excuse his indecisiveness on the morning of Baneberry. But the judge was not taken in. After tedious explanations that never got to the issue, the judge finally called the lawyers up to the bench and commented, almost in a whisper so it would not be on the record or heard by the expert, that he was "sure the witness meant well" but wanted the government to get to the point and move on. Of course the point was that

Cluff was befuddled and dawdled, and no amount of explanation by this expert could show anything else.

The government moved on. Lawyers tried to defend against the testimony of our geologist experts, Drs. Angino and Halepaska. Government employees wheeled into the courtroom a large, three-dimensional glass prism that purported to be a replica of the geology of the Baneberry site, depicting subsurface geologic formations, the shot point, and the vent path to the surface.

Although the government offered the display to assist the court in understanding the geology of the Baneberry site, we had never seen this two-by-four-foot wonder. When the court asked whether we objected, Alan and I were speechless. In fact, we were in awe, marveling at how much time and expense must have gone into preparing it. The judge allowed it into evidence with the caveat that it would not be marked or maintained as a trial exhibit but could be used by witnesses if it would help them explain the Baneberry geology.

The government wrapped up the defense of its decision to detonate Baneberry in the geologic medium displayed in the glass prism by calling to the stand Richard McArthur, the LLL geologist who selected the site. In his initial answers to questions from the government lawyer, McArthur was vague, suggesting that he did not truly realize the Baneberry device was placed in a water saturated montmorillonite clay formation or that there was a fault nearby.

But the judge had heard the testimony of our geologists, Drs. Angino and Halepaska. He cut in and asked McArthur pointedly if he was aware of clay deposits at the site. McArthur tried to evade the question, but when the judge repeated the question, he conceded he was. Similarly, McArthur tried to downplay his awareness of the Baneberry fault and its nearness to the shot point. But that claim was difficult to make, since the government's own display, the impressive prism in the middle of the courtroom, clearly depicted the Baneberry fault and showed that it nearly intersected the shot point.

The AEC spent part of a day showing segments of the films of the Baneberry venting and movement of the cloud. We had seen the films four years earlier under a protective order that precluded us from describing what we saw. Prior to trial, we demanded that the films be shown in their entirety at trial, but the government had exclusive control of the films. They acquiesced partially, showing selected portions during their case, ostensibly to make it appear that the films supported the defense.

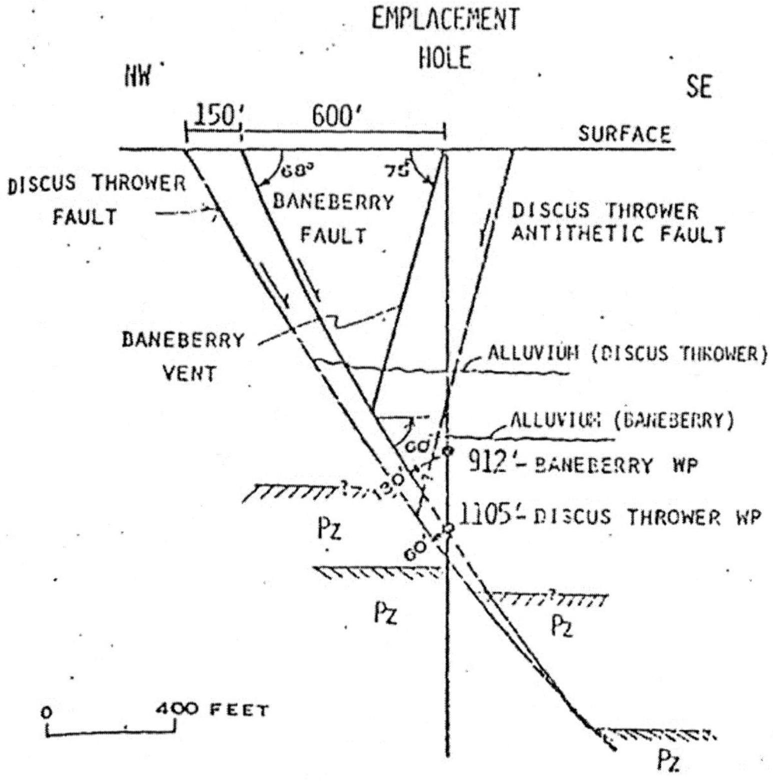

Figure 5.--Geometric comparison between the structure at Discus Thrower and Baneberry. WP, working point Pz, Paleozoic rocks.

Trial exhibit 37. Drawing of the Baneberry fault and vent path. Courtesy of the author.

Some of the films shown were from cameras around surface ground zero that showed the massive eruption of dust and smoke from the 300-foot fissure. They were interesting, but the films taken by cameras in the helicopter circling the Baneberry site that morning were spectacular. They confirmed the testimony and evidence of the eyewitnesses we called in our case and established that the vent cloud covered the Area 12 Camp while Roberts was carrying out the evacuation and Nunamaker was in the camp.

But the expensive and elaborate glass model that explained what happened 912 feet below the surface, and the films of the Baneberry cloud, paled in comparison to what the government spent on the all-day trip to NTS the day after the films were shown. We were not consulted about the trip. The judge, however, perked up and seemed pleased that the government wanted to take him out to the Test Site. We dared not object.

It was an all-day affair with members of the press tagging along. The judge and all the lawyers were flown out to NTS in an Air Force helicopter. As we flew into Test Site air space, the helicopter dropped altitude. We were told we had to fly low to avoid allowing us to peer into the highly classified Air Force facility in Area 51, just over the ridge on the northeast end of the Test Site.

Dorothy and Louise drove up and met us. After landing, we boarded limousines and were taken to CP-1, where the test manager and his panel were stationed on the day of Baneberry. We peeked into the control center, where Cluff and his advisors sat around a table watching the monitors on a wall that relayed the feed from cameras around the shot point.

From CP-1, we went over to the decontamination facility at CP-2, where Roberts and eighty-five others took showers and turned in their film badges and clothes throughout the afternoon and evening of the test. Next, we went to station BJY, the trailer where Dyer spent the long night before the shot and where he and Roberts watched the vent the following morning. We then headed north about nine miles to the rim of the Baneberry crater and from there to the platform overlooking the massive Sedan Crater, one of the main attractions at the Test Site.

Around noon, we arrived at Area 12 cafeteria. Alan and I ate lunch with Dorothy and Louise. From the cafeteria entrance, we had a panoramic view of Yucca Flat and looked down the hill to the house trailers on the east end of the camp, where Harley spent nearly an hour clearing out personnel. After lunch, we were driven up to T Tunnel, where Bill Nunamaker's shop was located. Louise teared up when she saw where Bill worked all those years. We returned to Mercury Medical and were flown back to town.

The elaborate tour might have made some sense if we were in a jury trial. In that case, it could have assisted a panel of jurors from different backgrounds, with no knowledge of the Nevada Test Site, to understand and sort out the activities of Harley Roberts and Bill Nunamaker on the day of Baneberry.

In our case, the judge had been to the Test Site and the maps, drawings, and extensive testimony about the events that day could not have been confusing to him. More important, there was no dispute about the time of the events. To Alan and me, from the helicopter ride to the all-day luxury limousine tour, it seemed an obsequious AEC effort to impress the judge.

Soon after, the AEC took the judge on another trip. We spent an afternoon at the U.S. Public Health building next to the UNLV campus. The purpose was to inspect a whole-body counter. A news reporter captured the event, snapping a photograph of government counsel John Thorndal lying on the whole-body machine while Justice Department lawyer Bill Elliott stood on one side and the judge on the other.[1] The purpose of the trip was meaningless, since neither Harley Roberts nor William Nunamaker were sent to the building for whole-body counts. The measurements taken of others exposed at Baneberry late in the afternoon of December 18, 1970, simply confirmed that radioactive iodine was still present in their bodies over eight hours after Baneberry. Like the Test Site trip, we were not consulted in advance, but it was arranged for the judge, and he appeared flattered by the lavish attention.

These displays preceded calling to the stand Mahlon Gates, Test Manager for the Nevada Operations Office in Las Vegas, the highest-ranking DOE official to testify. He oversaw the NTS and all its Nevada operations. After retiring from the military with the rank of general, he assumed a civilian position with the AEC in Nevada in 1972, two years after the Baneberry event.

As near as we could determine, Gates was called to discuss the chain of command in 1970, from the AEC's Test Site operation in Nevada right up to the president. But this seemed redundant, since we had already introduced an elaborate exhibit that included the chain-of-command information.

During his testimony through government counsel, the judge and the general engaged in a lively discourse about atomic testing at the Test Site, but when it came time for me to cross-examine General Gates about Baneberry and the issues and activities that related to our lawsuit, government counsel objected. The General, counsel acknowledged, knew nothing about Baneberry and had no role in the decisions made by his predecessor or those at the Test Site under his predecessor's command. Why then, we wondered, was he called to testify in the first place, other than to impress upon the judge the importance to the government of his decision in the Baneberry case.

Through these actions, the government had underwritten Mr. Elliott's pledge to "spend as much as it takes to win." The judge was visibly pleased with all the attention he was given, and we had no way of countering the effect it seemed to have on him. All these measures, we thought, were calculated to distract him from the negligent acts related to Baneberry itself and to minimize Baneberry as a small, insignificant mistake in the grand scale of the AEC's thirty-year Nevada Test Site nuclear program.

Notes

1. *Las Vegas Sun*, February 21, 1979.

[24]

Dr. Evans's Marvelous Cluster Theory

ALL THE GOVERNMENT'S RAZZLE-DAZZLE was sandwiched between a host of witnesses and evidence on radiation, along with the government's methodology for calculating the bone marrow doses for Roberts and Nunamaker.

Dr. Robley Evans, hired by REECo right after Baneberry vented, had eight years to prepare the government's defense. He also knew what Dr. Warren had said, having sat through his trial testimony. The government had nickeled and dimed and denigrated the widows' claims. Now it employed a similar tactic to reduce Roberts's radiation dose to the lowest possible amount to make it seem inconsequential and harmless, in fact, so harmless there had actually been no need for Roberts or any of the workers to undergo the ice-cold showers and decontamination procedures the afternoon and evening of Baneberry.

The government opened the radiation part of its case by calling REECo Rad-Safe managers to the stand. They began with a rudimentary discussion of the structure of the atom, describing electrons whirling around the nucleus. Uranium, the core element in a uranium bomb, contains a massive nucleus of neutrons and protons and layers and layers of circling electrons. A nuclear explosion splits the uranium atom, producing an enormous number of radioactive substances that have various decay periods, depending on the half-life ascribed to each.

The witnesses then discussed the film badges worn by NTS workers. One brought a Geiger counter of the type used by the Rad-Safe monitors who took radiation readings in the field. Alan and I had learned about radiation and the instruments at the time we began our investigation of Baneberry in 1971. We found the testimony elementary and were perplexed that the government turned the courtroom into a classroom, going over the same basic information that Dr. Warren had already explained to the judge.

We sat through several days listening to REECo personnel. We surmised that it must have been important to the government that these

REECo supervisors be allowed to testify, and they appeared proud to play a part in the trial. It was apparent that their sole purpose was to lay the groundwork for Dr. Robley Evans, the government's cleanup hitter, who sat through their testimony, frequently nodding his approval as they made their points.

After the Rad-Safe monitors had testified, Dr. Evans himself ascended the witness chair with as much aplomb as General Gates. His PhD was in physics from the California Institute of Technology with a subspecialty in mathematics. He taught physics at MIT from the 1930s until retiring in the early 1960s. He met Dr. Warren in the 1930s while Warren was teaching at Harvard.

We knew that Dr. Evans was hired in the early 1930s to reconstruct the doses of radiation delivered to the bones of young women who dipped their brushes in radium to illuminate watch dials. In the 1920s, health officials in New Jersey reported that the young women were suffering from bone cancers. The Radium Dial Company was forced to shut down its plant, and settlements were reached with the cancer victims.

Dr. Evans had served as a consultant to REECo since the mid-1960s, and was engaged by REECo immediately after the Baneberry event. He assisted REECo and the government throughout the eight years leading up to the trial, including preparation of Exhibit C-71, which REECo witnesses offered in evidence.[1] The exhibit, a sheet of graph paper with points depicting various radiation readings, included those taken from the darkened film in Roberts's badge, handwritten readings taken down at CP-1 from the Area 12 Camp probe, and readings of Roberts's clothing taken on December 21, 1971, three days after he was immersed in the cloud.[2]

Roberts's darkened film badge read 1,045 mR gamma. But Dr. Evans discredited that reading and revised it down to a maximum external gamma dose of 600 mR. Geiger counter readings of Roberts taken by field monitors were also discredited. Rad-Safe monitor Ellis took a reading on Stockade Wash Road at 9:45 am. His Geiger counter maxed out on the 200 mR scale. Dr. Evans stated the reading was unreliable and called Ellis's comment that Roberts was "hot as hell" gross hyperbole.

Rad-Safe monitor Virgil's reading of 300 mR gamma at Dead Horse Flats at around 11:00 am was also unreliable, since the needle on his instrument could only go as high as 200 mR gamma. Rad-Safe monitor Bill Earnest's reading at Dead Horse Flats at around 4:30 pm, when his instrument "pegged" at 200 mR gamma, was wrong, as was his estimate that Roberts's dose was probably around 1R gamma. It was growing dark, Dr. Evans opined, and Earnest must have misread his instrument or had the instrument on the lower scale, which peaked at 20 mR gamma.

Dr. Evans refused to accept any of Rad-Safe monitor Troy Ellis's readings when he took Roberts's measurements at the decontamination facility late that afternoon. Ellis's reading of over 200 mR gamma before Roberts entered the shower and his readings of 150 mR gamma after multiple showers could not be accurate, because Roberts's gamma readings should have decayed to much lower levels in the eight to nine hours after he left Area 12 Camp.

The 50 mR gamma reading of Roberts's hands when he arrived at the Mercury Medical facility, and the 25 mR gamma reading of his hands when he was released from Mercury Medical and issued rubber gloves to wear to bed also had to be discarded. His hands had been scrubbed multiple times; his readings should have dropped to imperceptible levels twelve or thirteen hours after he was in the Baneberry cloud.

If the readings of these monitors were given credence, they would not be consistent with the points on the graph upon which Dr. Evans relied in calculating Roberts's maximum external whole-body dose of 600 mR gamma.

The only Rad-Safe monitor who escaped criticism was Tom Hayes, whom the government recalled to the stand. Stationed on the road a quarter mile from Area 12 camp, Hayes never entered Area 12 Camp or took a single reading of Roberts on the day of Baneberry. In fact, Hayes did not take readings of any of the security force that evacuated the camp. The purpose in recalling him was to allow him to change the recorded readings he had taken at his station on the access road to Area 12 Camp. Hayes had testified that his Pic 6A device reached 800 mR gamma and stayed there during the hour he was at his station. Recalled to the stand, he claimed that his Pic6A reached 800 mR gamma between 8:25 am and 8:45 am and dropped significantly thereafter.

When we cross-examined Hayes, we pointed out that he had changed the report he prepared three days after Baneberry, and the testimony he gave at his deposition five years earlier.3 He also ignored the report prepared by Ron Perry, who stopped by Hayes's station at 9:00 am. All three clearly indicated that at 9:00 am Hayes's Pic 6A instrument registered 800 mR gamma and Ron Perry's Cutie Pie instrument registered 1,500 mR gamma. When confronted with his own report, deposition testimony, and Ron Perry's report, Hayes looked puzzled and said he did not remember seeing Ron Perry that morning. But he admitted that a monitor stopped by and took readings at around 9:00 am.

In our view, Dr. Evans's purpose in discrediting the readings taken by RadSafe monitors Ellis, Ernest, Virgil, and Perry, and the attempt to have Hayes reduce his readings, was to legitimize the readings from the only radiation instrument in the Area 12 Camp on the day of Baneberry: the probe at the cafeteria that peaked at 700 mR gamma at 8:40 am.

Relying upon the probe, Dr. Evans reduced the gamma dose recorded on Roberts's film badge, concluding that Roberts's maximum exposure while in the Area 12 Camp was 300 mR. This left 745 mR of the 1,045 mR gamma dose recorded on Roberts's film still to be explained. Dr. Evans reduced that reading to 300 mR gamma, claiming the film was contaminated and that the fur collar on the jacket Roberts wore for eight hours was the source of the 300 mR gamma reading.

Having reduced the whole-body film badge reading to 600 mR gamma, Dr. Evans then calculated Roberts's total bone marrow dose. He multiplied each of the 300 mR gamma doses by 70 percent, as Dr. Warren explained should be done, since the cortex of the bone would block about 30 percent of the gamma rays that struck the exterior of the body. Dr. Evans's final calculation was that Roberts's bone marrow dose was exactly 210 mR (70 percent × 300 mR), while Roberts was immersed in the Baneberry cloud, and exactly 210 mR (70 percent x 300 mR) from the fur collar on his jacket. Evans had come up with an extraordinary mathematical coincidence of exactly 210 mR from immersion in the cloud in Area 12 Camp and exactly 210 mR during the eight hours Roberts wore his radiation-infused fur collar.

Dr. Evans had effusive praise for REECo and its Rad-Safe personnel, even though nearly all the monitors in the field did not know how to read their instruments, did not realize the instruments had more than one scale, or did not know how to calculate or extrapolate the readings on their instruments.

His only criticism was directed at Harley Roberts and his employer WSI, because Roberts was issued and wore a jacket with a fur collar that collected radioactive material that continued to bombard him after he left the camp, doubling his gamma dose. Dr. Evans did not see fit to criticize REECo, whose monitors stood on the sidelines fully suited up in protective gear waving Roberts and the other guards into the cloud with their offending fur collars. He also could not blame the AEC for ordering Roberts and the security guards into a radiation zone, without any training and without coveralls, booties, hoods, or respirators, standard-issue protective gear for Rad-Safe monitors.

Dr. Evans then reviewed Roberts's thyroid readings. He was present in court when Dr. Warren explained that Roberts inhaled radioactive iodine in the Baneberry cloud that passed from his lungs into his blood stream and collected in his thyroid gland. While Dr. Evans could not argue with Dr. Warren that Roberts had inhaled the iodine, he minimized the 3,680 mR dose to Roberts's thyroid gland, opining that it added only 6 mR to his total bone marrow dose.

We were surprised at the remarkable mathematical precision of Dr. Evans's estimate of the bone marrow dose Roberts received and his certitude that it was exactly 426 mR. The judge appeared surprised as well, having listened attentively when Dr. Warren explained that in addition to the external gamma dose of around 1 R there would be some additional contribution from the 4,500 mR beta emitters and from inhalation. The judge interjected and referred to Dr. Warren's testimony on these matters on several occasions during Dr. Evans's testimony, but Dr. Evans stuck to his exact calculation.

After Dr. Evans arrived at his precise calculation of the bone marrow dose, the government lawyer tried to qualify him to offer an opinion regarding the cause of Roberts's acute myeloid leukemia. We objected on the basis that Dr. Evans, like our witnesses Dr. Arthur Tamplin and Dr. Rosalie Bertell, was not a medical doctor, and under well-established legal precedent not qualified to offer an opinion on the cause of anyone's leukemia. Government counsel argued vociferously that Dr. Evans should be allowed to offer an opinion on medical causation, but the judge sustained our objection.

Government counsel and Dr. Evans himself appeared crestfallen by the judge's ruling. But Dr. Evans was undaunted and shifted his testimony to a bizarre, nonmedical explanation to account for Roberts's leukemia and Nunamaker's as well. Dr. Evans called his alternative explanation the "theory of the clustering of rare events." Put another way, the occurrence of two simple events was a coincidence or an act of fate or God. He said he had written about his "cluster theory" but was unable to identify or pull out a single scientific publication by himself or anyone else that described the theory.

Dr. Evans asserted confidently that his cluster theory accounted for the occurrence of two acute myeloid leukemias in the group of eighty-six workers exposed at Baneberry. His explanation was as logically unsound as his bone marrow calculations were precise. He explained to the judge, "I will take a couple of examples from the newspapers, which I am sure you will remember, your Honor.

"There was a collision between two commercial airliners over the Grand Canyon some years ago, and the two airplanes involved were TWA and United. Not too long after those two, in Elizabeth, New Jersey, two commercial airliners collided, and it was again TWA and United. Now that is it. It hasn't happened since. In San Diego, last September, a commercial jet collided with a private plane, and there was a great deal of newspaper publicity, at least in Arizona, about the tremendous loss of life, which I think was one of the greatest in the continental United States.

"But, it did not come to much public notice that on January 31st over San Diego, there was another midair collision. It was between two Navy jets, an F-4 Phantom and an A-4 Skyhawk collided over San Diego. So, rare events cluster."

Unsolicited, Dr. Evans offered another example: two sets of triplets were born at Michael Reese Hospital in Chicago in June, and two more sets of triplets were born at the same hospital in September of the same year. These two sets of triplets were among 3,800 births at Michael Reese that year.

We were taken aback by the examples Dr. Evans gave to explain his cluster theory. Alan and I huddled, whispering that his theory was akin to the notion that if one Hollywood movie star dies, another star's death will follow soon after.

As I approached the podium to begin my cross-examination, Dr. Evans leaned back in the witness chair and grinned condescendingly. I asked him if he was a medical doctor. He admitted he was not but went on to explain that he had vast knowledge of medical issues based upon his studies. I asked if he was an epidemiologist, like Dr. Stewart, and qualified to offer an opinion there. He conceded that he was not an epidemiologist and had not given an opinion in that field.

I then referred to the two plane crashes and asked whether he had performed any calculations of the probabilities of the occurrence of the two airline collisions. "There was no way to calculate that. There is no way of telling," he admitted. I then asked whether the Federal Aviation Administration had determined the cause of the collision over the Grand Canyon or the cause of the collision in Elizabeth, New Jersey. He admitted, "Of course there would be a cause," and went on to state that there was "a cause for the triplets born at Michael Reese Hospital," as well.

When I asked whether radiation is a known cause of leukemia, he conceded that it was and had been known to cause leukemia since the 1920s. When I asked his opinion of Dr. Shields Warren in the field of radiation pathology, he stated, "He is superb."

After this last response, the judge interjected, "Doctor, I am still troubled with the cluster effect. It strikes me as being unscientific and philosophical." This provoked Dr. Evans into another discussion of his cluster theory.

> As you get sensitive to it, you will notice it more and more. As you drive to and from your work, I don't know how far that is in your particular case, but it is a few miles—I know that once we would become aware of this, that if a dog was in the street while we

were commuting to work. And it wouldn't be just one dog. If we saw one dog in front of us, very likely we were going to see another one that day but not the next day. Or it might be a child riding [running] in the street that day.

This response by Dr. Evans caused further inquiry by the court.

THE COURT: With my untrained mind, I would explain that as a coincidence.

DR. EVANS: Well, it is the same thing.

THE COURT: You don't think that there is a relationship between the events, only that they do cluster?

DR. EVANS: They do cluster.

THE COURT: Do they cluster the more rare they are? Is there a ratio there?

DR. EVANS: No, the fractional clustering is the same, regardless.

Dr. Evans had an interested audience of one and was not ready to give up an opportunity to continue the discussion. He asked and was granted permission to demonstrate his theory of the clustering of rare events. He explained that in his classes he would set a Geiger counter on his desk and the students would listen for a few minutes waiting to hear a "click-click-click-click-click" as gamma rays from space struck the instrument in rapid succession. He placed his Geiger counter on the judge's bench. The instrument was turned on and the entire courtroom sat breathlessly for what seemed an eternity, but probably around five minutes, waiting for the "click-click-click-click-click" Dr. Evans had foretold. Over the five-minute period, the silence was broken once or twice by a "click."

The experiment ended, but Dr. Evans persisted and wanted to give the judge another example. He asked permission to place a number of dimes on the judge's bench to demonstrate what he described as a periodic event, as opposed to a random one. The government lawyers seemed excited at this possibility and one after another fished in their pockets for dimes or other coins for the demonstration.

Judge Foley, however, had no patience for further demonstrations of the cluster theory. Visibly embarrassed, he declined the offer, thanked Dr. Evans for his testimony, and recessed the proceedings for the day.

Dr. Evans's professorial effort to convert nonsense to science was the humorous highlight of the trial. Certainly, it came at a stage where we sorely needed a bit of levity. We still wonder what the coin demonstration might have yielded and, in a way, wish Judge Foley had let him proceed. The irony was that the United States government had pledged to "spend as much as it takes" to defeat the claims of these two widows. Yet, with its top expert on the stand, the entire defense team was unable to come up with enough pocket change.

NOTES

1. *Baneberry Collection*, EX C-71.

2. Troy Ellis, the monitor at CP-2, took readings of Roberts's clothing when he checked in for decontamination around 5:30 pm on December 18, 1970. He wrote them down on a sheet of paper and placed them in the plastic bag with the clothing. He also wrote down Roberts's readings before and after he entered the showers, but the handwritten sheets with those readings disappeared. *Baneberry Collection*, TR: *Las Vegas Sun*, January 25, 1979.

3. *Baneberry Collection*, EX 16.

[25]

Emptying the AEC Laboratories

WHEN DR. EVANS ENDED his testimony, the government moved into the final phase of its defense. It called upon its own: men and women who were trained and had spent most of their professional careers in AEC-funded laboratories or affiliated hospitals. Three came from the AEC's Oak Ridge National Laboratory in Tennessee and its affiliated Oak Ridge Hospital, where Harley Roberts was sent in August 1973. Two came from the AEC's Brookhaven National Laboratory in New York. A final expert came from the Argonne National Laboratory's affiliated Franklin McLean Hospital in Chicago.

We were not surprised the government medical experts were all part of the AEC establishment and knew we would be unable to shake them from opinions that supported the AEC's threshold theory, the linchpin of the government's defense. As we began our cross-examinations, we stressed their relationship to the AEC and forced each to concede it supported most of their work. Some bristled at the implication that the relationship would influence their views. One even boasted that only 55 percent of his funding originated there.

Dr. Warren knew firsthand the importance of AEC funding and had laid the groundwork for this issue. He did so by emphasizing in his testimony that when he served as director of Biology and Medicine for the AEC from 1947 to 1952, one of his primary jobs was to assure adequate support for all the AEC's laboratories and hospital facilities, including the three laboratories mentioned here. He realized that his chief antagonist was Dr. Janet Rowley, the AEC's cytogeneticist, who worked at Franklin McLean Hospital.

When considering the testimony of a witness, particularly an expert witness, one must remember that his or her potential bias is as important as the testimony itself. In a jury trial, jurors are instructed before deliberations that, in assessing witness credibility, they may consider the witness's relationship or connection with a party to the lawsuit and whether that connection might influence testimony. If our case had been tried to a jury, we would have hammered the point that all the government's expert witnesses were biased in favor of the government because of their manifold professional relationship with the AEC. This was in contrast with our medical experts, Drs. Warren and Stewart, who were totally independent of both sides and had given opinions based upon the medical and scientific evidence. Drs. Tamplin and Bertell, who had conducted studies funded by the government, were ostracized when the results of their studies did not align with the AEC's position that low-level radiation did not cause adverse health effects.

The judge recognized why we questioned each of the government experts on this issue and, over objection by government counsel, allowed us to explore the matter with them. But he could not appreciate, as we did, the AEC's power over those dependent upon it for funding. Further, he did not know that the Justice Department had sought to disqualify Dr. Warren because his hospital received AEC funding. Nor would he, because Dr. Warren's principles precluded our mentioning or questioning him about a strategy he himself called "dirty pool."

The AEC's experts were, not unexpectedly, among those scientists who still clung to the threshold theory, some refusing to admit that a radiation dose less than 100 R—100 times the 1 R gamma dose recorded on Harley Roberts's film badge—could be shown to cause leukemia or cancer. Our only success was to get all of them, with one oddball exception, to agree with Dr. Warren that Roberts's acute myeloid leukemia arose within the time frame, or latency period, that one would expect if radiation from Baneberry were the cause. Most also admitted that Roberts's and Nunamaker's medical records contained no evidence of any blood abnormality, chromosome abnormality, or preleukemic condition prior to Baneberry. This admission from the government's experts contributed significantly to our case.

Since radiation at Baneberry stood out starkly as the only significant time connected event that could have caused these two leukemias, the government realized it could not rely entirely upon the threshold theory. Government counsel knew that Drs. Warren, Stewart, Tamplin, and Bertell had all testified that there is no safe radiation dose and had presented studies challenging the threshold theory. From the government's perspective, some explanation other than Dr. Evans's cluster theory, which came across as unscientific and frankly ludicrous, had to be offered to account for the leukemias. It called upon Dr. Janet Rowley.

Shifting from general radiation effects to specific effects upon human chromosomes, Dr. Rowley, a cytogeneticist from McLean Hospital, argued that radiation from Baneberry did not cause Robert's C-7 chromosome deletion. She began her testimony by explaining that her specialty, cytogenetics, is the field of medicine that deals with the study of chromosomes: the twenty-three pairs of rod-shaped particles found in the nucleus of the cell that contain all the human genes. The chromosomes are only visible during the brief interval when the cell divides. At that time, all forty-six chromosomes can be clearly seen under the microscope, as they line up to divide into two cells—referred to as daughter cells.

Dr. Rowley provided the court with an interesting history and overview of the advances in the field. Our knowledge of chromosomes in humans was so primitive that not until 1956 was the correct number of human chromosomes clearly determined. The first chromosome abnormality associated with a disease was discovered in 1959 by French physician Dr. Gerome Lejeune, who identified the extra chromosome, or trisomy, found in infants born with Down syndrome.

By the early 1960s, techniques for identifying each of the specific chromosomes had improved. But a banding technique to clearly identify each chromosome was not developed until 1972. This explained why, in July 1972, Dr. Kuhn at Loma Linda was unable to determine which C chromosome Roberts was missing in his bone marrow cells. In late 1973, however, using Dr. Caspersson's new Giemsa banding technique, the missing chromosome was identified as C-7.

The significance of Dr. Rowley's testimony was that prior to 1956 the type of detailed study performed on Roberts's chromosomes in 1974 was not possible. One could only wonder how many Japanese blast survivors who then died of acute myeloid leukemia within a few years also had the C-7 deletion, which Dr. Warren considered the hallmark and key to our case.

Dr. Rowley agreed with Dr. Warren that the C-7 deletion found in Roberts's bone marrow cells in June 1972 was the seminal finding and key to the causation of his leukemia and death. Dr. Warren had recognized the significance of the deletion in our first conversation with him in late February 1974 and confirmed it in his January 30, 1975, written opinion.

Dr. Rowley was hired by the AEC years later and issued her written opinion in February 1978—over four years after Dr. Warren had explained the importance of the C-7 deletion. In 1978, she stated she was "uncertain whether the radiation from Baneberry caused the C-7 deletion, but inclined to think not," because she felt his dose was too small and the interval from exposure to diagnosis of acute myeloid leukemia too short.[1]

When she came to testify at the trial a year later, her view had solidified. She was now convinced that the radiation dose was too low, embracing wholeheartedly the threshold theory, like the other government experts. But she had also modified her view regarding the latency period. At trial, she agreed with Dr. Warren that the latency period from Baneberry to the diagnosis of Roberts's leukemia was not too short for Baneberry to be the cause.

Dr. Rowley's complete agreement with Dr. Warren that the C-7 deletion initiated the blood disorder and caused Roberts's leukemia and death was a crucial concession. It demonstrated that in 1974 Dr. Warren was among the first in the field to recognize this significant finding, years ahead of his colleagues. The only remaining issue was the cause of the missing C-7 chromosome identified in Roberts's bone marrow cells in July 1972. By 1979, when the trial began, there were only thirteen reported cases of patients with this rare C-7 deletion—not including the Roberts case. Dr. Warren had reviewed all thirteen cases published in the medical literature, several of which were Dr. Rowley's own cases. From his review, Warren concluded that radiation could not be ruled out as the cause in any of them, because the medical records in some of the cases did not include sufficient information on the patient's history to determine radiation exposure prior to the detection of the C-7 deletion. As Dr. Warren aptly put it, "You can't prove a negative."

Dr. Rowley claimed initially that radiation was not the cause of any of the C-7 deletions in the thirteen cases. But the judge, who remembered Dr. Warren's testimony, queried her on this point.

> THE COURT: I'm not clear in one area. What is the relationship in your experience between patients that were given radiation doses, such as you just described, and chromosome aberrations like the missing C-7? Is there a relationship?
>
> DR. ROWLEY: Well, we have too few patients to say that specifically, because only two of our patients had radiotherapy. And they had abnormalities of chromosome 7.

This admission by Dr. Rowley seemed to fully confirm Dr. Warren's testimony and debunk any suggestion that radiation was not a known cause of the C-7 deletion. Dr. Rowley must have realized that she had given ground on this very significant point. She then fell back upon the threshold theory to argue that Roberts's radiation dose was too low to have caused his C-7 deletion.

Next, she advanced another explanation for the deletion, relying upon a study by Dr. Felix Mitelman, a Swedish physician. Dr. Mitelman studied fifty-six people diagnosed with acute myeloid leukemia who had been exposed to solvents, insecticides, and petroleum products. His preliminary and tentative view was that such exposures might be related to their leukemias. Dr. Rowley claimed that Dr. Mitelman's study was evidence that Roberts's leukemia was more probably related to his exposure to petroleum products when he ran his filling station in Bicknell, Indiana, in 1960, or when he delivered soda pop and dairy products ten years prior to Baneberry.

Judge Foley interrupted and inquired whether the fifty-six people studied by Dr. Mitelman had been exposed to radiation. All Dr. Rowley could say was that per the study, anyone exposed to radiation was excluded. Our assumption was that the judge was somewhat skeptical that none of the fifty-six, mostly middle aged or older, had ever had an x-ray or other diagnostic procedure. We thought he must also have been influenced by Dr. Rowley's admission that two of her own cases were ones in which radiation was linked to the C-7 abnormality and would consider that evidence much more significant than the Mitelman report.

I thought Judge Foley's comments left Dr. Rowley vulnerable and asked her to abandon her opinion and reliance upon the report. But she dug in her heels and was adamant that Mitelman was solid evidence that Roberts's leukemia was more likely caused by his exposure to petroleum products. Her insistence forced me to go through the report and the specifics about the fifty-six study subjects. She stated that Dr. Mitelman classified twenty-three as having exposure to solvents, insecticides, or petroleum products; thirty-three had no apparent exposure. Only three of the fifty-six had a missing C-7 as their only chromosome abnormality, as Roberts had. Dr. Rowley further admitted that no patient who had been exposed to petroleum products had a C-7 deletion as the only chromosome abnormality.

I then focused upon the seven persons in the Mitelman study who were exposed to petroleum products. Since there was no information regarding the work history of the seven, Dr. Rowley could not explain specifically how they were exposed to petroleum products or the extent of their exposures. Of the seven, four were males twenty-three to forty-six years of age, none of whom had any chromosome abnormality at all. Only one of the seven had a C-7 deletion. He died at age thirty-two and had other chromosome abnormalities along with the C-7 deletion. Although Dr. Rowley had no specific information about this male, how he was exposed, or the extent and duration of his exposure, she remained resolute. For her, this single case in the Mitelman's study provided scientific support that Roberts's work a decade before Baneberry was the more likely cause of his C-7 deletion.

In his testimony, Dr. Warren had ruled out any relationship between Roberts's service station work ten years before Baneberry, because, as he pointed out, once the C-7 deletion occurs, it produces blood abnormalities within two to three years at most. Therefore, if the C-7 deletion occurred in the early 1960s, Roberts would have had blood abnormalities when he began at the Test Site in 1966 and certainly by 1970, when Baneberry occurred.

To emphasize Dr. Warren's testimony on this point, I asked Dr. Rowley how long, in her opinion, it took after the first C-7 deletion occurred to produce a blood abnormality. She hesitated and was unwilling to give any time frame, realizing that pinning herself down to an interval shorter than ten to twelve years would rule out her petroleum products theory.

I concluded my cross-examination by asking whether she felt the Mitelman study offered a sound basis for her opinion, since Dr. Mitelman acknowledged that his study was tentative and preliminary and had urged others to carefully review work histories to determine whether solvents, insecticides, and petroleum products were associated with chromosome abnormalities in patients diagnosed with acute myeloid leukemia. She conceded his study was preliminary and not conclusive but would not abandon her opinion.

In our view, Dr. Rowley had failed to counter Dr. Warren's testimony. In fact, her testimony confirmed his opinions. Judge Foley's questions to Dr. Rowley were significant, forcing her to admit that radiation in two of her own cases had caused C-7 abnormalities and challenging the relevance of the Mitelman study. We did not see how the judge could give any credence to Dr. Rowley's petroleum products theory as the cause of Roberts's C-7 deletion, where Dr. Mitelman himself had admitted that his findings were preliminary.

After the government's case ended, we believed Dr. Warren's careful analysis and opinion had withstood all the challenges of the AEC medical men and women. It boiled down to a matter of credibility, and Dr. Warren, unlike all the government witnesses, was not beholden to the AEC establishment.

Dr. Warren's opinion in the Roberts case was but a continuation of his life-long curiosity about radiation and, in this instance, his quest for the truth about its effects upon human chromosomes. The AEC invoked its threshold theory, and, when it became patently inadequate to deal with alteration of chromosomes in the process of cell division, shifted to Dr. Rowley's "petroleum products" theory in a feeble effort to explain away Roberts's C-7 deletion.

NOTES

1. Janet Rowley to Buford Allen, ERDA counsel, February 7, 1978, with attached *Analysis of Data, Opinion in the Case of Harley Roberts, and Comments on the Opinion of Shields Warren,* M.D. Copy in author's possession.

[26]

Not with a Bang But a Whimper

WE CONCLUDED OUR CASE by calling Dr. John Gofman.1 Dr. Gofman received his PhD in nuclear physical chemistry from UC Berkeley in 1943 and was deeply involved in the Manhattan Project. Among other duties, Robert Oppenheimer assigned him to utilize the cyclotron to produce 1.2 milligrams of plutonium. After World War II, he earned his medical degree at UC San Francisco in 1946. In 1947, he was appointed to the Division of Medical Physics, Department of Physics at Berkeley, became a full professor in 1954, and retired in 1973.

He taught the methodology and use of radioactive substances and the biological effects of radiation. In 1954, Ernest Lawrence, inventor of the cyclotron and founder of the Lawrence Radiation Laboratory (later LLL) appointed Dr. Gofman medical director, and in 1963 Gofman founded and became first director of the Biomedical Research Division there. The new position fulfilled a request from the AEC to LLL to conduct research into the health effects of radioiodine upon persons living downwind from atmospheric tests at NTS in 1962. This last résumé item refreshed the court regarding Dr. Tamplin's testimony about the study and its impact upon the AEC.

Dr. Gofman had reviewed Dr. Evans's calculations of the Roberts and Nunamaker bone marrow doses and found it "virtually impossible" that the doses could be so low," because

> they are based upon external gamma dose and they neglect totally the major source of exposure that these individuals would have had. Given the circumstances, I would estimate that the doses from this sort of blast, and I cannot give you exact dose simply because no one has given me the exact composition of the cloud and all of the radioactive substances in the cloud these men were exposed to, but, the external dose [Roberts] measured was 1 Rem, or take Robley Evans's four tenths (4/10) Rem to the bone marrow . . . and one tenth (1/10) for Mr. Nunamaker. It would be my opinion, based upon

my work in this field, that the true dose must have been one hundred (100) times higher to the bone marrow of each of these individuals.

Dr. Gofman explained his statement by pointing out that the Baneberry cloud would have contained "short-life radionuclides in the first one to two hours when Roberts and Nunamaker were exposed to the cloud, and they would have decayed in the bodies of Mr. Roberts and Mr. Nunamaker, because they were not cleared from the site."

Dr. Gofman supported the opinion of Drs. Warren and Stewart that the radiation Roberts received caused his leukemia, even if he had to accept Dr. Evans's bone marrow dose, which he was convinced was wrong. He also supported Dr. Stewart's opinion that Nunamaker's leukemia was caused by Baneberry, in part because it was a statistical certainty, but also because there was no evidence of any medical problems prior to and for several years after his exposure until he was diagnosed in 1974 with leukemia.

Dr. Gofman reviewed the work history of each man. When asked about Dr. Rowley's opinion that Roberts's leukemia was caused by his exposure to petroleum products in 1960, he replied, "I find it rather absurd that the casual exposure to solvents and fumes in gasoline station operators could be regarded as a dominant cause of leukemia. . . . It is speculative; it is not science."

Finally, Dr. Gofman stated that there was no evidence to support the threshold theory upon which the government experts relied, and that the linear theory was accepted by most scientists in the field, supporting Drs. Warren, Stewart, Bertell, and Tamplin.

When the trial testimony ended, the denial of an opportunity to sum up the case was disappointing to me. Alan had given the opening statement, and we had agreed I would make the closing argument. Now there would be no final act in the Baneberry tragedy that had played out in the courtroom over the past three months. I would have no chance to say a final farewell to Harley Roberts and try to honor his deathbed request to "make the bastards pay."

Instead, the judge read in open court the posttrial schedule. The court reporter would prepare the transcript of the three-month trial, and we would then file briefs discussing nine separate issues.2 After he gaveled the end of the trial and exited the courtroom, we glanced over at Mr. Elliott and Mr. Thorndal, packed our files, trial exhibits, and legal pads into briefcases and boxes and carted them out of the courtroom.

The end of a trial is a time for reflection and, regardless of the result, evokes a sense of relief. But the Baneberry trial ended like a funeral procession, Alan and I pallbearers carrying the Baneberry casket filled with records and documents to be placed in a crypt until a final decision was handed down.

When we got back to the office, we talked to Dorothy and Louise. Louise, the more vocal of the two, asked bluntly why Judge Foley, who listened to the same testimony they heard day after day, could not simply decide the case and end it. Surely, he understood the evidence. Why was it going to take a year or more for him to make up his mind? Dorothy nodded in agreement, and both looked straight into our eyes for answers.

We had none. All we could say was that Judge Foley was a federal judge with the power to do whatever he wanted. To console them, we pointed out that he recognized it was an important case and that we had presented strong evidence, or he would have ruled against us at the close of the trial. Neither Dorothy nor Louise seemed satisfied.

Alan and I were anxious to get home but lingered for half an hour reflecting on what Alan called "the fine mess" I had gotten him into. We talked about the financial drain the case had brought upon us and would continue to impose upon our small law practice. We were not looking forward to spending hundreds of hours reading thousands of pages of trial transcripts, combing through the trial exhibits, reliving the last three months, and preparing drafts of lengthy legal briefs. We had lost count of the costs and time already expended and were fatigued at the prospect of the additional time and expense required to push the Baneberry case to a conclusion.

As former prosecutors, we envied the salaried lawyers from the Justice Department, their extensive support staff, the U.S. Attorney's office, and the AEC's local office. But what galled us more was that John Thorndal and his private law firm, which had already made hundreds of thousands of dollars over the eight years leading up to the trial and untold thousands for the three-month trial, would now have a steady stream of income preparing legal briefs for Judge Foley and briefs if the case was appealed. Baneberry had been and would continue to be a boon to him and a bane to us.

NOTES

1. In early March 1979, Dr. Gofman testified as the chief medical causation expert for the plaintiffs in the Silkwood v. Kerr-McGee trial in Oklahoma City, Oklahoma.

2. *Las Vegas Review-Journal*, April 8, 1979.

[27

Justice Delayed Is Justice Denied

WHILE WE HUNKERED DOWN in trial from January 16 through April 5, 1979, the AEC was being shellacked with adverse publicity about the effects of its nuclear testing program. The downwinders, whose first claims were filed with great fanfare by Stewart Udall on December 22, 1978, were headline news in Las Vegas on February 8, 1979: "Fallout to kill for 5,000 years." The article claimed the "government knew its atomic tests in Nevada would kill some people but lied to a public of 'guinea pigs' [who] will suffer the consequences for 5,000 years."[1]

On February 11, 1979, Stanley Jaffe, an army veteran exposed to radiation at the Test Site in 1953, won his appeal in the Third Circuit Court of Appeals. Jaffe's victory was followed by a March 5, 1979, story in the *Los Angeles Times*: "Pentagon disregard of A-test peril told." It reported that recently declassified documents disclosed that Dr. Shields Warren, AEC director of Biology and Medicine, had warned military officials about placing soldiers too close to A-bomb blasts.[2]

On February 15, 1979, the Bulloch family and other Utah sheep ranchers, who lost their case against the government in 1956, were again in the news. The *Las Vegas Review-Journal* reported, "Utah charges energy commission negligent." The article disclosed that 400 recently released documents showed their sheep were exposed to radioactive iodine doses 1,000 times the maximum allowable human dose, contributing to if not causing the deaths of the sheep, and that the government had refused to investigate.[3]

In late February, while the government was calling experts from its DOE funded hospitals to challenge Dr. Warren's opinion in the Roberts case, the *Las Vegas Sun* headline read, "Feds to probe fallout of Nevada nuke tests." The House Oversight Subcommittee "would begin a full-scale investigation into all phases of health effects from radiation."[4]

On March 8, 1979, *Silkwood v. Kerr-McGee* opened in Oklahoma City. Dr. John Gofman was the first witness to testify. He told the jury about Karen Silkwood's exposure to plutonium while she worked at the Kerr-McGee plant.[5] Just three days later, Bill Elliott crowed that the government would "spend whatever it takes to win [the Baneberry case]."[6] And on the same day, Drs. Gofman and Martell told the *Silkwood* jury that the plutonium Karen Silkwood ingested would have caused her to develop cancer.[7]

On March 24, 1979, as the government was winding down its defense of our case, Stewart Udall filed another hundred tort claims bringing to 547 the number of downwinders' claims.[8]

On March 28, 1979, after the government ended its case in Baneberry and we were in recess preparing our rebuttal, radioactive steam leaked from the Three Mile Island nuclear power plant.[9] By March 30, 1979, thousands were fleeing the area as 2.5 million curies of radioactive steam poured out of the Three Mile Island tower.[10]

The Baneberry trial ended on April 5, 1979, when the judge read the schedule of proceedings.[11] On April 8, 1979, our local press covered the nine issues he ordered us to brief.[12] But the *Baltimore Sun* focused on the precedential effect our case might have: "Nev. suit may set precedent for fallout claims."[13] Also, on April 8, 1979, members of both houses of Congress discussed the effect the Three Mile Island incident could have on the nation's nuclear power industry.[14]

News coverage about the effects of nuclear testing was not confined to U.S. citizens and military personnel. Earlier, we had learned of the trust fund set up for Marshall Islanders in an article that appeared in the *Las Vegas Review-Journal* on June 4, 1975. On March 27, 1978, Walter Pincus detailed the plight of the islanders. He recounted the latest chapter in the tragic tale of the natives exposed to fallout from the 1954 *Bravo* hydrogen bomb test: "Marshall Islands still affected by 1954 blast."[15]

On May 8, 1979, Dr. George Voelz, eminent radiation pathologist and chief of medical services at Los Alamos Scientific Laboratories (LASL), testified for defendant Kerr-McGee. He told the jury his autopsy on the remains of Karen Silkwood showed she only had 8.8 nanocuries of plutonium in her body, much less than the maximum lifetime safe exposure limit of 40. Dr. Voelz, called to counter Dr. Gofman's testimony, proclaimed that this small amount of plutonium in Karen's body "would have no adverse effect upon her health."[16]

On May 13, 1979, a *Las Vegas Sun* article, "They expect to talk until all survivors are dead," featured residents of St. George, Utah. It discussed recent congressional hearings in Salt Lake City and Las Vegas investigating the downwinders' claims.[17]

Except for coverage of the Baneberry case, the publicity from early 1978 through May 1979 was predominantly critical of the government, helping to create a nationwide concern that the AEC might have deliberately sacrificed U.S. citizens in the course of promoting its nuclear testing program.

But the bombshell came on May 18, 1979, when a jury in Oklahoma City arrived at a verdict in the *Silkwood* case. It found in favor of Karen Silkwood's three minor children and awarded them $10.5 million in damages against KerrMcGee.[18] It was a stunning victory for the Silkwoods, their attorney Gerry Spence, and Dr. John Gofman, whose testimony the jurors found more persuasive than LASL's radiation expert, Dr. George Voelz.

In our minds, the *Silkwood* verdict, handed down by a jury of ordinary Oklahoma citizens, exemplified the stark difference between trial by jury and our trial before a federal judge under the FTCA. Two trials that involved exposure to radiation levels that government experts dismissed as too little to cause leukemia or cancer ended within a month of each other. Karen Silkwood's children were accorded speedy justice by a jury that rejected the opinions of the AEC scientists. But justice was not swift for Harley's widow and Bill's widow. They would wait another six years for the federal judge to enter judgment in their case.

Because the Baneberry trial did not end in April 1979, Alan and I could not extricate ourselves from the posttrial schedule Judge Foley imposed. But we did not foresee a six-year delay before judgment was entered or a seventeen year delay before the case would end.

During those seventeen years, we became embroiled in litigation on behalf of 220 other NTS workers who believed, as we did, that they were just as entitled to seek compensation for their cancers as Roberts and Nunamaker, downwinders, uranium miners, atomic veterans, Karen Silkwood's heirs, Marshall Islanders, Rocky Flats workers,[19] Hanford workers,[20] and others.

When the trial ended in April 1979, we returned to the practice of law and had little time to think about Baneberry, until September 15, 1980, when the court reporter filed the last volume of the 5,404-page trial transcript. We scrambled to review the transcript and trial exhibits and filed our posttrial brief on November 28, 1980, then waited for the government to file theirs.

But the government did not file their posttrial brief as the court had scheduled. Instead, on January 30, 1981, it filed a motion for summary judgment, asking the court to dismiss Roberts's and Nunamaker's actions on the basis that the plaintiffs' exclusive remedy for their radiation-induced leukemias was to pursue a worker's compensation proceeding against their respective employers, WSI and REECo.[21]

In preparing our opposition to the motion, we contacted the Nevada Industrial Commission (NIC) and discovered that the AEC had made an agreement with it in June 1956, pursuant to which AEC contractors at NTS were not required to pay premiums into the state industrial fund to cover injuries or diseases caused by radiation exposure. Under the terms of the agreement, which we labeled a sweetheart contract, if a worker employed by an AEC contractor filed a claim for a radiation-related disease, the AEC would decide whether the claim had merit. If the AEC approved the claim, it agreed to reimburse the NIC for any benefits paid, if federal appropriations were available.

We realized instantly why the AEC had sent lawyers to Nevada in early 1956 to steamroll the NIC into signing the sweetheart contract on June 1, 1956. In 1956, the *Bulloch* case was nearing trial in Salt Lake City.[22] If Federal Judge A. Sherman Christensen found that the radiation that fell on sheep in the 1953 A-bomb tests had caused their lesions and deaths, it might occur to citizens in Utah and eastern Nevada, exposed to fallout from the same tests, or to Nevada Test Site workers, or soldiers at Camp Desert Rock, that they too might be in peril of developing cancer.

But in 1956, when *Bulloch* was tried, the AEC managed to silence scientists who disagreed with the experts they mustered to testify before Judge Christensen. The government won. When Judge Christensen learned, twenty-three years later, that the AEC had stifled all who might have testified against the government, he reopened the case on the basis that the government and its lawyers had perpetrated a fraud on the court.[23] But the government appealed his ruling to the Tenth Circuit Court and won again.[24]

The filing of the motion on January 30, 1981, was ironic in a way. Joe Carter, who worked as a laborer at NTS in the early 1950s, died of brain cancer in 1980. While we were investigating his medical history, we learned that Carter was one of four workers exposed to excessive radiation in a plutonium dispersal experiment on January 18, 1956.[25] Oral Epley, one of the four, died on February 1, 1956. On August 17, 1980, the circumstances of his death were on the front page of the *Las Vegas Sun*.[26] The article discussed my inquiry to LASL about Oral Epley's organs, which were sent to LASL for examination following his autopsy on February 1, 1956. It also mentioned assurances by Test Site supervisors, who visited Epley's family while he was in the hospital, that there was a $50,000 life insurance policy. But after Epley died, the $50,000 policy, like the organs sent to LASL, could not be found.[27] The rest of the story, not covered in the article, was that I called the mortuary in Oklahoma and spoke to the ninety-three-year-old mortician who received Epley's remains for burial. He told me he was contacted by someone from the government who directed him not to touch Epley's body because it was contaminated with radiation.

Judge Foley denied, for the second time, the government's motion to dismiss the Baneberry case based on the worker's compensation exclusive remedy defense. He also denied the government's identical motion filed in the companion *Prescott* case, which we filed in 1980.[28] The government appealed his decision in the Baneberry case and his decision in Prescott. In 1984, the Ninth Circuit Court of Appeals affirmed the rulings.[29]

We waited for the court to rule on Baneberry. On June 8, 1982, Judge Foley entered a six-page *Partial Decision—Negligence Issues*, setting forth the salient facts and finding, "Plaintiffs have proven by a preponderance of the evidence that employees of the United States were negligent in the manner in which persons were evacuated post-shot from Area 12 and in the manner in which persons who have been exposed to radiation were attempted to be decontaminated."

We would have been stunned if Judge Foley had ruled otherwise, since the evidence of Cluff 's negligent conduct was overwhelming. Now, the only remaining issue was whether he would accept the opinion of Dr. Warren and find that the radiation Roberts received was sufficient to cause a C-7 deletion and leukemia. If he found for Roberts, he might also find in favor of Nunamaker.

After he handed down the ruling on negligence in June 1982, we believed the judge would want to make his final ruling before the downwinders' case, *Allen v. United States*, went to trial in Salt Lake City in September 1982. A ruling on Baneberry, filed eight years before *Allen*, could influence the *Allen* case and give Baneberry some precedential value.

But Judge Foley did not act. The *Allen* trial began before U.S. District Judge Bruce Jenkins. Dale Haralson, lead counsel for the downwinders brought to court twenty-four test cases: eight died of leukemia and sixteen others died or were diagnosed with various cancers. Press coverage of the trial was extensive in our newspapers through its conclusion in November 1982.

On January 20, 1983, four years after our trial began, Judge Foley issued a two-sentence ruling. He found that Roberts received 426 mR to his bone marrow and Nunamaker 100 mR to his bone marrow and ruled we had not presented evidence to support causation of the two leukemias. He directed the government lawyers to write the decision for him and to prepare the findings of fact.

In our view, it was a travesty. Judge Foley had a responsibility to measure the evidence presented at trial and render a reasoned decision based on that evidence. He had not only missed an opportunity to hand down a landmark decision that might have become a beacon for others who suffered because of AEC recklessness, he abdicated his responsibility as a jurist. In two sentences, he unceremoniously washed his hands of Baneberry and turned Roberts and Nunamaker over to government lawyers.

When we tried to explain Judge Foley's ruling to Dorothy and Louise, they could not understand why he had sat on the case for nearly four years and then insulted them with a piece of paper that said almost nothing. If the case was as simple as his ruling seemed, he should have had the guts to end it in April 1979. At least they would have been spared the misery of waiting. We were as shocked and baffled as they and could only conclude he had become so overwhelmed and weary of the burden of the Baneberry case that he simply took the safe course and ruled in favor of the United States government.

We knew what the government lawyers would do with carte blanche to write their own decision in the case. They would craft findings that absolved the AEC, slanted to portray the government and its agency as blameless. We knew they would make it appear as if Dorothy and Louise had needlessly put an innocent government agency, the AEC, through an expensive trial.

The government lawyers took a year to prepare the final document, which stretched Judge Foley's two-sentence ruling to proportions even we could not have imagined. It was eighty-eight pages long. And, as expected, it was a scathing and slanderous assault upon all our experts. It validated virtually every proposition, fact, and theory offered by the government and cleared the AEC of any wrongdoing or responsibility for Harley's or Bill's leukemias and deaths.

Dr. Warren earned a modicum of respect, more in the nature of a backhanded and condescending commentary. The government lawyers acknowledged his eminent qualification as a historic and revered figure upon whom the AEC had bestowed its highest awards. But they denigrated his well-reasoned opinions and made them appear as obsolete as their threshold theory truly was. The resurrected threshold theory became the centerpiece of their case and ultimate proof that no leukemia could possibly be caused by radiation that did not exceed their arbitrary exposure level of 100 R. Alan and I were relieved that Dr. Warren was no longer alive to review their comments and wondered whether they would have been so brazen if he were.

While discounting Dr. Warren's expertise, the government adopted wholesale Dr. Rowley's petroleum products theory. For the government lawyers, Dr. Rowley's reliance upon a single study by Dr. Felix Mitelman was incontrovertible proof that Roberts's C-7 deletion came from his earlier exposure to petroleum products. But one item that the government lawyers decided to omit was Dr. Evans's "cluster theory" as an explanation for the occurrence of these two leukemias. Even they must have recognized that no one, including the judge, gave any credence to such a bizarre argument.

On April 16, 1984, we filed our objections challenging most of the Findings of Fact and Conclusions of Law. And on May 4, we filed a motion to reopen the action or for a new trial. In support, we supplied an affidavit of Dr. Karl Z. Morgan, who, in January 1984 at our request, reviewed the trial testimony and trial exhibits that Dr. Robley Evans relied upon to calculate Roberts's bone marrow dose. In a comprehensive affidavit, Dr. Morgan attested that Dr. Evans had failed to consider the bone marrow dose Roberts received from inhaling radioactive isotopes present in the Baneberry cloud during the first one to two hours after the detonation.[30]

Dr. Morgan was the leading expert in the world on internal dose calculations. In 1947, he published the first paper showing how to calculate internal dose from radionuclides deposited in the body. Considered by many the father of health physics, he founded and served as president of the *Health Physics Society*, was editor of Health Physics Journal, and served as director of health Physics at Oak Ridge National Laboratory from 1943 until 1972. He was chairman of the Internal Dose Committee of the International and National Commissions on Radiation Protection (ICRP, NCRP) that set the standards and published the handbooks used to determine maximum permissible radiation doses.

Dr. Morgan identified twenty-eight radioactive isotopes that would have been in the Baneberry cloud in the first several hours after the device detonated. He calculated the dose each would have delivered to Roberts's bone marrow after it was taken into the lungs and irradiated the rib cage, where a substantial portion of the red bone morrow is located. He relied upon Dr. Evans's trial testimony and the King Tables in the leading internal dose handbook to calculate dosage. He concluded that Roberts's total bone marrow dose from inhalation of the twenty-eight radionuclides was 7,100 mR, which, when added to the bone marrow dose derived from external gamma readings on the film badge, showed total bone marrow dose at 7,830 mR.

Dr. Morgan's affidavit established that Dr. Warren had been right all along. Warren had stated that Roberts's bone marrow dose would have included inhaled radionuclides, "the ashes of the explosion, a quite wide range of radioactive isotopes." In fact, Dr. Morgan confirmed Dr. Warren's long stated opinion that Roberts's "bone marrow dose was somewhere between Dr. Evans's low estimate of less than half a rem and my initial estimate of 15 rem."

Based upon Roberts's properly calculated bone marrow dose of 7.83 R (7,830 mR), Dr. Morgan calculated the probability of leukemia causation.

Relying upon the BEIR III report, he determined that the probability that Roberts's leukemia was caused by Baneberry ranged from a low of 38.3 percent to a high of 78.9 percent.[31]

Another basis for our motion was the discovery of an article published in the *Lancet*, by Dr. Felix Mitelman in December 1979, eight months after Dr. Rowley testified at trial. In the *Lancet* article, Dr. Mitelman now stated, "Furthermore, exposure to petroleum products seems to be associated with normal chromosomes, in contrast to exposure to chemical solvents and insecticides."[32] Dr. Mitelman repudiated Dr. Rowley's reliance upon an earlier paper that suggested a possible relationship between exposure to petroleum products and the C-7 deletion.[33]

We contended the court should reopen the action since Dr. Morgan had obliterated Dr. Evans's bone marrow dose calculations, and Dr. Rowley's petroleum products theory had been discredited by Dr. Mitelman, whose preliminary and narrow suggestion she had relied on entirely at trial.

On May 10, 1984, six days after we filed our motion, Judge Bruce Jenkins's 500-page Memorandum decision in *Allen* was released.[34] In stark contrast to Judge Foley, Judge Jenkins analyzed the facts presented by the lay and expert witnesses called to testify at his trial, included an elegant legal analysis of the arguments presented by counsel for the government and the plaintiffs, and found in favor of the heirs of eight persons who died of leukemia. He also found in favor of one woman who died of breast cancer and a young woman who survived, living with thyroid cancer. The judge awarded a total of nearly $2.5 million to the ten plaintiffs who prevailed.

The Jenkins decision was a thrilling victory for Dale Haralson, who led the team of lawyers for the plaintiffs and was a crushing defeat for the AEC. For over three decades, the AEC had insisted that not one single cancer or leukemia had been caused by radiation from its aboveground atomic testing program.

On June 1, 1984, we supplemented our motion to reopen, citing the *Allen* decision as compelling evidence that low-level radiation, which ranged from .36 rem to 3.7 rem, had been found by Judge Jenkins sufficient to cause the eight leukemias.[35]

In the government's opposition to our motion, it tried to defend Dr. Evans and Dr. Rowley. Dr. Evans supplied an affidavit in which he acknowledged that Dr. Morgan had "mechanically" tabulated the list of radionuclides present in the Baneberry explosion, but "fractionation" prevented those twenty-eight radionuclides from reaching the surface and entering the radioactive cloud. Somehow, unlike the radioactive iodine that was also present in the explosion and measured in Roberts's thyroid gland, these radionuclides were trapped below ground. However, Dr. Evans admitted that he could not support his "fractionation" position, because to do so would require actual measurements of the radioactive cloud in Area 12 Camp, and he knew none were taken.[36]

We filed a reply urging the court to reopen the case to allow Dr. Morgan to testify and to strike Dr. Rowley's petroleum products theory. Having waited over five years for the court's decision, we could see no reason why Judge Foley would deny us an opportunity to present evidence that would correct erroneous findings and could lead to a just decision in the case.[37]

On January 4, 1985, in a minute order and without explanation, the judge denied our motion.[38] We viewed this as a second act of abdication to the government. We could only conclude that the judge had resolved to stand by the government, despite clear evidence that Dr. Evans had not accurately calculated Roberts's bone marrow dose and that the petroleum products theory was as absurd as Dr. Evans's cluster theory. Instead, we hoped he would recognize Dr. Warren's opinion as credible and correct.

On January 5, 1985, six years after the Baneberry trial, Judge Foley adopted every proposed finding offered by the government, or as we would contend, rubber stamped the government's decision and entered judgment against Dorothy Roberts and Louise Nunamaker. We appealed the judgment and his denial of our motion to reopen.

On December 24, 1986, the three-member Ninth Circuit panel, headed by Chief Judge Browning, entered an Order of Limited Remand, sending the case back to Judge Foley directing him "to explain his reasons for denying Roberts's and Nunamaker's motion to reopen or grant a new trial to receive new evidence contained in three affidavits by Dr. Karl Z. Morgan and in recently published articles [Mitelman's paper] which Roberts sought to introduce."

On June 24, 1987, Judge Foley made findings and denied the motion to reopen. He ruled that Dr. Morgan could have been consulted and offered his opinion at trial or at some point earlier than his affidavits were offered. He also found that reopening the case would require considerable time and additional witnesses. Of interest to us, he observed that, since Dr. Morgan's testimony was offered to bolster Dr. Warren's testimony that Roberts's bone dose was sufficient to cause leukemia and Dr. Warren was deceased, the court would be denied the benefit of Dr. Warren's reassessment.

We appealed that ruling, and our appeal was reinstated in the Ninth Circuit in 1988. There was one final legal hurdle we had to overcome: the discretionary immunity defense that harkened back to Dalehite v. United States and the Texas City fertilizer explosion of April 1947.

By 1988, the Baneberry case and our companion Test Site case, *Prescott v. United States*, were the only FTCA radiation cases that had survived this defense. And if the government had its way, both cases would join all others: in *Allen v. United States* (downwinders), Judge Jenkins's decision had been reversed in the Tenth Circuit;[39] in *Begay v. United States* (uranium miners), the lower court's dismissal of the claims brought by uranium miners was affirmed in the Ninth Circuit;[40] in *Bulloch v. United States* (sheep case), the Tenth Circuit reversed Judge Christensen's ruling that reopened the case;[41] and in *Consolidated United States Atmospheric Testing*, the Ninth Circuit ended the atomic veterans' litigation for radiation related injuries.[42]

But despite the apparent odds, we won the legal battle in the Ninth Circuit. Our appeal in *Roberts and Nunamaker* was reinstated, and we soldiered on. We also defeated the governmental immunity defense in the Ninth Circuit in the companion case, *Prescott v. United States*.[43] The victory in Prescott allowed us to try six test cases. In 1994, we lost and did not appeal that decision.

By the time the discretionary immunity defense was swept aside by the Ninth Circuit in *Roberts and Nunamaker v. United States* and *Prescott v. United States*, the Radiation Exposure Compensation Act, RECA, had been signed into law. It offered compensation to eligible uranium miners, downwinders, and NTS workers who contracted leukemia and certain cancers—if they could demonstrate radiation exposure during aboveground tests in the 1950s or from radiation released into the atmosphere from the Plowshare tests in 1962.[44]

RECA was prefaced with an apology from the United States government for exposing its citizens to radiation. It was the last of a series of congressional efforts to provide compensation for those exposed to atmospheric radiation. The first effort began in 1979: "Bill aids nuke test victims,"[45] spawned by highly publicized investigations that began during the Baneberry trial and resulted in the publication of *The Forgotten Guinea Pigs Report, August 1980*, by the House Subcommittee on Oversight and Investigations.[46] The first proposals had only offered compensation to radiation victims living downwind from NTS.

In 1988, Congress enacted legislation to afford atomic veterans relief under the Radiation Exposure Veterans Compensations Act (REVCA). With the passage of REVCA and the Tenth Circuit's 1987 decision in *Allen* reversing Judge Jenkins's award, it was only a matter of time before Congress would act.

In 1990, the Radiation Exposure Compensation Act was signed into law. When it was passed, its sponsor, Senator Orrin Hatch, stated that he did not want it to be "a playground to benefit the lawyers," and it severely limited the fees attorneys hired to assist claimants could receive.[47] As of March

2015, 3,578 Test Site workers, 18,087 downwinders, and nearly 8,000 uranium miners or their widows and children have been awarded $2 billion in compensation for leukemias and cancers linked to the AEC nuclear testing program.

Many of our Test Site clients were eligible for benefits, and we handled a few claims for workers who fit the criteria, including Keith Prescott, who died of multiple myeloma, a cancer of the bone marrow. We also filed a claim on behalf of the daughters of Kenny Case, the Atomic Cowboy who appeared on the television show *What's My Line* in New York City in 1961. Kenny was an ardent supporter of the Test Site workers, led by Bennie Levy, as they pursued their lawsuit in federal court. At that time, Kenny was in excellent health and thought the radiation he received in the 1950s would have no long-term effects. He was wrong. In 1985, he died of leukemia. We assisted his five daughters in their claim, each receiving one-fifth of the $75,000 award.

In late 1982, just prior to issuing his two-sentence ruling in January 1983, Judge Foley took senior status and reduced his federal caseload, though he continued to handle *Roberts and Nunamaker* and the *Prescott case*.

In 1985, after the government wrote Judge Foley's decision and he had denied our motions to reopen the case, the federal building, where Dorothy and Louise had relived Baneberry in a fruitless search for justice, was named the Foley Federal Building to honor Judge Foley, his father, who preceded him on the federal bench, and the Foley family of attorneys.

Judge Roger D. Foley died in January 1996, before the final appeal of his ruling was heard in the Ninth Circuit Court. Near the end of his life, he realized that the Baneberry trial was the most significant legal case in which he had been involved, and one of the longest and most important in Nevada history. He arranged to deposit Baneberry trial material into the archival collections of the University of Nevada–Las Vegas. Alan and I were invited to the dedication ceremony. With considerable reluctance, we went with our wives, not to celebrate Judge Foley's decision in favor of the AEC, which we were convinced was wrong, but out of respect for Harley and Dorothy Roberts and Bill and Louise Nunamaker. By 1993, when we attended the dedication, Judge Foley's 1985 decision in favor of the AEC was of little consequence. It delayed but did not hold back the truth about the human consequences of the AEC atomic testing program.

During the Baneberry trial, a news reporter, aware of government lawyer Bill Elliott's pledge to "spend whatever it takes to win," asked Alan and me why we had pursued the case, knowing that it would require so much personal and financial sacrifice. Even now, it remains difficult to explain our commitment to Harley Roberts, our faith in Drs. Warren and Stewart, and our belief that the bane and curse of Baneberry might end favorably in a federal courthouse in our hometown. But the explanation may be no more complicated than Robert Browning's inspiring line,

> Ah, but a man's reach should exceed his grasp,
> Or what's a heaven for?

Sadly, and prophetically, Baneberry began and ended ever-faithful to its name. While it made sure that the widows of the two men who breathed its lethal radioactive gases received no compensation, it also played a part in awakening the public to the dangers of low-level radiation and helped to end the Nevada nuclear testing program. The AEC and its successor, the Department of Energy, left the Test Site a barren and toxic wasteland pockmarked from the Baneberry crater and countless others. A gravestone embossed with the odd-shaped Baneberry cloud should be erected at the National Atomic Testing Museum in Las Vegas engraved with the AEC's pledge as an immortal epitaph: "The government will spend whatever it takes to win."

And a memorial should be erected at the entrance to the Nevada Test Site to remind future generations of a tragic period in American history. As President Eisenhower warned the American people in his January 1961 farewell address, there are dire consequences when "a government contract becomes virtually a substitute for intellectual curiosity" and "public policy becomes the captive of the scientific-technological elite."

NOTES

1. *Las Vegas Review-Journal*, February 1, 1979. This was the first reference we can recall to the downwinders as "guinea pigs" and may have inspired *The Forgotten Guinea Pigs Report*, issued in 1980. Copy in author's possession.
2. At the meeting with Dr. Warren in Tucson in March 1975, he told me about his disagreement with the military and his resignation in June 1952, because he did not want responsibility for the health effects that might result.
3. The Bulloch family, lead plaintiffs, took the case to trial in federal court in Salt Lake City, Utah, in 1956 and lost. *Bullock v. United States*, 145 F. Supp. 824 (D. Utah 1956). See chapter 6.
4. *Las Vegas Sun*, February 27, 1979; *Las Vegas Review-Journal*, February 27, 1979.
5. *Las Vegas Sun*, March 8, 1979.
6. *Los Angeles Herald Examiner*, March 11, 1979.
7. *Las Vegas Sun*, March 11, 1979.
8. Ibid., March 24, 1979.
9. *Las Vegas Review-Journal*, March 28, 1979.
10. Ibid., March 31, 1979.
11. Ibid., April 6, 1979.
12. Ibid., April 8, 1979.

13. *Baltimore Sun*, April 8, 1979.

14. *Las Vegas Sun*, April 8, 1979.

15. *Las Vegas Review-Journal*, March 27, 1979. In 1981, the Marshall Islanders filed administrative claims seeking billions of dollars for injuries and deaths they claimed were caused by tests in the Pacific. *Las Vegas-Review Journal*, April 23, 1981.

16. *Las Vegas Sun*, May 8, 1979.

17. Ibid., May 13, 1979.

18. *Las Vegas Review-Journal*, May 18, 1979.

19. See *Krumbach v. Dow Chemical Co.*, 676 P.2d 1213 (Colo. App. 1983). Dr. Alice Stewart came to Las Vegas in 1980 and then Denver to testify that Leroy Krumbach's cancer was caused by his exposure to radiation at the Rocky Flats nuclear weapons plant in Colorado.

20. Dr. Thomas Mancuso's study of excess cancers among the Hanford workers swirled in controversy, even after, and perhaps because, Drs. Stewart and Kneale joined him early in 1978. See John Findlay and Bruce Hevly, *Atomic Frontier Days* (Seattle: University of Washington Press, 2011), for a comprehensive discussion of the history, politics, and billions of dollars spent to clean up Hanford.

21. DS 210. On July 23, 1976, the defendants filed the identical motion. On December 27, 1976, the motion was denied. DS 256. The defendants did not appeal that ruling. Defendants filed the identical motion in *Prescott v. United States*, the action we filed in 1980 on behalf of Keith Prescott and 220 other NTS workers who joined later. Judge Foley denied the motion. Prescott v. United States, 523 F. Supp. 918 (1981). The government appealed and the Ninth Circuit Court of Appeals affirmed his ruling. *Prescott v. United States*, 731 F.2d 1388 (9th Cir. 1984).

22. *Bulloch v. United States*, 145 F. Supp. 824 (D. Utah, October 26, 1956).

23. *Bulloch II*, 95 F.R.D. 123 (D. Utah 1982).

24. *Bulloch v. United States*, 763 F2d. 115 (10th Cir. 1985).

25. *United States Nuclear Tests*, July 1945 through September 1992, DOE/NV-209-REV 15, December 2000, pp. 6–7; *Las Vegas Sun*, January 19, 1956; *Las Vegas Review-Journal*, January 22, 1956. The January 18, 1956, test was the fourth and final test in "Operation Project 56, No. 4, Plutonium Dispersal in Area 11d.

26. *Las Vegas Sun*, August 17, 1980.

27. Ibid.

28. *Prescott v. United States*, 523 F. Supp. 918 (D. Nev. 1981).

29. *Prescott v. United States*, 731 F.2d. 1388 (9th Cir. 1984).

30. DS 520. Motion to Reopen Action or for a New Trial, May 4, 1984. Copy in author's possession.

31. *BEIR III, Biological Effects of Ionizing Radiation* (Washington, D.C.: National Academy Press, 1980).

32. *Lancet*, December 1, 1979, 1195.

33. *Baneberry Collection*, EX B-20; Felix Mitelman, "Relation among Occupational Exposure to Potential Mutagenic/Carcinogenic Agents, Clinical Findings, and Bone Marrow Chromosomes in Acute Nonlymphocytic [myelogenous] Leukemia," *Blood 52*, no. 6 (1978): 1229–37.

34. *Allen v. United States*, 599 F. Supp. 247 (D. Utah 1984).

35. DS 522. Supplement to Motion. Copy in author's possession.

36. DS 526. Defendant's Response to Motion. Copy in author's possession.

37. DS 536. Reply in Support of Motion. Copy in author's possession.

38. DS 538. Minute Order denying motion to reopen or for new trial.

39. *Allen v. United States*, 816 F.2d 1417 (10th Cir. 1987).

40. *Begay v. United States*, 768 F.2d 1959 (9th Cir. 1985).

41. *Bulloch v. United States*, 763 D.2d 1115 (10th Cir. 1985).

42. *Consolidated United States Atmospheric Testing Litigation*, 820 F.2d 982 (9th Cir. 1987). Pat Broudy's case was consolidated with the others and dismissed.

43. *Prescott v. United States*, 973 F.2d 696 (9th Cir. 1992).

44. *Radiation Exposure Compensation Act, 42* U.S.C. Sec. 2210.

45. *Las Vegas Sun*, September 25, 1979.

46. *The Forgotten Guinea Pigs Report, August 1980*, Subcommittee on Oversight and Investigations (Washington, D.C.: U.S. Government Printing Office). Copy in author's possession.

47. I have been unable to source the news article, but that statement is emblazoned in my memory.

Epilogue

THE TWENTY-FIVE-YEAR Baneberry odyssey ended in 1996, but the high and low points of the adventure are as fresh today as they were then.

The most exhilarating moment: Dr. Shields Warren's spell-binding explanation of the Roberts case, supported by Dr. Alice Stewart and Dr. John Gofman at trial, and his bone marrow dose estimate, vindicated posttrial by Dr. Karl Morgan's startling revelation that Dr. Evans had hoodwinked us all.

The most painful moment: watching Harley Roberts struggle to breathe, but determined to fight for justice with his last breath.

The most humorous: Dr. Evans's preposterous effort to sell his cluster theory to Judge Foley.

The most depressing: learning that Judge Foley had telescoped our eight years of preparation and forty-one-day trial into a two-sentence ruling, followed by a somber meeting with Dorothy and Louise.

The most insulting: a journalist questioning our motives for taking on our own government, which in turn was committed "to spend whatever it takes to win."

The irony of Baneberry is that two brothers, who held the AEC in high esteem when it came to town in 1951, became its enemy, unmasking a pattern of deception, cover-up, and intimidation we learned had been standard for decades prior to Baneberry.

On the Baneberry trail, we met many other atomic testing victims, whose stories and travails have been told, and told so well, by academics, historians, lawyers, and journalists.

In 1976, we learned about the mysterious death of Karen Silkwood. We followed the lawsuit closely and reveled in Gerry Spence's stunning victory in May 1979. The Silkwood story was told by Richard Rashke in 1981,[1] humorous anecdotes from the trial by Gerry Spence in 1982,[2] and made into a movie in 1983.[3]

In April 1982, on the eve of the downwinders' trial in Salt Lake City,

Harvey Wasserman and Norman Solomon published a shocking exposé about persons exposed to atomic radiation beginning with U.S. soldiers who entered Japan in September 1945 and ending with the Three Mile Island meltdown in 1979.[4] It was the first of many books about radiation effects after our Baneberry trial ended and was highly publicized in Las Vegas.[5]

In 1978, we met Janet Gordon and other residents of southern Utah, who were collecting records of cancer deaths among people exposed to radiation from 1950s atomic tests.

The same year, we met MacArthur Wright, an attorney from St. George, Utah, and Dale Haralson, a lawyer from Tucson, Arizona. They were investigating cancer deaths among people living downwind from NTS. Haralson, Wright, and Stewart Udall filed federal tort claims for downwinders in December 1978.

In 1982, Dale Haralson led a team of lawyers who tried the Allen case in Salt Lake City. I was told there was not a dry eye in the courtroom when he ended his closing argument.

Dale Haralson's victory is embodied in Judge Bruce Jenkins's 500-page Memorandum Decision. The downwinders' story is told by Howard Ball, Phillip Fradkin, Richard L. Miller, and A. Constandina Titus.[6] Titus also chronicled Nevada's role in the atomic testing program from 1951 forward: the politics, legal issues, claims, court cases including Baneberry's role, and the early compensation efforts that led to REVCA and RECA.

In December 1978, we read of Martin "Butch" Bardoli, the Nevada boy who lived at the Twin Springs Ranch that borders the Test Site. Martin was exposed to radiation from the early 1950s aboveground tests and died of leukemia in 1956, at age 7.[7] His story was retold in greater detail on April 27, 1979, with a picture of little Martin and his classmates.[8] Martin Bardoli was very probably the first Nevadan to die of leukemia from atomic testing at the Nevada Test Site.[9] But he was not the last.

After Martin Bardoli's mother's complaints were derided,[10] and after Judge Christensen exonerated the AEC for the sheep deaths in October 1956,[11] there was little concern in Las Vegas about the health effects of atomic testing, until Baneberry vented in December 1971.

From July 1972 until April 1974, we watched Harley Roberts progress to the final stages of his leukemia and death. In 1976, we learned that Bill Nunamaker died of leukemia in December 1974.

In 1981, Gloria Gregerson, who watched the early 1950s radioactive clouds shower her home in Bunkerville, Nevada, called me from her hospital bed. Diagnosed with terminal leukemia at forty-one, she was told she was

too old for a bone marrow transplant. Gloria was aware Dr. Alice Stewart was in Las Vegas and asked if I would bring her to visit. Dr. Stewart was delighted to meet Gloria, but nothing could be done. Gloria died a few months later.[12]

In 1985, Kenny Case, a Nevadan the AEC proudly dubbed the Atomic Cowboy, was dying of leukemia.[13] I visited him a few weeks before his death.

As Nevadans, Alan and I were primarily concerned with the plight of Nevada Test Site workers. We lost the court cases, but remain convinced of two things. First, Dr. Warren was correct in his conviction that Harley Roberts's bone marrow dose from radiation at Baneberry caused his death. Second, our lawsuits on behalf of Roberts, Nunamaker, Prescott, and 220 other NTS workers helped assure that Nevada Test Site workers were included in RECA when it passed in 1990.

The ultimate irony is that Harley Roberts, who gave his life for the cause, was not eligible for RECA benefits.

NOTES

1. Richard L. Rashke, *The Killing of Karen Silkwood* (Boston: Houghton Mifflin, 1982).
2. Gerry Spence, *Gunning for Justice* (New York: Doubleday, 1982).
3. *Silkwood*, directed by Mike Nichols (December 1983; Los Angeles, CA: 20th Century Fox).
4. Harvey Wasserman and Norman Solomon, *Killing Our Own* (New York: Delacorte Press, 1982).
5. *Las Vegas Sun*, *Las Vegas Sun Magazine*, April 25,1982, "Nuclear test coverups revealed in explosive book."
6. Howard Ball, *Justice Downwind* (New York: Oxford University Press, 1986). Phillip Fradkin, *Fallout* (Tucson: University of Arizona Press, 1989). Richard L. Miller, *Under the Cloud* (New York: Free Press, 1986). A. Constandina Titus, *Bombs in the Backyard* (Reno: University of Nevada Press, 1986; 2nd ed., 2001), Baneberry, 105.
7. *Las Vegas Sun*, December 17, 1978.
8. *Las Vegas Valley Times*, April 27, 1979.
9. Richard L. Miller, *Under the Cloud* (New York: Free Press, 1986), 147, 199–203.
10. Ibid.
11. *Bulloch v. United States*, 145 F. Supp. 824 (D. Utah 1956).
12. We would learn in the early 1980s that Utah children exposed to radiation from the early 1950s atomic tests also died of leukemia. Karlene Hafen died on November 17, 1956, age fourteen, three and one-half years after her home in St. George, Utah, was blanketed with fallout on May 19, 1953, from test *Harry*. Sheldon Nisson, who lived in Washington, Utah, near St. George, died of acute myelogenous leukemia on July 6, 1959, age thirteen, six years after he was exposed to radiation from Harry. See *Allen v. United States*, 597 F. Supp. 247 (D. Utah 1984)
13. Kenny Case, the Atomic Cowboy, is prominently featured at the National Atomic Testing Museum in Las Vegas, Nevada. But there is no mention of the fact that he died of leukemia.

Notes to Sources

THE BANEBERRY STORY BEGAN as a memoir, recollections and ramblings about events that happened decades earlier. But Harley Roberts's and Bill Nunamaker's sacrifice required more. And Dr. Shields Warren, Dr. Alice Stewart, Dr. John Gofman, and Dr. Karl Morgan deserved a detailed and accurate rendition of the scientific and medical issues they presented so elegantly in the Baneberry lawsuit.

Therefore, I opened boxes and bins filled with musty news clippings, pleading files, the 5,400-page trial transcript, trial exhibits, posttrial briefs, posttrial motions, appellate briefs, correspondence files, and the pleadings and documents in *Prescott v. United States*, *Allen v. United States*, *Begay v. United States*, *Silkwood v. Kerr-McGee*, *Bulloch v. United States* (reopened), *Broudy v. United States*, and *Krumbach v. Dow Chemical*.

Our Baneberry correspondence files enabled me to back up statements about settlement discussions and trial preparation but also to refresh mental impressions of the events.

All documents filed with the court clerk in *Roberts and Nunamaker v. United States*, including nearly sixty depositions, are identified in the clerk's docket sheet. This was important, because we kept only a few depositions and discarded many documents filed in the case.

However, we did preserve the three posttrial motions to reopen the case in 1984, with Dr. Morgan's affidavits attached and Dr. Felix Mitelman's December 1979 publication that discredited Dr. Rowley's reliance upon his earlier paper.

After the Baneberry trial ended in 1979, I read publications by scholars and journalists about the history of nuclear testing and those exposed to radiation from nuclear tests: Wasserman and Solomon, Ball, Titus, Fradkin, and Miller. For Nevadans, Titus captured our unique role in the continental testing program.

The backstory—the politics behind the atomic testing program—came to light after the trial ended in 1979. It has been described by Wasserman and Solomon, Ball, Titus, Fradkin, and Miller, among others. In addition, I was given an in-depth tutorial into those matters by Mary D. Wammack, PhD, who shared with me her doctoral dissertation.[1]

In writing about Baneberry, I strived to tell the story as it unfolded and consciously avoided reliance upon source material collected by others after the Baneberry trial ended. My purpose was to place Baneberry in context and to focus on the bone marrow dose Harley Roberts received and the genesis of his leukemia as understood at the time. Because Dr. Warren and others explained the scientific and medical issues involved in the case, I did not prepare a comprehensive glossary of terms.

The 5,404-page trial transcript and trial exhibits are housed in the *Baneberry Collection* at UNLV. In the possession of the author are: the trial transcript, trial exhibits, newspaper articles, pleadings, correspondence files, court decisions, posttrial motions, posttrial briefs, the clerk's docket sheet, and briefs filed in the Ninth Circuit Court of Appeals.

NOTES

1. Mary D. Wammack, "Atomic Governance: Militarism, Secrecy and Science in Post-War America, 1945–1958," PhD diss., Dept. of History, University of Nevada, Las Vegas, 2010.

Glossary

AEC: Atomic Energy Commission, created in 1946. In 1975, it was renamed the Energy Research and Development Agency (ERDA). In 1977, it was renamed the Department of Energy (DOE).

Area 12 Camp: Base camp in Area 12 where Harley Roberts and security guards carried out emergency evacuation of 900 Test Site workers after Baneberry vent (see NTS map and Area 12 Camp map).

Baneberry: AEC code name for the underground nuclear test detonated at NTS on December 18, 1970 (see NTS map).

Baneberry vent: Baneberry test released nearly 7 million curies of radiation into the atmosphere in a hammerhead-shaped cloud (see photos of vent cloud).

Beta radiation: Of the three common types of emissions from radioactive materials, beta particles have the medium penetrating power and can generally be stopped by a thin layer of metal or plastic.

BJY: WSI security trailer where Dyer, Roberts, and security force was located at 7:30 am on December 18, 1970, when Baneberry was detonated (see NTS map).

CP-1: Operation control point where Baneberry Test Manager Frank Cluff and panel of advisors were located (see NTS map).

CP-2: REECo Rad-Safe decontamination facility where Harley Roberts and eighty-five other Test Site workers were decontaminated (see NTS map).

Gamma radiation: Extremely penetrating photon energy, produced by nuclear reactions. Gamma is higher wavelength than x-rays, and unlike alpha and beta radiation does not consist of particles. Gamma radiation, or rays, can be recorded on film badges and measured with Geiger counters.

Geiger counter: Portable instrument issued to Rad-Safe monitors to measure gamma rays.

IGAN: Independent Guard Association of Nevada, guard union that represented security guards employed by Wackenhut Services Inc. (WSI) at the Nevada Test Site.

LASL: Los Alamos Scientific Laboratory, designed and conducted the first nuclear test Trinity on July 16, 1945, as well as the first A-bomb test at NTS on January 27, 1951, and the majority of the 1,030 U.S. nuclear tests.

LLL: Lawrence Livermore Laboratory, founded by Nobel Laureate Ernest Lawrence in 1952 as Lawrence Radiation Laboratory (LRL). LLL Designed and detonated nearly one-half of the nuclear tests at NTS, including the Baneberry test.

NTS: Nevada Test Site, named Nevada Proving Grounds when atomic testing began in 1951, changed to NTS in 1955 (see map).

NVO-95: Sixty-four-page *Baneberry Summary Report*, issued January 1971. A sixteen page edited version of *Baneberry Summary Report* was issued by the AEC on May 14, 1971.

REECo: Reynolds Electrical and Engineering Company, Inc. From 1952 through Baneberry, REECo employed directly or through subcontractors most NTS workers.

Rad-Safe: REECo Radiation Safety Division employed personnel who issued and recorded film badge readings, took radiation readings, and decontaminated the eighty-six men exposed to radiation released in Baneberry vent cloud.

USGS: United States Geological Survey, Department of the Interior, issued USGS 474-14, Results of Exploration of the Baneberry Site, Early 1971.

WSI: Wackenhut Services, Inc., employed security guards at NTS.

CHARACTERS

Alice Stewart, MD: British hematologist and epidemiologist who testified that exposure to radiation at Baneberry caused the deaths of Harley Roberts and Bill Nunamaker in 1974.

Bill Cleghorn: IGAN president who initiated the filing of the lawsuit on behalf of thirteen security guards exposed to radiation at Baneberry.

Bill Nunamaker: REECo employee exposed to radiation at Baneberry who died of leukemia in December 1974. In 1976, his widow, Louise Nunamaker, filed a lawsuit, consolidated and tried with Dorothy Roberts's case in 1979.

Ernie Dyer: WSI sergeant in charge of emergency evacuation of Area 12 after Baneberry vent and brother-in-law of Harley Roberts.

Frank Cluff: AEC test manager for Baneberry at CP-1.

Harley Roberts: WSI security guard exposed to radiation while carrying out emergency evacuation of Area 12 Camp. Filed a lawsuit in February 1972, and died in April 1974; his widow, Dorothy Roberts, brought the litigation to trial in 1979.

Janet Rowley, MD: Cytogeneticist at AEC's Mclean Hospital in Chicago, testified for the AEC that Harley Roberts's C-7 chromosome deletion was not caused by Baneberry but by exposure to petroleum products ten years prior to Baneberry.

John Gofman, MD, PhD: UC Berkeley professor of medicine (emeritus). As rebuttal witness, testified that leukemia deaths of Harley Roberts and Bill Nunamaker were caused by Baneberry, that Robley Evans's bone marrow did not include internal exposure, and that Janet Rowley's opinion that Roberts's leukemia was caused by exposure to petroleum products was not supported by scientific evidence.

Karl Morgan, PhD: Health physicist reviewed Robley Evans's bone marrow dose calculations and supplied posttrial affidavits that inhalation of radionuclides increased Roberts's bone marrow dose twenty times Evans's trial estimate.

Robley Evans, PhD: MIT physicist who had studied radiation effects and testified for the government. He performed calculations of Harley Roberts's bone marrow dose and offered his theory of "the clustering of rare events" as an explanation for the occurrence of two leukemias among eighty-six men exposed at Baneberry.

Roger D. Foley: U.S. district judge who presided over the Baneberry trial in 1979 and issued his judgment in 1985.

Shields Warren, MD: Harvard Professor of Medicine (emeritus). Testified at trial that Harley Roberts's exposure to radiation at Baneberry caused the deletion of chromosome C-7 that resulted in Roberts's leukemia and death in 1974.

About The Authors

LARRY C. JOHNS

Larry C. Johns was born in Las Vegas, Nevada, on December 23, 1944, the youngest (along with his twin sister) of five children of Ray M. Johns and Helen H. Johns, longtime schoolteachers who retired from the Clark County School District in the 1970s. Larry attended elementary school, junior high, and Las Vegas High School, graduating in 1962. He attended college at North Texas University his freshman year, then transferred to the University of Arizona, where he completed his BA in 1966 (French/history) and Juris Doctor degree in 1968 at the College of Law.

He married Mary Pratt on June 4, 1966, in Tucson, Arizona. They have four children, Charles Johns, Laura (Johns) Bolhouse, Julianna (Johns) Cumiskey, Jason Johns, and seven grandchildren.

He returned to Las Vegas in 1968 and was admitted to practice law in Nevada in October 1968, Nevada Bar #1895. He served as Deputy District Attorney for Clark County, where he tried many felony cases. In 1971, he and coauthor and brother, Alan Johns, formed a law partnership, Johns and Johns, Ltd. From 1971 to present, he and Alan tried hundreds of civil and criminal cases (primarily jury trials), as well as the Baneberry and Prescott cases. He has briefed and argued over two dozen cases in the Nevada Supreme Court and the Ninth Circuit Court of Appeals and filed Petitions for Certiorari in the United States Supreme Court.

From 1998 to the present, in addition to his private law practice, he has been appointed by the Clark County District Court to serve as an Arbitrator and Short Trial Judge in over a hundred civil cases.

He joined the Nevada Trial Lawyers Association and the Association of Trial Lawyers of America (ATLA) in 1975 and was active until 2002. In 1993, he was selected to membership in the Nevada American Inns of Court, Lloyd D. George Chapter, and remained active until 2005.

ALAN R. JOHNS

Alan R. Johns was born in Dalton, Nebraska, on September 8, 1938. He came to Las Vegas with his parents, Ray and Helen Johns, his elder sister, Judy Johns, and younger brother, Ronald Johns, in August 1942. The primary author of the book, Larry C. Johns, and his twin sister, Linda, were born in Las Vegas.

After graduating from Las Vegas High School in 1956, Alan obtained his BA degree and Juris Doctor degree at the University of Colorado. He was admitted to practice law in Colorado in 1962 and in Nevada in 1963.

In 1963 Alan joined the Army Reserves, completed his basic training, and was honorably discharged in 1969. He married Loretta Jung on June 6, 1964 in Las Vegas, and they have three sons, Tristram Johns, Gregory Johns, and Brian Johns, and eight grandchildren.

Alan served in the Clark County District Attorney's office and was chief criminal deputy from 1963 to 1970. From 1974 through 1975 he served as Special Prosecutor for Clark County. He has practiced both criminal and civil law before all Nevada courts and administrative agencies, the U.S. District Court, Ninth Circuit Court of Appeals, and the U.S. Supreme Court. He has also served as an Arbitrator, Mediator, Judge Pro Tempore, and Supreme Court Settlement Judge.

INDEX

Made in United States
Cleveland, OH
05 November 2026

47664316R00131